ON THE

SOCIAL ORGANIZATION

AND

MODE OF GOVERNMENT

OF THE

ANCIENT MEXICANS.

BY

Ad. F. BANDELIER.

[From the Twelfth Annual Report of the Peabody Museum of Archæology and
Ethnology, Cambridge. 1879.]

NEW YORK
COOPER SQUARE PUBLISHERS, INC.
1975

Originally Published 1879
Published 1975 by Cooper Square Publishers, Inc.
59 Fourth Avenue, New York, N. Y. 10003

Printed in the United States of America

Library of Congress Cataloging in Publication Data

Bandelier, Adolph Francis Alphonse, 1840-1914.
 On the social organization and mode of government
of the ancient Mexicans.
 "From the twelfth annual report of the Peabody
Museum of Archaelogy and Ethnology, Cambridge, 1879."
 Reprint of the 1879 ed. printed at the Salem Press,
Salem.
 1. Aztecs. 2. Indians of Mexico—Tribal govern-
ment. 3. Indians of Mexico—Social life and customs.
I. Title.
F1219.B224   1975   970.3   84547
ISBN 0-8154-0504-9

ON THE SOCIAL ORGANIZATION AND MODE OF GOVERNMENT OF THE ANCIENT MEXICANS.

By Ad. F. Bandelier.

Two previous papers have already been devoted to some of the most prominent features of the life of the ancient Mexicans, namely: warlike customs, and their mode of distributing and occupying the soil and their rules of Inheritance.[1] The conclusions of both essays were chiefly negative, in so far as they tended to establish the non-existence of a condition which has, for three centuries, been regarded as prevailing. Thus, in the first, we have attempted to disprove the existence of a military despotism[2], and in the second, the existence of feudalism[3] among the natives of Mexico. More positive results were, however, foreshadowed in both instances by the suggestion, if not by the demonstration, that aboriginal society in Mexico rested on a democratic principle. The present essay is intended to show—if the organization of the natives of Mexico was *not* as it is commonly represented—what that organization really was, according to our conception, and what status

[1] *Tenth Report of the Peabody Museum:* " *On the Art of War and Mode of Warfare of the Ancient Mexicans.*" *Eleventh Report:* " *On the Tenure and Distribution of Lands among the Ancient Mexicans, and the Customs with Respect to Inheritance.*"

[2] "*Art of War,*" pp. (127, 128, and 161).

[3] " *Tenure of Lands,*" (pp. 418 and 448). In both instances, as well as in the present discussion, the works of the Hon. L. H. Morgan have furnished to the writer his points of departure and lines of investigation; besides, the distinguished American ethnologist has watched with more than friendly solicitude the progress of all these essays. If I seize the opportunity to recall here the debt of gratitude under which I stand toward him, it is coupled with the wish to express heartfelt thanks to several of my friends, to whose liberal assistance these and the preceding pages owe their existence, nearly as much as to my individual work. Let me name here, Mr. F. W. Putnam, Curator of the Peabody Museum, Col. Fred Hecker, of Summerfield, Illinois, Dr. G. Bruhl, of Cincinnati, Ohio, and the officers of the Mercantile Library at St. Louis, Missouri. Lastly, because most remote, though certainly not least, am I deeply indebted to the great documentary historian of the City of Mexico, Sr. Don Joaquin Garcia Icazbalceta for nearly all information which could not be obtained from the usually known sources.

of progress in Institutions can be assigned to the remarkable tribe which has become so prominent in history. In other words, our object is to reconstruct the mode of government of the ancient Mexicans, the nature of its offices and dignities, and especially the principles ruling and guiding their social agglomeration.

The distinguished Mexican scholar, Manuel Orozco y Berra, explains, as well as qualifies, the condition of the aborigines of Mexico in the following manner:

"If, from the boundary-lines of the empire [of Mexico, according to his views] we now turn to the races peopling its area, we find it to be a truth undeniable that no common nor mutual tie connected these numerous and diverse tribes. Each one was independent under its chiefs.[4]"

[4] "*Geografia de las Lenguas y Carta Etnográfica de México*," por *Manuel Orozco y Berra*, Mexico, 1864, (Tercera Parte, IX México, p. 252). "Si de las demarcaciones del imperio pasamos â considerar las razas que lo poblaban, encontraremos como una verdad innegable que tanta tribu diversa no tenia un lazo comun de union. Cada una era independiente bajo el mando de sus señores. Las ambiciones particulares encendian la guerra, y la misma familia se fraccionaba. A su semejanza, cada pueblo tenia un gefe que de nombre reconocia al señor principal, y todas las provincias estaban subdividas hasta formar un sistema bajo algunos puntos semejante al feudal. Rencores y odios apartaban las tribus, y la guerra era constante, porque siendo una de sus principales virtudes la valentía, no podian verse sin combatirse, ä imitacion de los orgullosos animales que sirven de diversion en los palenques. Por instinto ó porque las generaciones son arrastradas aun ä su pesar por la corriente de los tiempos, los Mexicanos emprendieron la tarea de reunir en un solo haz todos aquellos pueblos, de formar de ellos una nacion, y de asimilar sus intereses con los intereses del imperio. Para llevar ä cabo semejante tarea era preciso, la fuerza para poder triunfar; un sistema proseguido con tino, y con tenacidad, y el tiempo bastante para que el odio se bórrara y dejara nacer las simpatías. Pero la unidad que solicitaban los Mexicanos llevaba ä las tribus al mas espantoso de los despotismos; el imperio era muy nuevo para haber alcanzado otra cosa que reducir ä la servidumbre, sin poder contar con el amor de sus vasallos; de manera que en lugar de amigos, tenia enemigos solapados, y su grandeza era solo engañosa appariencia. En esta sazon se presentaron los conquistadores españoles. Cualquiera fuerza extraña habia de hacer vacilar al coloso; as tribus, mal halladas con la servidumbre, vieron en los invasores ä quienes podrán salvarles del yugo; en su juicio rencoroso no quisieron advertir, que por alcanzar una estéril venganza aventuraban su propia existencia, y corrieron de tropel ä colocarse bajo las banderas de los estranjeros." It may be interesting to compare this weighty authority with my remarks on the same subject in "*Art of War*," (pp. 100, also note 17), and "*Tenure of Lands*," (pp. 416, 417, and 418, and annotations.) The difference consists in that Sr. Orozco y Berra ascribes to the ancient Mexicans a decided tendency to "nationallize," so to say, the aboriginal people of their conquered area, to force uniformity of customs and organization upon them, and establish a true despotism. To this I beg leave to suggest in reply:—

(1). That the Mexicans, *alone*, formed only a *part* (two-fifths in amount of tribute) of that power which is commonly termed "an Empire" (El Imperio) and which was but the Nahuatl confederacy of the Mexican valley. In evidence of it I will take the liberty to quote his own words, (same part and chapter, pp. 240, 241): "El reino de Acolhuacan era el segundo en poderío; su capital era Tetzcoco, ä la orilla del lago de su nombre. Pequeña hoy y sin material interes, en lo antiguo fué rival de México y

This eliminates at once the notion of a Mexican state or empire, embracing in the folds of political society [5] all the groups of abor-

la segunda poblacion de las del Valle." Farther on, quoting *Juan Bautista Pomar*, " *Relacion de la ciudad de Tezcuco*," (MSS., belonging to Sr. Icazbalceta, and dated 1582) who says of Tezcuco: "La extension del reino era desde el mar del N. á la del Sur, con todo lo que se comprende á ia banda del Poniente hasta el puerto de la Vera Cruz, salvo la Ciudad de Tlachcala y Huexotzinco," the learned ethnographer adds, (p. 242), " Juan B. Pomar fija las limites del reino con toda la exaggeracion que puede infundir el orgullo de raza. Por nuestra parte, hemos leido con cuidado las relaciones que á la monarquía corresponden, y hemos estudiado en el plano los lugares à que se refieren, y ni de las unas ni de las otras llegamos á sacar jamas que los reyes de Acolhuacan mandaron sobre las tribus avecindadas in la costa del Pacifico, no ya à la misma de México, sino aun á menores latitudes." He then enters upon a discussion of the number and names of settlements which gave tribute exclusively to Tezcuco. We can only refer to it in general here, as one of the most valuable contributions to Mexican history, and based upon authorities which ought to be published as soon as possible, some of which we mention for the benefit of students :—

(1). " *Memorial dirigido al rey por Don Hernando Pimentel Nexcavualcuyutl, cacique y gobernador de la provincia de Tezcuco, etc.*" This is the celebrated Report used by Torquemada and Fernando de Alba Ixtlilxochitl, and which the Cavaliere Boturini Benaducci owned.

(2). " *Relacion de Senpuhuala del corregidor Luis Obregon*," 1580, MSS.

(3). " *Relacion de Epazoyuca por el corregidor Luis Obregon*," 1580, MSS.

(4). " *Relacion de Tetliztaca por el corregidor Luis Obregon*," 1580, MSS.

(5). " *Relacion de Meztitlan por el alcalde mayor Gabriel de Chavez*," 1589, MSS.

(6). " *Relacion de Atengo por el corregidor Juan de Padilla*," 1579, MSS.

(7). " *Relacion de Atlatlauca por el corregidor Gaspar de Solis*," 1580, MSS.

(8). " *Relacion de Acapiztla por el alcalde mayor Juan Gutierrez de Liebana*," 1580, MSS.

(9). " *Relacion de Culhuacan por el corregidor Gonzalo Gallego*," 1580, MSS.

(10). " *Relacion de Iztapalapa por el corregidor Gonzalo Gallego*," 1580, MSS.

Since most of these valuable MSS. are the property of Sr. J. G. Icazbalceta, an early publication thereof may be hoped for.

Sr. Orozco y Berra now reaches the important conclusion :

(*a*). That Aculhuacan or Tezcuco had settlements tributary to it alone, (p. 246).

(*b*). That the " Empire " had tributaries of itself.

(*c*). That certain pueblos paid tribute both to Tezcuco and to Mexico, (p. 246), Epazoyuca, "pertenecieron tambien á Tetzcoco, y en el reinado de Itzcoatl quedaron por mitad para México y para Tetzcoco, á fin de que de alli sacaran los imperiales las navajas para sus macanas." Taken probably from Relacion 3.

The "Imperiales" were, therefore, the confederates, and the "Imperio" the confederacy. But, if, within the area conquered by these confederates, each one of them received its share of tributary tribes, how could it be their task or tendency to unify or nationalize, since each of the three associates composed but a part of that power, and their association was a voluntary one ?

(2). None of the confederates exercised any power over the others, beyond the exclusively military direction delegated to the Mexicans proper. " *Rapport sur les différentes classes de chefs de la Nouvelle Espagne, Par Alonzo de Zurita*," translated from the Spanish original by Mr. Ternaux Compans, and printed in 1840, by him in his " *Voyages Relations et Mémoires origina aux pour servir à l' histoire de la découverte de l' Amérique*," (p. 11). " La province de Mexico était soumise á trois principaux chefs : celui de Mexico, celui de Tezcuco ct celui de Tlacopan, que l'on nomme aujourd' hui Tacuba. Tous les chefs inférieurs relevaient de ces souverains et leur obéissaient. Les trois chefs supérieurs formaient une conlédération et se partageaient les provinces dont ils s'emparaient. Le souverain de Mexico avait au dessous de lui ceux de Tezcuco et de Tacuba pour les affaires qui avaient rapport à la guerre; quant á toutes les autres, leurs puissances étaient égales, de sorte que l' un d' eux ne se mêlait jamais du

igines settled within the area tributary to the valley-tribes. Consequently we need not look beyond the tribe, for any *larger group*

gouvernment des autres," (p. 16). "Chaque souverain confirmait l' election de ses vassaux, car, ainsi qu' on l' a déja dit, leur jurisdiction était indépendante pour les affaires civiles et criminelles."

Fray Toribio de Motolinia, " Historia de los Indios de Nueva España," in Vol. I, of Sr. Icazbalceta's " Coleccion de Documentos, etc."(Epistola proemial, p. 5). "Despues el señorio de Tetzcoco fué tan grande como el de México." (Id. p. 11) ʻʻ Los de Tetzcoco, que en antigüedad y señorio no son menos que los Mexicanos." (Tratado III, Cap. VI1, p. 182) " Esta cindad de Tetzcoco era la segunda cosa principal de la tierra, y asimismo el señor de ella era el segundo señor de la tierra; sujetaba debajo de si quince provincias hasta la provincia de Tuzapan, que está ă la costa del Mar del Norte. . . . . . ă la parte de Oriente tiene México Tenuchtitlan ă una legua la ciudad ó pueblo de Tlacopan, adonde residia el tercero señor de la tierra, al cual estaban sujetas diez provincias:, estos dos señores ya dichos se podrian bien llamar reyes, porque no les faltaba nada para lo ser. (p. 183) ʻʻ Las de las provincias y principales pueblos eran como señores de ditado ó salva, y sobre todos eran los mas principales los dos, el de Tetzcoco y el de Tlacopan; y estos con todos los otros todo lo mas del tiempo residian en México, y tenian corte ă Moteuczoma." We know, however, that the fact of *residence* of the head-war-chiefs of Tezcuco and Tlacopan at Mexico, is not true,. though their frequent visits there on military business, and their protracted stay after the Spaniards had entered the pueblo, may explain the error. The latter passage is amended by the good father (Trat. III, cap. VIII, p. 187), as follows: "y si de esto algun señor tenia exencion era el de Tetzcoco."

Fernando Cortés, Carta Segunda, (In *Vedia's " Historiadores primitivos, etc."* Vol. I, p. 29). Speaking of Cacamatzin, he says: ʻʻ é segun lo que despues dél supe, era él muy cercano deudo de Muteczuma, y tenia su señorio junto al del dicho Muteczuma; cuyo nombre era Haculuacan." Cortés further relates that when Cacamatzin threatened to take up arms, he requested Montezuma to direct him to come to Mexico, but the chieftain of Tezcuco refused, saying, "that if they wanted something of him, they might come over on his land, where they would find out who he was, and what kind of obedience he was held to." Montezuma even was afraid, upon this reply, to suggest open violence, dissuading Cortés from it altogether. This shows clearly that the Mexicans had no authority over the Tezcucans, and even were loth to assail them.

Francisco Lopez de Gomara. Conquista de Méjico (In Vedia, Tom. I, p. 346). " Habia asimesmo otros muchos señores y reyes, como los de Tezcuco y Tlacopan, que no le debian nada, sino la obediencia y homenaje." Also, on the treacherous seizure of Cacamatzin, he confirms Cortés (p. 355), " La prision de Cacama, rey de Tezcuco." (Id. p. 433), " a Chimapopoca sucedió el otra su hermano, dicho Izcona. Este Izcona señoréo ă Azcupuzalco, Cuanhnau, Chalco, Couatlichan y Huexocinco, mas tuvo por accompañados en el gobierno ă Nezaualcoyocin, señor de Tezcuco, y al señor de Tlacopan, y de aqui adelante mandaron y gobernaron estos tres señores cuantos reinos y pueblos obedecian y tributaban ă los de Culúa; bien que el principal y el mayor dellos era el rey de Méjico, el segundo el de Tezcuco, y el menor el de Tlacopan."

Bernal Diez de Castillo. Historia verdadera de la Conquista de Nueva-España. (Vedia, Vol. II, Cap. C, p. 100.) " Como el Cacamatzin, señor de la ciudad de Tezcuco que despues de Méjico era la mayor y mas principal ciudad que hay en la Nueva España." Also on the seizure of Cacamatzin, confirmatory of Cortés and of Gomara (pp. 101 and 102).

Gonzalo Fernandez de Oviedo y Valdés. Historia natural y general de Indias. Madrid, 1853 (Lib. XXXIII, cap. VIII, pp. 294 and 295). The entire chapter is devoted to the seizure of Cacamatzin, and is almost a verbal copy of the report made by Cortés (Lib. XXXIII, cap. LII, p. 539). It contains a letter written to Oviedo, by the vice-roy of Mexico, Don Antonio de Mendoza, under date of 6 October, 1541, in which this functionary says: " Y lo de aqui no es tan poco que no podays hacer libro dello, é no será pequeño; porque aunque Monteçuma é México es lo que entre nosotros ha sonado,

of social organization. The confederacy of tribes, as we have already shown, carried no influence whatever on the organization.

no era menor señor el Caconci de Mechuacan, y otros que recenoscian al uno ni al otro." We quote this passage merely as a general illustration.

Fray Bernardino de Sahagun. Historia general de las Cosas de Nueva-España, published by Sr. C. M. de Bustamante, in 1829 (Vol. II, lib. VIII, cap. III, p. 276), "El cuarto señor de Tezcoco se llamó Netzahoalcoiotzin, y reinó setenta y un años, y en tiempo de esto se comenzaron las guerras, y tuvo el señorio de Tezcoco siendo señor del de México Itzcoatzin, y estos entrambos hicieron guerra ã los de Tecpaneca, de Atzcaptzalco, y ã otros pueblos y provincias, y el fué fundador del señorio de Tezcoco in Aculhoacan." (Id. Vol. III. lib. XII, cap. XLI, page 59, close of chapter.)

Fray Diego Dúrán. Historia de las Yndias de Nueva España é Islas de Tierra Firme. Published by Sr. José Fernandez Ramirez at Mexico, in 1867, (Cap. XIV, p. 123). "El rey Itzcoatl, aunque mal dispuesto, holgó de la victoria y dió las gracias ã todos los señores y principales, al qual, agrauándosele la enfermedad, entendiendo de se acertarsele la muerte, mandó llamar al Señor de Tezcuco, Neçaualcoyotl, pariente cercano suyo, y aconsejóle que no tuviese guerra con los Mexicanos, sus parientes y amigos, sino que antes se hiciese con ellos y fuese en su favor siempre: y dexó ordenado que desde en adelante fuese de Tezcuco el segundo rey de la comarca y el tercero el de Tacuba, ã quien llamauan el rey de Tlaluacpan. . . ." (p. 124). " . . . y solo estos tres reynos mandaron y governaron la tierra, de hoy en adelante, siendo el de México sobre todos ellos, y casi como emperador y monarca del nueuo mundo." Nearly the whole of Cap. XV is devoted to the formation of the confederacy, but cannot be inserted here. The editor, Sr. J. F. Ramirez, appears to incline to the opinion, however, that there was a confederacy on equal terms, (note 2, p. 130). The same author also states repeatedly that the head-chiefs of Tezcuco and Tlacopan sacrificed (slaughtered) captives at the chief teo-calli of Mexico, on very solemn occasions, together with the head-chief of Mexico, thus showing equal rights. (Cap. XXIII, p. 197 and others.) But his plainest statement is found (Cap. XLIII, p. 347), and reads as follows: "Algunos han querido decir quel reyno de Tezcuco era libre de todo reconocimiento y parias al monarca, y que en nada le era sujeto, lo qual allo al coutrario en esta ystoria Mexicana; porque aunque ã la verdad no tributauan ã Mexico mantas ni joias ni plumas ni cosas de comida, como otras provincias tributauan, hallo empero ã los Mexicanos metidos en las tierras tezcucanas donde sembraban y cogian, y algunos dellos hechos terrazgueros' de los señores de México; y allo que en ofréciéndose estas fiestas y solenidades, daban tributo desclauos para ella, de lo qual ninguno estaua esento ni reservado. Tambien allo que ofréciéndose dar guerra ã alguna ciudad y provincia, al primero que llamauan y acudian para que apercibiese sus gentes, era al rey de Tezcuco, y como abemos, notado en esta ystoria, le hacian venir ã Mexico todas las veces que se ofrecia ocasion, loqual no era poca sujecion, dado que tuviese sus préeminencias y libertades de rey y señor de aquella provincia de Aculuacan; . . . ."

Fernando de Alvarado Tezozomoc. Crónica Mexicana. (9th Vol. of Lord Kingsborough's "Antiquities of Mexico.") This author agrees so closely with Durán in most instances, that we can dispense with full quotations. See Cap. XIX and XX, on the pretended conquest of Tezcuco by the Mexicans. Tezozomoc is very positive on the question of joint sacrifice (Cap. LXIX, p. 117). A singular remark is, however, found (Cap. XCVII. p. 172). After the Huexotzincas had sent delegates to Mexico to sue for peace, the Mexican council was called together: "dijo zihuacoatl resoluto: Senor, como será esto, si no lo saben vuestros consegeros de guerra los reyes de Aculhuacan-Nezahualpilli, y el de Tecpanecas Tlaltecatzin? hagase entero cabildo y acuerdo: fue acordado asi." This important incident shows that not even the Mexicans had the right to treat alone with a power hostile to the three tribes, consequently that the other two were their *confederates*, and *not their feudal vassals*. Fray Durán confirms the incident in chapter LX, p. 473, of his work, precedingly quoted.

Joseph de Acosta, Historia natural y moral de las Indias, Madrid, 1608, derives his information from the same source as the two preceding, namely: the Codex Rami

It was only a partnership, formed for the purpose of carrying on the business of warfare, and that intended not for the extension of

rez, now in process of publication at Mexico. Acosta mentions and describes (Lib. VII, Cap. XV, p. 490), the traditionary war between the Mexicans and Tezcucans concluding: " Con esto quedó el Rey de Mexico por supremo Rey de Tezcuco, y no quitandoles su Rey, sino haziendole del supremo Censejo suyo." (Cap. XVI, p. 490.) Both chiefs, of Tezcuco and of Tlacopan, are mentioned by him as " electors " of the Mexican head-chiefs.

Sebastian Ramirez de Fuenleal, Bishop of San Domingo and President of the Royal Audiencia at Mexico. " *Lettre . . . ă sa majesté Charles V*," translated by Mr. Ternaux-Compans in his " Premier Recueil de Piéces relatives ă la Nouvelle-Espagne," and bearing date 3 Nov., 1532 (p. 254). " Les souverains de Tezcoco, de Tacuba, qui étaient trés puissants dans cette contrée, agissaient de méme que Mutizuma. Ils partageaient entre eux et ce souverain le fruit de leurs conquĕtes; cependant les souverains de Mexico étaient les plus puissants, et ils eurent toujours une plus grande différence." The same words about are repeated in the " *Second Recueil,*" printed 1840, (the first " Recueil" appeared in 1838), on p. 222. The Report is therein stated to be by the President *and* the Audiencia.

" *Lettre des Chapelains Frére Toribio et Frére Diego D'Olarte ă Don Luis de Velasco* etc.," date : St. François de Cholula, 27 Aõut, 1554. (Ternaux, " Recueil," 1, p. 403), "Toutes les autres obéissaient ă Montezuma, au souverain de Tezcuco, et ă celui de Tlacopa. Ces trois princes étaient étroitement confédérés; ils partagaient entre eux tous les pays qu'ils subjuguaient. Montezuma éxerçait la toute-puissance dans les affaires relatives ă la guerre et au gouvernment de la confédération."

Fray Géronimo de Mendieta. " *Historia ecclĕsiastica Indiana,*" published by Icazbalceta in 1870. After having mentioned (Lib. II, cap. XXVI, p. 129) that the chiefs of Mexico and Tezcuco sent challenges to foreign tribes to recognize " the chief of Mexico " as their superior, and to give him tribute, he says (Cap. XXVIII, p. 134), "Es de saber que los señores de México, Tezcuco y Tacuba, como reyes y señores supremos de esta tierra. . . . ." (Cap. XXXVII, p. 156.) " Los señores de las provincias ó pueblos que inmediatamente eran subjetos ă Mexico, iban luego alli ă s'er confirmados en sus señorias, despues que los principales de sus provincias los habian elegido, y con algunos. . . . . En los pueblos y provincias que inmediatamente eran subjetos ă Tezcuco y ă Tacuba tenian recurso por la confirmacion ă sus señores; *que en esto y otras cosas estos dos señores no reconocian superior.*" Italics are my own.

Antonio de Herrera. " *Historia general de los hechos de los Castellanos en las Islas y la Tierra-Firme del mar Oceano.*" 1726, Madrid. (Dec. II, lib. VII, cap. XII, p. 190). He almost copies Gomara, and in regard to the seizure of Cacamatzin he not only confirms Cortés, Gomara, and Bernal Diez, but is much more detailed and positive yet. (Dec. II, lib. IX, cap. II, pp. 217, 218.) Finally he asserts: (Dec. III, lib. IV, cap. XV. p 133). " Con Mexico estaban confederados los Señores de Tezcuco, i Tlacopan, que aora llaman Tacuba, i partian lo que ganaban, i obedecian al Señor de Mexico, en lo tocante ă la guerra, i tenian algunos Pueblos comunes en sucesion, asi de los Señorios, como de los Maiorazgos, i haciendas."

We now turn to an author who plainly takes an opposite view of the question, claiming, in place of a *Mexican* " Empire," the supremacy for the *Tezcucans*, or an ancient " Empire" of the Chichimecas. The latter claim has already been discussed in " *Tenure of Lands* " (p. 394, note 10). This assumption,— which strongly combats the view that there was anything at all like an Empire, while it implies the existence of a mere confederacy,— is set forth by the following well known Tezcucan native author.

Fernando de Alba Ixtlilxochitl. " *Histoire des Chichimèques ou des anciens Rois de Tezcuco.*" This is the french translation of the original " Historia de los Chichimecos, etc., etc.," contained in Lord Kingsborough's 9th volume. Since abstracts might prove too lengthy, I merely refer to (Cap. XXXII), on the formation of the confederacy as containing some very plain and remarkable passages (pp. 218, 219, and 220), among

territorial ownership, but only for an increase of the means of subsistence.[6]

which is one : " ces trois dynasties gouvernaient la Nouvelle-Espagne jusquă l'arrivée des
chrétiens. Cependant, quoiqúelles fussent égales en rąng, en puissance et en revenu,
il y avait de certains tributs dont le roi de Tlacopan ne recevait qu 'un cinquiéme, tan-
dis que ceux de Mexico et de Tezcuco en recevaient chacun deux." See also (Cap.
XXXIV, cap. XXXVI, pp. 245 and 246; cap. XXXVIII, pp. 269 and 273; 2d vol., Cap. LXXI,
pp. 109 and 110), and others. Nevertheless, Ixtlilxochitl reproaches bitterly Monteznma
with having usurped the leading power which belonged to the Texcucans (according
to him), and having taken the direction of the confederacy into his hands. (Cap.
LXXV, p. 128, to XXVI, p. 132, etc.). These charges are violently repeated in his other
and more extensive work: " *Relaciones historicas*." Also in Vol. IX of Lord
Kinsborough. As a specimen, I refer to the ' Venida de los Españoles " translated also
by Mr. Ternaux under the title of " *Cruautés horribles des conquérants du Méxique*."
In regard to the war between Tezcuco and Mexico, in which he, of course, attributes the
fullest victory to the former see also " *Undécima Relacion*" (Kingsborough, IX, pp. 407
and 408). Ixtlilxochitl is seconded and followed by his illustrious contemporary. *Fray
Juan de Torquemada. " Los veinteiun Libros Rituales i monarchia Indiana*, etc., etc.'
Edition of 1723. This distinguished ecclesiastic is such a consistent advocate of feudalism, that he even assigns the division of Tenochtitlan into four quarters to an
"edict" of the "Chichimecan Emperor" Techotlalatzin (Lib. II, cap. VIII, pp. 88
and 89), or to an order of Mexican "Lords" (Lib. III, cap. XXIV, p. 295). Still he is very
plain about Tezcuco being equal and not subject to Mexico. Compare for instance
(Lib. III, cap. XXVII, p. 304), " nunca perdió su antigua estimacion, y'siempré tuvo
Rei, y Señor legitimo, que la regia, y governaba, y era igual con el de Mexico," (Lib. II,
cap. XXXIX, p. 144), about the confederacy; (Cap. XI, p. 146). About the pretended
war between the two tribes (Cap. XLII, p. 149. "Y no solo no es verdad; pero es
directamente contra ella." On the supposed intrigues of Montezuma against the Tezcucans (Lib. II, caps. LXXXIII, LXXXIV, etc., etc.), until the first passage of Cap.
LXXXVII, (p. 227), " muerto el Rei Neçahualpilli de Tetzcuco, y entrando en su lugar su
Hijo Cacama . . . . · corrió la confederacion de los Reies, como hasta entonces lo
avian acostumbrado . . . ." also (Lib. XI, cap. XXVI, p. 353), " . . . . nó deja de ser
su igual, y semejante el de Tetzcuco . . . . ." (Cap. XXVII, p. 356; cap. XXVIII, p. 361.)
Copy of Mendieta. About warfare of the Confederates (Lib. XII, cap. VI, p. 382;
Lib. XIV, cap. I, p. 533; Cap. II, p. 537). Division of Spoils and of Tributes Idem.
(cap. VIII, pp. 546, 547 and 548), " porque cierto es asi, qne el Rei de Mexico no era maior
en Autoridad, que el de Tetzcuco . . . . ." From these, but especially from Torquemada's history of the conquest, which occupies the entire fourth Book (Vol. I), enough
can be gathered to show that this cumbrous but important authority admits no Mexican
Empire, but only a confederacy of Mexicans, Tezcucans, and Tlacopans.
Fray Agustin de Vetancurt, " *Teatro Mexicano,*" (Edition of 1870), admits the supremacy of the Mexicans (Parte IIa, Trat. 1°, cap. XIV, p. 291), "y remataron la fiesta que
dando Izcohuatl por rey supremo del imperio tepaneca, por ser primero que nezahualcoyotl, y este por rey de los aculhuas, y al de Tacuba le hicieron rey de la parte de
mazahuacan, etc. . . . . .". But the confederacy " liga," of the three chiefs is acknowledged everywhere. (Also Trat. II°, cap. III, p. 382), " cuando los Mexicanos, los tezco-
canos ó de Tlacopan (que eran los reyes que estaban confederados para las guerras,
etc. . . ."
To this lengthy collection of quotations many others might be added, from the same
period as well as of a later date. They appear to justify the proposition advanced,
namely : none of the confederates exercised any power over the others, beyond that of
exclusively military leadership, which had been awarded to the Mexicans proper.

The conquerors never interfered with the government, organization, and mode of
life of tribes whom they had overpowered. No attempt, either direct or implied, was
made to assimilate or incorporate them.

My friend *Dr. G. Brühl,* author of the highly interesting and conscientious work

Our investigations are therefore confined to the limits of the single tribe, and we have selected for that purpose the Mexicans

"*Die Culturvoelker des alten Amerika*" (Cincinnati, 1876, '77, '78), has, in regard to the statements made in "*Art of War*" (p. 100, note 17; p. 133, note 152), and in "*Tenure of Lands*" (pp. 412 and 413, also note 56; pp. 417 and 418, also note 69), called my attention to a passage from *Sahagnn*, "*Historia general*" (Lib. VIII, cap. XXIV, p. 313), "Habiendo pacificado la provincia, luego los señores del campo repartian tributos á los que habian sido conquistados, para que cada un año los diesen al señor que les habia conquistado, y el tributo era de lo que en ella se criaba y se hacia, y luego elegian gobernadores y oficiales que presidiesen en aquella provincia, no de los naturales de ella, sino de los que la habian conquistado." The author himself, however, gives the explanation of what he intends to designate by such "governors and officials who should preside in said province." In his 12th Book, (Cap, II, p. 5, Vol. III), he says: "La primera vez que parecieron navios en la costa de esta Nueva-España, los capitanes de Moctheuzoma que se llamaban *Calpixques* que estaban cerca de la costa luego fueron á ver que era aquello que vino, que nunca habian visto navios, uno de los cuales fue el calpixque de Cuextecatl que se llamaba Pinotl: llevaba consigo otros calpixques uno que se llamaba Yaotzin, que residia en el pueblo de Mictlanquauhtla, y otro que se llamaba Teozinzocatl, que residia en el pueblo de Teociniocan, y otro que se llamaba Cuitlalpitoc, este no era calpixque sino criado de uno de estos calpixques, y principalejo que se llamaba Tentlil." In this Sahagun about agrees with *Tezozomoc* (*Crónica*, Cap. CVI, CVII, CVIII, CIX), inasmuch as the latter also states the officers to have been calpixques, th. is, "Stewards" or *gatherers of tribute*. Compare *Alonzo de Molina*, "*Vocabulario*," (Parte IIa, p. 12.)

The names of these Indians who received Cortés are found nearly alike in all the authors, but we are struck by the fact that many of them call the natives "governors" of Montezuma. I quote *Bernal Diez de Castillo* (Cap. XXXVIII, pp. 32 and 33, Vedia, Vol. II) *Gomara* (pp. 312, 313, 314, etc., Vedia I). *Ixtlilxochitl* ("*Histoire des Chichiměques*," Cap. LXXIX, p. 160). "*Cruautés horribles*," (p. 3.) *Herrera* (Dec. II, lib. V, cap. IV, p. 116; Cap. V, p. 117). *Torquemada* (Lib. IV, cap. XVI, p. 387; Cap. XVII, p. 389, etc.). *Vetancurt* (Vol. II, cap. IV, p. 43). *Fray Joseph Joaquin Granados y Galvez*, ("*Tardes Americanas*" Mexico, 1778, 9th evening, p. 234). *Abbate F. X. Clavigero* ("*Geschichte von Mexico*," Leipzig, 1790, a german translation of the Italian original which appeared at Cesena in 1780. Vol. II, Lib. VIII, cap. V, p. 16). These *governors* therefore were but "calpixques," in other words *collectors of tribute*. This is already stated by *Oviedo y Valdés* (Vol. III, Lib. XXXIII, cap. I, p. 259), speaking of Cempoal, "porque los indios è ministros, que alli estaban para mandarlos, eran oficiales è mayordomos de la cibdad de México." The "*Real Ejecutoria de S. M., Sobre Tierras y Reservas de Pechos y Paga perteneciente á os Caciques de Axapucso, de la Jurisdiccion de Otumba*," (Col. de Doc's, Vol. II, Icazbalceta, p. 5), calls all the Indians in question "enviados por el gran Montezuma."

This explains the evident contradictions of Sahagun.

It is a singular fact, but one amply proven by the records of the conquest, that nowhere did the Spaniards, on their whole march from the coast to Mexico, meet with Mexican *administrators* or *rulers* of subjected tribes. Quotations are useless, we only refer to the remarkable description furnished by Bernal Diez of the events at Quiahuiztlan (Vedia II, Cap. XLVI, pp. 40 and 41), which culminated in the violence done to the "recaudadores de Montezuma." This scene, which is highly characteristic, has been beautifully "remodeled," through a few omissions, by our own great *W. H. Prescott* ("*History of the conquest of Mexico*," 1869, Book II, chap. VII, p. 349). There is, finally, abundant proof of the fact that neither the Mexicans, nor any of their confederates, ever attempted to change or subvert the organization and mode of government of any of the tribes whom they overthrew. I refer to *Oviedo y Valdés* (Lib. XXXIII, cap. XLVI, p. 502). *Torquemada* (Lib. XIV, cap. VIII, p. 547). *Ixtlilxochitl* (*Histoire des Chichiměques*, (Cap. XXXVIII, p. 273). *Andrés de Tâpia* ("*Relacion sobre la Conquista*

proper, who dwelt, as elsewhere established by us, on the partly artificial islands in the lagune of the Mexican valley.[7] Besides the prominence acquired by them in the annals of history, it may safely be assumed that, in a general manner, their Institutions are typical of those of other sedentary tribes.[8]

Tribal society, based according to Lewis H. Morgan upon KIN, and not *political* society which rests, according to the same author, upon TERRITORY and PROPERTY, must therefore be looked for among the ancient Mexicans. It remains for us to establish its degree of development, its details, and the manner of its working.

In order to comprehend the true nature of these questions, we should secure as much information as possible of the *past* of the tribe under consideration. Institutions are never wilfully or accidentally created, but evolved; in other words, they are the result of growth in knowledge and experience.[9] The great difference existing between tribal society and political is explained as a dif-

---

de México," Col. de Doc., Vol. II, Icazbalceta, p. 561, and especially p. 592), " México tenia en su tiempo en el hacer guerra esta órden; que yendo ǎ la guerra, al que se daba de paz no tenia sobre él tributo cierto, sino que tantas veces en el año lo llevaban presente ǎ su discrecion del que lo llevaba; pero si era poco mostrábales mal rostro, y si mucho agradeciaselo. Y en estos no ponia mayordomo ni recaudador ni cosa; el señor se era señor. Los que tomaba de guerra decian *tequitin tlacotl,* que quiere decir, tributan como esclavos. En estos ponia mayordomos y recogedores y recaudadores; y aunque los Señores mandaban su gente, eran debajo de la mano destos de México . . . . ." *Motolinia* (Trat. III, cap. VII. p. 185), *Granados y Galvez.* (5th night, p. 168), a singular picture of purest feudality, for which Gomara may be responsible in part. *Ramirez de Fuenleal* (*Letter of 4th Nov.,* 1532, 1st; " *Recueil,*" (pp. 245, 246, and 247). *Zurita* " *Rapport,*" (p. 16), to be compared with Mendieta and Torquemada.

Consequently there was no tendency towards unification or nationalization in all the successful and extensive raids which the Nahuatlaca of the valley of Mexico carried on for a full century. No organic body, larger than the tribe, resulted from these sanguinary forays; because the confederacy itself was not the end, but the beginning of these undertakings. This justifies the view which I shall hereafter advocate in regard to the nature of that confederacy namely: as a mere partnership to carry on the business of warfare the latter in turn being part of the mode of subsistence.

[5] " Based upon territory and property " according to L. H. Morgan, in contra-distinction to tribal-society, based upon " Kin." (" *Ancient Society,*" chapter II, page 62).

[6] "*Art of War,*" p. 95.

[7] "*Art of War,*" p. 150. " *Tenure of Lands,*" pp. 421, 422.

[8] " *Ixtlilxochitl* (*Histoire des Chichimĕques,*" Cap. XXXVI, p. 245). "Ainsi, tout ce qui se dit de Tezcuco doit s'entendre aussi des deux autres, ..." *Gomara* (p. 440, Vedia, I). "To speak of the Mexicans, signifies as much as speaking of all New Spain." The title of the section is: " Costumbres de los hombres," and the original text reads: "Hablando de méjicanos, es hablar en general de toda la Nueva-España." Although *Zurita* (p. 5) insists upon the variety of customs among the aborigines,— changing from settlement to settlement, from tribe to tribe,—his own report furnishes the proof of the contrary, and it is evident from the text that he alludes principally to the diversity in languages and dialects.

[9] *Morgan* (" *Ancient Society,*" Chap. I, p. 6).

ferent state of progress. But Institutions have grown out of the relations between the sexes, and the increase of the human species and its propagation. Had political society existed in Mexico, we should be entitled to find there a plain and definite conception of the family.[10] Whether such is the case a glance at the system of consanguinity of the ancient Mexicans, as far as it may be possible, will tell us.

Among American aborigines of low culture, in fact over the widest area once held by the "Indian" race, "mother-right" ruled supreme. The tangible fact, coarsely expressed, that a child was always sure of his *mother*, whereas it might not be equally certain of his *father*,[11] created in course of time and with increased numbers a tendency to aggregate into clusters whose basis was certainty of descent in common. These clusters were the KINS, significantly termed "lineages" by Spanish authors. Such as traced back their descent to a common mother therefore composed one of these, regardless of their male procreators. The family— consisting of a group which includes children as descendants of *both* parents—was not yet recognized, and the kin took its place for all purposes of public life. It formed the *unit of social organization*. With the growth of knowledge and experience however, and a corresponding increase of wants, the importance of man rose correspondingly. "Mother-right" began to yield ; female descent to change to "descent in the male line." Nevertheless the kin remained the unit of social agglomeration, with the only difference that it was reckoned through males instead of by females. It required the final overthrow of the kin as a public Institution to bring about the present shape of that intimate group, the family, among the most highly advanced nations.[12]

The two extremes of growth of the family, as characterized by the inception of the kin, and by the family after the obliteration

---

[10] (*Ancient Society*," Chap. II, p. 78.) For the so-called "Descriptive System of Relationship," compare. *L. H. Morgan* ("*Systems of Consanguinity and Affinity of the Human Family*," Chap. II, pp. 16, 12, 13).

[11] This assertion is found in various authors. I shall quote but one: *Gregorio Garcia*, ("*Origen de los Indios de el Nuevo Mundo e Indias Occidentales*," second edition, 1729, Madrid, Lib. IV, Cap. XXIII, p. 247).

[12] Although it is entirely out of the line of these researches to enter upon a discussion of Primitive Marriage, I was compelled to refer to the question of kin in such a manner as to explain at least the importance of that group in the history of society. For anything else, the works of Mr. Morgan, Sir Henry S. Maine, John F. Mc Lennan, and some publications of Dr. Ad. Bastian, should be consulted, besides a great number of others too numerous to mention here.

of the former, are distinguished by the terminology of relationship. In the case of the former, relatives are at once classified ; in the latter instance, they are merely described. Now, our investigations of the customs of Inheritance among the ancient Mexicans have led us to the conclusion that they had already achieved progress to *descent in the male line*.[13] *Actual* family existed among them in its incipient form at least.

But we meet here with a singular feature in designating relationships. *Ascending* from the " Ego," as point of departure, we find the following terms in the Mexican (Nahuatl) language.

Father : " tatli "—" teta." [14]

Brother of father or mother (paternal or maternal uncle) : " tlatli " — " tetla." [15]

Grandfather : " tecul." Granduncle : " tecol." [16]

Great-grandfather : " achtontli." [17]

---

[13] " *Tenure of Lands* " (p. 429, note 106).

[14] *Molina* (" *Vocabulario*." Part Ia, p. 91 ; IIa. pp. 106, 91). Besides the plural " tetatzin," the names, " yzcacauhti," " teizcacauh," are also mentioned (I, p. 91). The former is defined (II, p. 48) as " natural father." It derives from " Izcalia " or " ninoizcalia " — " to give life " and " acauhtli." The latter evidently is an abbreviation or corruption from " nitla teachcauhaia " — " to be preferred in what is distributed, or in a distribution " (II, p. 2), which in turn is at the root of " teachcauhtin " — " elder brother " (II, p. 91). It is superfluous here to quote authorities in support of the fact that " ach " is frequently corrupted to " ac," or the inverse. In Cakchiquel: " Tata " See *Brasseur de Bourbourg* (" *Grammaire de la Langue Quichée, etc.*" pp. 217, 218). The root " Ta " is also found in other Indian idioms, See: *Gatschet* (*Zwölf Sprachen aus dem Südwesten Nordamerikas*," p. 137).

[15] *Molina* (I, p. 180; II, p. 140.) All the difference consists in the insertion of the letter " l " after the " t." " Tetla " is but an abbreviation of 'Te-tatli," from " Tehuatl" thou, p. 94, and father, which is also shown in the alteration of " tatli " to " tayta " or " tata ; " the name given by children to their father (p. 91, II). Corresponds to the qquiché " tat " (*Brasseur de Bourbourg*, " *Grammaire, etc.*" p. 218), and to the Muysca " Ze paba " (" Pába " father). *Morgan* after *Uricoechea* (" *Systems of consanguinity*," p. 265).

[16] *Molina* (II, p. 94; II, p. 93). Here again the change from " u " to " o " appears, which is so frequent among older authors. For inst., *Tezcoco* and *Tezcuco*, *Ometochtli* and *Ometuchtli*, *Tlacopan* and *Tlacahuapan*, *Olli* and *Ulli*, etc. etc. Such changes are very excusable, they proceed from the Indian pronunciation of vowels. On this subject compare, although it concerns properly but the Qquichua idiom of Peru, the excellent essay of Señor Don *Gavino Pacheco y Zegarra* of Puno, entitled " *Alphabet phonétique de la langue Qquichua*," published in the 2nd volume of the " *Compte Rendu du Congrès International des Américanistes*," at Nancy, in 1875. He says (p. 303) " D'autre part, le kehua différant essentiellunent des langues romanes, surtout en ce qui concerne les sons élémentaires, il est impossible de donner une idée exacte de ces sons au moyen du seul alphabet latin. . . ." In regard to " O " and " U," see pp. 306, 307, 308. etc. What the author says of the Qquichua applies exactly to the Nahuatl also. See *Molina* (" Prologo y Avisos," 3d page " Aviso septimo").

[17] *Molina* (I, p. 117; II, p. 2). Literally, " little preferred one." Compare *Sahagun* (Lib. X, cap. I, p. 5, 3d Vol).

Mother : " nantli " — " tenantzin " — " teciztli." [18]

Aunt : " auitl "—" teaui." [19]

Grandmother as well as grand-aunt : " citli." [20]

Great-grandmother " piptontli." [21]

Descending from the " Ego."

Son : "tepiltzin," " tetelpuch." But the women (mother, sisters, etc.), call him " noconeuh." [22]

[18] *Molina* (I, p. 80; II, pp. 63, 92, 98). "Ciztli" is probably the same as " Citli,"— hare, or grandaunt. The fact that the same name should be given to a near female relative or even to the mother, and to a fleet, timid, quadruped, is very singular. It may be that the timidity of the animal has given occasion to bestow the name, or, since hare's hair was frequently woven into fine mantles, together with feathers, that this also may have given rise to it. The latter is first mentioned by *Peter Martyr, of Anghiera, " De nouo Orbe,"* or the " *Historie of the West Indies, etc., etc.*" London, 1612. An English translation by Michael Lok and Richard Eden, of the famous " Decades," also entitled " *De Rebus Oceanicis,*" (Dec. V, cap. X, p. 229), he mentions having seen among the objects brought to the court of Spain by Juan de Ribera, garments; "they compact of Conies haire, and they set these feathers in such order between the Cony haire, and intermingle them between the thriddes of the cotton, and weave them in such difficulty, that we do not well understande how they might do it." *Sahagun* (Lib. XI, Cap. 1, p. 157) mentions another animal to which the name " cioatlamacazqui" is given, which he translated "little old woman," basing upon its other designation of " tlamaton."

The reverend father is, however, in error. The first name signifies literally, " woman medicine-man," or " female doctor " (Indian notion of course), and the second "little medicine-man," from " ciuatl " woman, Molina, II, p. 22, "tlama "—medicine-man, (II. 125). This animal seems to be the Raccoon, as the following quotations prove: *Joannis Eusebius Nieremberg,* (" *Historia naturæ maxinæ peregrime,*" Antwerp, 1635 Lib. IX, Cap. XLII, p. 175). "Antra canitates montium atque collium Tzozocolci hospitatur animal peregrinum, quod cuncta manibns praetentat. Mapach ab Indis dicitur, sed non firmo nomine; alij illamaton seu vetulam appellant, alij maxtle seu gossypinum cìngulum, alij cioatlamacazque seu sacerdotissam." *Oviedo y Valdés* (Lib. XII, Cap. XXXIX, p. 422), he calls "Coçumatle," an animal which is probably the Coati, makes no mention of the "mapach," but *Clavigero* (Lib. I, Cap. X, p. 76) treats of this animal fully.

The naming of a female relationship, " Citli" appears the more strange, as this name is given, in the Mexican mythological tales, to a *god* who tried to compel the sun to move, and lost his life in the attempt. This story is due to *Andrés de Olmos,* neither Sahagun nor Motolinia mention the occurrence in this manner. Compare *Sahagun* (Lib. VII. Cap. II, p. 245, etc., etc.); *Mendieta* (Lib. II, Cap. I, pp. 77, 78) and *Torquemada* (Lib. VI, Cap. XLI, p. 76). Both refer it to his authority. We shall refer to it in our essay on " Creed and Belief."

[19] *Molina* (I, 113; II, 9, 91).

[20] *Molina* (I, 113; II, 22). See note 18.

[21] *Molina* (I, p. 117; II, 82). There is also, " nipipinia"—"pararse flaco de vejez," and " Pipinqui ynacayo"—"viejo flaco y arrugado." The affix "tontli" is a diminutive.

[22] *Molina* (I, p. 71). A singular etymology is shown here: The *man* says,

$\begin{Bmatrix} \text{" Thy "} \\ \text{" Their"} \end{Bmatrix}$ boy" or $\begin{Bmatrix} \text{" Thy "} \\ \text{" Their"} \end{Bmatrix}$ youth." ("Te-piltzin"—"Te-telpuch"$\begin{Bmatrix} \text{from " Tehuatl"} \\ \text{or "Te"} \end{Bmatrix}$

$\begin{Bmatrix} \text{" thou "} \\ \text{" their "} \end{Bmatrix}$ and " Piltzintli," child, male or female, (II, p. 82,) and "Telpochtli," youth, (p. 96). The *woman,* however calls: " *my* child " (or boy, since the same name is for both

Daughter: "teichpuch," "tepiltzin." Women call her "teconeuh." [23]

Grandson or granddaughter, male or female cousin, are called alike, to wit: "yxiuhtli"—"teixiuh." [24]

Nephew and niece are called: "machtli"—"temach" by the males. The females however address them: "nopilo." [25]

This brings to light some very curious facts.

In the first place, the following grades of consanguinity are called by the same names respectively: grandfather and grand-uncle, grandmother and grand-aunt, father and uncle, grand-daughter, grandson and cousin, nephew and niece.

---

sexes), from "conetl"—"niño o niña" (II, p. 24), and the possessive pronoun "no" according to *H. H. Bancroft,* "*Native Races of the Pacific States,*" (Vol. III, Cap. IX, p. 734), or "noca"—"of me" (*Molina,* II, 72). These are, however, not the only appellations. We have besides:

Children of both sexes and grandchildren, collectively: "tepilhuan, teixhuan" (I, p. 71). The first one is easily decomposed into "te" theirs, "piltzuitli" child, and a possessive affix "huan" *Bancroft* ("*Native Races,*" Vol. III, Cap. IX, p. 732).

Oldest son or daughter "teyacapan" "yacapantli" (p. 71, I). From "nicyacatia," to be the first or leader (II, p. 22), "yacatl"—nose probably on account of its protuberance, (II, p. 22).

Second son or daughter, "tlacoyeua" "tetlamamallo" (p. 71, I). The first one might possibly derive from "centlacol"—one-half (I, p. 83), since Molina adds (II, p. 118), "el segundo hijo ó hija, o de tres o quatro engendrados ó nacidos." The etymology of the other, if correct, would be singular. It is either from "tetla" uncle, and "tetlan nina mamali" "hender, meterse entre mucha gente" (II, p. 52), or from "te" their and, "Tlamama" carrier of a load (II, p. 125). In both cases it indicates an inferior position.

Youngest son or daughter "xocoyotl" "texocoyouh" (I, p. 71). Definitions too doubtful. Finally, there are the surnames, or caresses, like, "cuzcatlquetzalli"—collar of changing green hues,—"tecuzcauan"—"tequetzalhuan" (I, p. 71), which all have the same significance, in a general way, of "precious gem" or "jewel." These metaphorical names are found profusely in *Tezozomoc* ("*Crónica Mexicana.*")

The fact, above noticed, that while men, if strangers, address boys, "their boy," while women call them "my boy," is perhaps significant. It might be a lingering remnant of "mother-right."

[23] *Molina* (I, 71), derives from "Ichpocatl" (girl, II, p, 32.) So far teichpeuh,—the other two are already explained.

[24] *Molina* (I, pp. 88, 98). But there is also. "Nieto ó nieta dos vezes," "ycutontli" "teicuton." Now, according to the same authority (II, p. 34), the older brother or sister calls the younger "n. icuh" ("n" as abbreviation to "no"). Consequently, the signification would be, "little younger brother or sister."

[25] *Molina* (I, p. 109; II, 51, 73). In this case the woman again calls them "my child" ("no" my, and "piltzintli" child). The custom of giving different names to relationships, by women and by men, is found in Peru among the Qquichua and Inca. Compare *Garcilasso de la Vega,* "*Histoire des Incas Rois du Pérou.*" (French translation from the original Spanish, by J. Baudouin, Amsterdam, 1704. Lib. IV, Cap. XI, Vol. I, pp. 359, 360). *J. J. von Tschudi* ("*Peru*" *Reiseskizzen,* St. Gall, 1846, an excellent book. Vol. II, Cap. X, p. 380). A similar custom also appears in New Granada among the Muysca. *L. H. Morgan* ("*Systems of Consanguinity, etc..*" p. 265, after *Uricoechea*).

Secondly, the relationships in the descending scale are more closely described than those in the ascending scale.

Thirdly, in some instances women give different names from those given by men.

It results from it, that the classificatory system still, to a great extent, predominated in the ancient Mexican nomenclature for relationship, while the more modern descriptive system appears in a minority of cases only. This leads to the inference that the Mexican family itself was yet but imperfectly constituted. It was not yet so established as to form a definite group and hence cannot be expected to exercise any influence in the matter of public social life. We are, therefore, again justified in looking to the *kin* as the unit of social organization, within the limits of that widest aggregate, the tribe.[26]

Traditionary tales about the earliest settlement of man in Mexico as well as in Central America, distinctly ascribe it to " lineages " or relationships. The tribe is merely implied, and appears in a definite form only *after* this settlement has already occurred.

The " Popol-Vuh," or gathering of the cosmological and traditionary records of the QQuiché tribe of Guatemala, after enumerating the four wives of the four first men created, even says: " These [their spouses], engendered mankind, the large and small tribes : and they were the stock of us, of the QQuiché tribe." This indicates, perhaps, descent in the female line at a very early date.[27]

---

[26] *Dr. Adolphus Bastian,* " *Ueber die Eheverhältnisse,*" ("*Zeitschrift für Ethnologie,*" Berlin, Vol. V, 1874) presupposes a family, definite and distinct: "Aus der Ehe, als erster Kreisung der Gesellschaft geht die Familie hervor, in ausgedehnter Peripherie als gens (unter Erweiterung durch die Agnaten) aus ursprusnglichen Patriciern; wo der Clan unter Aufuahme fictiver Venrwandten und zugehörigen seinen abschluss unter den Patriarchen bewahrt." Such views offer a sufficient explanation, when applied indiscriminately to the inhabitants of *all* the continents, why the organization of some aborigines of this continent is still regarded as monarchical. The nature and functions of the Indian kin are completely misunderstood and proportionately misrepresented. (See also Id., p. 396.)

[27] " *Popol-Vuh* " (Translated from the original QQuiché by the *Abbé Charles Etienne Brasseur de Bourbourg,* Paris, 1861, Part III, cap. III, p. 205). " E pogol vinak, chuti amag, nima amag; are cut u xe kech, ri oh Queche-vinak; tzatz cut x-uxic ri Ahqixb Ahqahb; mana xa E cáhib chic x-uxic, xere cahib ri qui chuch oh quiche vinak." Mr. Brasseur translates " vinak " alternately as men, tribes, and nations. According to his own vocabulary, however, it means but " man " or " the increase " (See " *Grammaire QQuiché,*" p. 233). In his translation of the " *Rabinal-Achi*" ("*Grammaire*" First Scene, pp. 27 and 35, and other places), " vinak " is also rendered as chief. But the true QQuiché word for tribe is " amag " ("*Grammaire,*" p. 167). This alters the sense to the extent that instead of "QQuiché tribe " it should read "men of QQuiché" or rather "QQuiché

The first settlement of Chiapas is ascribed, in the tale of Votan, to *seven families*.[28] But there is still another and more remarkable tradition connected with it. Like the Aborigines of Mexico of *Nahuatl* stock, the *Tarasca* of Michhuacan, the *Maya* of Yucatan, and the *QQuiché, Cakchiquel* and *Zutuhil* of Guatemala, the Aborigines of Chiapas had a month composed of twenty days, bearing each a particular name. It is positively asserted by very old authority, that these twenty days were named after as many chiefs of an equal number of lineages or kins, the latter being the earliest settlers of the country. Furthermore, among these twenty names, four are everywhere prominently distinguished.

men." The last words " xere cahib ri qui chuch oh Quiché vinak," are literally: " though four these (which, who) certainly (surely) mother us (we) QQuiché men." The note by the celebrated Abbé (p. 207, note 3), in which he states that "mother" is often applied to chief, finds a parallel in many passages of *Tezozomoc* when the tribe is also addressed as father and mother. Also *Durán* (Cap. XV, p. 127).

The creation of these four men and four women immediately precedes, in the Popol-Vuh, the tale of the first sacrifice and the distribution of the idols, and is distinctly stated as having occurred during the time of obscurity, the morning star being their only guide and most brilliant luminary (" *Popol-Vuh*," pp. 209, 211, and 213). Now an analogous tale is told by *Sahagun* (Lib. VII, cap. II, p. 248, etc.), about the first appearance of both sun and moon. The Gods disputed about the place where the two celestial bodies would rise, and *four* of them, together with *four* women, looked to the *east* for their coming. The QQuiché tradition (p. 207), places the coming of these first people also in the East. It appears to be, therefore, a tradition originally common to the " Nahuatl " and to the " QQuiché," and its bearing upon the question at issue becomes still more prominent.

[28] The two leading sources on Chiapas namely: *Nuñez de la Vega* (" *Constitution diocesana del Estado de Chiapas*, Roma, 1702), and *Fray Antonio de Remesal* (" *Historia de la Provincia de Chyapa y Guatemala de la Orden de Santo Domingo*," 1619), not being at my command now,—I can but refer the student to them, and to the following works besides: *Lorenzo Boturini Benaducci* (" *Idea de una Nueva Historia General de la America Septentrional*," Madrid, 1776, § XVI, p. 115, copying *Nuñez de la Vega*, 34, § XXX), *Mariano Veytia y Echeverria* (" *Historia antigua de Méjico*," 1836, by Ortega, Vol. I, cap. II, p. 15). *Clavigero* (Lib. II. cap. XII, pp. 164 and 165). *Paul Felix Cabrera* (" *Teatro critico Americano*," german translation by Lieut. *General J. H von Minutoli*, incorporated in the latter's book. " *Beschreibung einer alten Stadt, die in Guatimala (Neuspanien) unfern Palenque entdeckt worden ist*," p. 30. etc., after Vega also). *Brasseur de Bourbourg* (" *Popol-Vuh*" Introduction, pp. LXXIII, LXXXVII, CXII, etc.). *Alex. von Humboldt* (" *Vues des Cordillères et monuments des peuples indigènes de l' Amérique*," 1861, Vol. I, pp. 382 and 383; II, pp. 356 and 357). *Bancroft, H. H.*, (Vol. III, cap, X, pp. 450 and 454; and especially Vol. V, cap. III, from p. 159 on). As usual, very full and valuable, although he does not mention any source older than Nuñez de la Vega. Finally, *A. Bastian* (" *Die Culturlaender des alten Amerika*," 1878, Vol. II, pp. 360 and 362). The latter says that Votan found Chiapas already peopled. This is not confirmed by what I know of Vega and of the other (later) authority *Don Ramon Ordoñez y Aguiar* (" *Hisotria de la Creacion del Cielo y de la Tierra*" MSS. at the " Museo Nacional " of Mexico). Votan was " sent to divide and distribute the land " *Cabrera* says (" *Beschreibung, etc.*," " *Teatro*," p. 33), basing upon verbal communications of *Ordonnez y Aguiar*: " He (Votan) assures, that he brought seven families to this continent, of Valum Votan, and assigned land to them."

They not only indicate the first day of each "week" of five days, but they also designate the years of the calendar. It is well-known that the largest authentically established cycle of Central American and Mexican natives consisted of 52 years, that is of a thirteen-fold recurrence of the same series of four, named alike, respectively as one of the four initial days of the weekly indictions. This peculiarity, coupled with the positive description furnished in the "Popol-Vuh" of the segmentation of four original kins into a number of smaller ones, and with the fact that nearly every aboriginal settlement, at the present time, divides into four principal groups of inhabitants, becomes suggestive of the inference, not only that the consanguine group was the original type of social organization at the remotest period, but that the ethnography of Mexico and Central America may even be derived from a segmentation of primitive kins, and reassociation of these fragments into tribes, under the influence of time and mutation of residence, dialectical variation aiding.[29]

[29] Without quoting superfluously to prove well-known facts — household words so to say, in Mexican and Central-American archæology — we will place side by side the names of the days of the Mexican, Nicaraguan, Yucatecan, QQuiché, Chiapanecan, and Tarascan month.

NAHUATL.			MAYA.		TZENDAL. Chiapas and Soconusco.
Mexican.	Niquiran.	Tarascan.	Maya.	QQuiché.	
Cipactli,	Cipat,	Inbeari,	Ymix,	Imox,	Imox,
Ehecatl,	Ecat or Hecat,	Inthaati,	Yk,	Ig,	Igh,
Calli,	Cali,	Inbani,	Akbal,	Akbal,	Votan,
Cuetzpalin,	Quespal,	Inxichari,	Kan,	Qat	Chanan,
Cohuatl,	Coat,	Inchini,	Chicchan,	Can,	Abah,
Miquiztli,	Missiste,	Inrini,	Quimij,	Camey,	Tox,
Mazatl,	Macet, ˙	Inpari,	Manik,	Quich,	Moxic,
Tochtli,	Toste,	Inchon,	Lamat,	Ganel,	Lambat,
Atl,	At.	Inthahui,	Muluc,	Toh,	Molo,
Ytzcuintli,	Yzquindi,	Intzini,	Oc,	Tzy,	Elab
Ozomatli,	Ocomate,	Intzoniabi,	Chuen,	Batz,	Batz,
Malinalli,	Malinal,	Intzimbi,	Eb,	Ci,	Evob,
Acatl,	Acato,	Inthihui,	Been,	Ah,	Been,
Ocelotl,	Oçelot,	Inixotzini,	Gix,	Itz,	Hix,
Quauhtli,	Oate,	Inichini,	Men,	Tziquin	Tzibin,
Cozcaquauhtli,	Coscagoate,	Iniabi,	Quib,	Ahmak,	Chabin,
Ollin,	Olin,	Intaniri,	Caban,	Noh,	Chic,
Tecpatl,	Tapecat,	Inodon,	Edznab,	Tihax,	Chinax,
Quiahiutl,	Quiaüit,	Iniubi,	Cauac,	Caok,	Cahogh,
Xochitl.	Sochit.	Inettuni.	Ajau.	Hunahpu.	Aghual.

The four leaders (as I may be permitted to call them), are respectively: In Mexico, *Tochtli, Acatl, Tecpatl, Calli.* In Michhuacan, *Inchon, Inthihui, Inodon, Inbani.* In Chiapas, *Votan, Lambat, Been, Chinax.* In Guatemala, *Akbal, Ganel, Ah, Tihax.* Finally in Yucatan, *Kan, Muluc, Gix, Cauac.*

I have not the means of discussing the Tarascan calendar of Michhuacan; it is suf-

.It is not surprising therefore if, of the earliest traces which are
met with concerning such Aborigines as spoke the "good sound"

ficient for my purpose to establish its identity, in system, with the others. The Nicaraguan days are corruptions of the Mexican names, the "Niquiran" being a "Nahuatl"
dialect.

Taking now the four remaining groups, we place opposite to each word its translation or interpretation so far as I can trace it, which is of course not always possible.

Mexican.	*QQuiché.*	*Maya.*	*Chiapaneco.*
Cipactli, *Marine mon-ster.*	Imox, *Swordfish.*	Ymix. *Dragon.*	Imox.
	Ig, *Breath.*	Yk, *Breath or wind.*	Igh.
Ehecatl, *Wind.*	Akbal, *chaos* (?).	Akbal, (See below).	*Votan.*
Calli, House.	Cat, *Lizard.*	*Kan. Snake.*	Chanan, *Snake.*
Cuetzpalin, *Lizard.*	Can, *Snake.*	Chicchan.	Abah, *Stone* (?).
Cohuatl, *Snake.*	Camey, *Death.*	Quimij, *Death.*	Tox.
Miquiztli, *Skull.*	Quich, *Deer.*	Manik, (See below).	Moxic.
Mazatl, *Deer.*	Ganel, *Rabbit.*	Lamat.	*Lambat.*
Tochtli, Rabbit.	Toh, *Shower.*	*Muluc.*	Molo.
Atl, *Water.*	Tzy, *Dog.*	Oc.	Elab.
Ytzcuintli, *Dog.*	Batz, *Monkey.*	Chuen. (See below).	Batz, *Monkey* (?).
Ozomatli, *Monkey.*	Ci, *Broom.*	Eb, *Staircase.*	Eoob.
Malinalli,*Knot or twist*	Ah, *Cane.*	Been.	*Been.*
Acatl, Cane.	Itz, *Wizard.*	*Gix, Wizard.*	Hix.
Ocelotl, *Wild cat or tiger.*	Tziquin, *Bird.*	Men, *Builder* (?).	Tzibin.
	Ahmak, *Owl.*	Quib, *Gum or wax.*	Chabin.
Quauhtli, *Eagle.*	Noh, *Temperature.*	Caban.	Chic.
Cozcaquauhtli, *Vul-ture.*	Tihax, *Obsidian.*	Edznab.	*Chinax.*
	Caok, *Rain.*	*Cauic.*	Cahogh.
Ollin, *Motion.*	Hunahpu, *Shooter out of a tube.*	Ajau, *Chief.*	Aghual.
Tecpatl, flint.			
Quiahuitl, *Rain.*			
Xochitl, *flower.*			

For the interpretation, as above attempted, I have consulted the following very
limited number of authors: — *Brasseur de Bourbourg* (" *Relation des choses de Yuc
atan, etc.*" " *Popol-Vuh,*" " *Grammaire Quiché,*" " *Ruines de Palenqué,*") H. H. *Bancroft,*
(Vol. II and III). *Orozco y Berra,* (" *Geografia de las Lenguas,*") and other sources.
Mr. Bancroft translates the QQuiché "akbal" by *chaos.* I would suggest " *household,*"
båsing upon the following note of Mr. Brasseur: (" *Chronologia antigua de Yucatan,
etc.,*" por *Don Juan Pio Perez* in "Choses de Yucatan," p. 375). "*Akbal,* mot vielli qu'
on retrouve dans la langue Quiché avec le sens de marmite, vase, peut être le même que
le mot *con* ou *comitl* des Mexicains." Sr. Perez says about the word: "desconocido:
tambien se halla entre los dias chiapanecas, escrito *Aghual,*" (p. 374). In this the learned
Yucatan is mistaken, for Aghual corresponds to the Maya and QQuiché "Ajau" or
"Ahau." Now the pot or rather kettle, was distinctly connected with the housewife,
and the word "Akbal" being, as the Abbé tells us, out of use, the suggestion that it
may have been used to indicate something like the Mexican "Calli"—house,—is at
least permitted.

I have deliberately translated "Kan" by snake, instead of by "cord of hennequen"
as Pio-Perez has it (p. 372). Compare note 1 by the Abbé.

Manik is interpreted by Pio-Perez as follows: " es perdida su verdadera acepcion;
pero si se divide la espresion man-ik viento que pasa, quizá se entenderia lo que fué."
If this is accepted, then the signification might be: " fleetness," " swiftness," or "rap-
idity,"— some of the attributes of the *deer,* which is the corresponding sign in both the
Mexican and QQuiché.

Chuen, for the reasons indicated by Brasseur (note 3, p. 372 of " *Chronologia, etc.,*")
should be " monkey," as well as in the three other idioms.

In regard to "Gix" *Sr. Orozco y Berra* (Part II, V, p. 103), copies the three inter-
pretations of Don Pio-Perez, one of which amounts to " the act of plundering or rob-

or " Nahuatl " language in Mexico, we gather the information that they started off in bands constituting "lineages" or kins. This

bing a tree." Might there be any vague connection between this and the Mexican " Ocelotl " or beast of prey?

The word " Cauac " is mentioned as " desconocido " or disused. Still the analogy in sound with the QQuiché " Caok " rain, is striking, as well as with the Tzendal " Cahogh " and finally also with the Mexican " Quiahuitl."

In regard to the calendar of Chiapas, I regret to say that the material at my command is by far too limited to venture much of an interpretation. Not one of the few Tzendal vocabularies or Grammars yet existing is within my reach. Still I must note here: " Chan " in Tzendal signifies *Snake*, therefore my translation of " Chanan." *Brasseur de Bourbourg* (" *Recherches sur les Ruines de Palenqué*," Cap. II, p. 32, notes 4 and 5).

" Abah " probably *Stone* (" *Palenqué*," p. 65, note 5).

" Batz " as *monkey*, is identified with the three other signs of the same day by *Brasseur* (" *Popol-Vuh*," Introd. p. CXXXV, note 5, Part II, cap. I, p. 69, note 4).

Furthermore, the signs Imox, Igh, Hix, and Cahogh are, in sound at least, analogous, if not identical, with the corresponding signs of the QQuiché and Maya calendars, and the signs Lambat, Molo, Been, and Aghual, are nearly alike to those of the same days of the Maya alone, whereas, Tzibin reminds of the Tziquin in QQuiché.

Taking now the Mexican calendar as a basis, we cannot fail to notice:

(1). That fifteen of its signs are identical with those of the QQuiché.

(2). Three are absolutely identical with signs of the Maya, and five more are presumably identical also.

(3). Two are identical with signs of the Tzendal, and two more presumably so.

Therefore our assumption appears justified, that:—

(1). The Mexican and QQuiché names of the days have a common origin.

(2). That the same is likely in regard to the Maya, since the Maya and QQuiché are regarded as belonging, linguistically, to the same stock.

(3). That a presumption in favor of a similar relation towards the Tzendal of Chiapas may be admitted since, besides the four signs recognized as common to both calendars, there are at least eight more which, in sound, are identical with others of the Maya and QQuichè.

I feel authorized, consequently, to conclude:—

(1). That the names of the days given by the four linguistical clusters above stated, were probably, originally identical.

(2). That these names, therefore, *had a common origin*.

This origin is stated as follows:—

Mendieta (Lib. IV, cap. XLI, p. 537), "and these Indians affirmed, that in ancient times there came to this land twenty men, and the chief of them was called Cacalcan. . . . . This writes the bishop of Chiapas. . . ." This bishop of Chiapas was *Fray Bartolomé de Las Casas*, who, in the MSS., " *Historia apologética de Indias*" (Vol. III, cap. 124), appears to be more detailed. I quote Las Casas from *Brasseur* and from *H. H. Bancroft*, (Vol. 3, p. 465), where he says (Cap. 123),—the MS. itself not being accessible to me. Now it is commonly admitted, and this admission (whether correct or not) is so general, that no quotations are needed in evidence, that Cuculcan or Cocolcan is identical with the Mexican Quetzalcohuatl. To Quetzalcohuatl, however, is attributed the formation of the *Mexican Calendar*. (*Torquemada*, Lib. VI, cap. XXIV, p. 52. *Mendieta*, Lib. II, cap. XIV, pp. 97, 98.)

In regard to the origin of the Tzendal Calendar, the tradition is very clear. *Boturini* (" *Idea*, etc.," § XVI, pp. 115 to 121). Quoting *Nuñez de la Vega* (32, § XXVIII of the " *Constitucion Diocesana* ") " y prosigue el Prelado diciendo, que *al que llamaban Coslàhuntox (que es el Demonio, segun los Indios dicen, con trece potestades) le tienen pintado en Silla, y con hastas en la cabeza como de carnero*, quando dicho Coslahúntox se ha de corregir en Ymos, ó Mox, y no está puesto en el Kalendario por Demonio,

was the case with the so-called "Toltecs," [30] and with all their successors, such as the "Tezcucans," "Tecpanecans," and others, *including the ancient Mexicans.*[31]

sino por cabeza de los veinte Señores, Symbolos de los dias de el Año, y assi viene ă ser el primer Symbolo de ellos." (See also Idem, pp. 118, 119, quoting Nuñez de la Vega, 33, 34, and 35). "concuerda el Systema de los Kalendarios de Chiàppa, y Soconùsco con el Tultéco, ... pues en lugar de los quatro Caractéres Tècpatl, Calli, Tóchtli, Acatl, se sirven los de Chiăppa de quatro Figuras de Señores, Votan, Lambat, Bèen, y Chinax, etc., etc."

Clavigero (Lib. II, cap. XII, p. 164). "The Chiapanecs, if we can place any reliance upon their traditions, were the first settlers of the New World. They claim that Votan, the grandson of the venerable old man who built the great ark in order to save himself and his family during the deluge, and who was one of those who erected the high building that reached into the clouds, set out by special command of God, to people the country." Adopted and quoted also by Señor Don *Francisco Pimentel,* (" *Cuadro Descriptivo y Comparativo de las Lenguas Indigénas de México,*" 1865, Vol. II, p. 232.) *Clavigero* (Lib. VI, cap. XXIX, p. 412, Vol. I) "The Chiapanecs . . . . instead of the figures and names of the rabbit, cane, flint, and house, used the names Votan, Lambat, Been, and Chinax, and instead of the Mexican names of the days, they adopted those of twenty celebrated men of their ancestry, among which the four names above mentioned took the same place as among the Mexicans the Rabbit and the others." Compare also, in the appendix to the same volume, p. 633, the " *Letter of the Abbé Don Lorenzo Hervas,*" Cesena, 31 July, 1780. *Clavigero* (Vol. II, "Dissertations, etc.," Cap. II, p. 281). After recalling the tradition of Votan, quoting from Nuñez de la Vega, he adds in note b, "Votan is the name of the leader of the 20 celebrated men, after which the 20 days of the month of the Chiapanecs are named."

These statements, which rest upon the writings of Nuñez de la Vega and of Ordonnez y Aguiar, are adopted, among later writers, by :—

Brasseur de Bourbourg (" *Popol-Vuh,*" Introduction, § V, p. LXXII. " *Chronologia,*" in " *Relation des choses du Yucatan,*" p. 374, note 4).

The identity of the twenty days of the Chiapanecan months with the names of twenty leaders of as many kins, is very likely, therefore; and since we have found the close resemblance of the Chiapanecan Calendar with that of the Yucatecan Maya, it is not unreasonable to suggest: that the names of the Maya days originally denoted the same twenty kins also. If such is the case (as the tale of Cuculcan and of his nineteen followers also seems to indicate), then the twenty signs of the QQuiché have a similar origin and finally, the actual identity of the QQuiché Calendar with the Mexican or Nahuatl proper leads to the inference that the twenty names of days of the Tzendal, Maya, and Nahuatl groups of sedentary Indians in Mexico and Central America, indicate *a common origin of these three clusters, from twenty kins or clans, or gentes,* at a remote period.

Within these twenty kins there appear *four* more prominent than the other. This again may indicate a *still older* derivation from *four,* out of which the remaining sixteen sprang through segmentation. How such segmentation may occur is plainly stated in the " *Popol-Vuh,*" and has been fully referred to by me in " *Ténure of Lands*" (p. 391, 392, note 7), to which, in addition to the Indian authority, and to Mr. Morgan's "*Ancient Society*" (Part II, Chapter IV), I beg leave to direct the " curious reader." In regard to the actually prevailing division of Indian settlements into four quarters, it is asserted by *Brasseur de Bourbourg* (" *Popol-Vuh,*" Introduction, p. 117), " Enfin, presque toutes les villes ou tribus sont partagées en quatre clans ou quartiers, dont les chefs forment le grand conseil."

I give the above as mere suggestions, begging for their acceptance in a kindly way, since they are not intended to be thrust upon the reader as "results." But I cannot resist the temptation to submit some remarks here, on other peculiarities exhibited

About the middle of the thirteenth century the Mexicans
while on a migration towards more southern regions, made

by the so-called calendars just named, which peculiarities may throw some light on
the questions raised, as to whether they originally denoted kins or not.

With a single exception (Cipactli), the Mexican and allied calendars contained the
name of not one object, or phenomenon, which might not be met with *somewhere* over
the wide area which the three linguistical stocks occupied at the time of the Conquest.
Still, as Sr. Orozco y Berra strikingly proves (" *Géografia de las Lenguas*," Parte IIa,
Cap. V, p, 107), the Mexican month contains the names of animals unknown to the
ultimate home of the tribe as well as to more *northern* regions. Thus the *monkey*
("Ozomatli") is not found on the high central tableland. In regard to the sign
Cipactli, I shall elsewhere refer to this sign, which may perhaps denote a " cuttle-fish "
of monstrous dimensions.

Supposing now (since we have no proof yet to the contrary), that this "marine
monster" was also an inhabitant of tropical seas, it must strike us that the twenty
signs for the days of the aboriginal calendars under consideration

    (1). Represent types and phenomena which are met with, *not exclusively, but still
        all*, within the area of Mexico and Central America.

    (2). That some of the animal types are limited to tropical and low regions only.

    (3). That none of the animals belong exclusively to the temperate zone of North
        America.

Consequently, that these signs are of a meridional origin, and even, taking into
account that the monkey is not found in the valley of Mexico, that they originated to
the *south* of it. Still, the four " Leaders," as I have called them (the first signs of
each " week " of five days), namely: Rabbit, cane, flint, and house,—might as well
have been selected at the *north*.

It is a fact abundantly proven, that the kins or gentes composing the tribes of North
America are named after a principle identical with that found in the naming of the
days among the aborigines of more southerly latitudes, namely : after objects and
natural phenomena. Mr. Morgan has given the names of the gentes of at least thirty
tribes, consisting in all of two hundred and ninety-six gentes. Of these two hundred
and ninety-six names, ninety-eight are signs of the Mexican days, repeatedly found in
the different tribes. These signs are as follows :—

Itzcuintli. Dog, mostly found, however, as wolf	22 times.
Quauhtli, Eagle	12 "
Cozcaquauhtli, Hawk (although it is the "ringed vulture")	8 "
Mazatl. Deer, Elk, Caribou, Antelope	20 "
Cohuatl, Snake	9 "
Atl, Water (also as " Ice," " Sea," etc.)	4 "
Miquiztli, Skull (as " Head ")	1 time.
Ollin (as " many seasons " and " Sun ")	2 times.
Calli. House (as " high village " and " lodge ")	3 "
Tecpatl. Flint (as " knife ")	2 "
Ocelotl, Tiger (also as " panther " and " wild cat ")	5 "
Ehecatl, Wind	1 time.
Acatl. Cane (also as " Indian corn ")	3 times.
Tochtli, Rabbit (also as " hare ")	3 "
Cuetzpalin. Lizard ("frog ")	1 time.
Xochitl. Flower (as " Tobacco ")	1 "
Quiahuitl, Rain	1 "

I beg to observe, that if I have added " Cozcaquauhtli " to this list, supposing it to
be the equivalent of " Hawk," this is a mere suggestion, and not an affirmation on my
part.

Thus sixteen, if not seventeen, of the twenty signs of days of the Mexican month,
are found in North America as " *totems* " *probably of aboriginal clans or kins.*

It is further interesting to note, that of the nine clans composing the Moqui tribes
of Arizona, the names of seven correspond to signs of Mexican days, ("*Ancient
Society,*" Part II, p. 179). What little is known of the Laguna Indians foreshadows a
similar result (p. 180), thus permitting the query, whether the pueblo Indians of the

their first appearance in the northern sections of the former republic of Mexico, as a cluster of seven kins, united by the bond of common language and worship.[32] The names of these seven kins are distinctly stated and it is not devoid of interest to notice that some of these names were perpetuated as late as 1690 among the numerous "Indian wards" of the present City of Mexico.[33] We may as well add here, that these

central west might not perhaps show a closer connection yet between the very ancient Mexican kins as denoted by their days, and the gentes composing their own tribes.

After these speculations, which I submit for what they may be worth, and with the distinct reserve that I do not attach any value to them save as hints and queries for further investigation, I beg leave to state, that in my fourth paper "On the Creed and Belief of the Ancient Mexicans," I intend to discuss all these points with more thoroughness, and, I hope, with the aid of more suitable material than that now at my command.

[30] *Ixtlilxochitl* ("*Relaciones historicas*" "*Segunda Relacion*," Kingsborough, Vol. IX, p. 323) "y casi el ultimo de estos años se juntaron dos cabezas principales y los otros cinco inferiores à tratar si se quedarian en esta tierra ó si pasarian mas adelante." Also "*Noticias de los Pobladores y Naciones de esta Parte de America llamada Nueva-España*" ("*Tercera Relacion de los Tultecas*," Kingsborough, IX, p. 393), "Estos siete caudillos . . . . . con todas sus gentes viniéron descubriendo y poblando por todas las partes que llegaban." ("*Histoire des Chichimèques*," Cap. I, p. 13), "Ils avaient sept chefs, et choisissaient alternativement un d'entr'eux pour les gouverner." In addition to authorities quoted on the Toltecs in "*Tenure of Lands*" (p. 388, note 7, to p. 392). I refer to *Vetancurt* ("*Teatro Mexicano*," Vol I, Part II, Trat. I. Cap. IV, p. 234). *Granados y Galvez* (2a Tarde, p. 31).

[31] "*Tardes Americanas*" (p. 31), "bien es que los mapas de estos no nos pintan tierras, sino familias: y como estos vaguearon sin fixeza alguna por tan varios rumbos. . . . . ." It is superfluous to quote authorities in full, I but refer to "*Histoire des Chichimèques*" (Cap. V, pp. 38, 39; X, p. 70). *Sahagun* (Lib. X, cap. XXIX). The whole chapter is very important. *Durán* (Cap. II, pp. 10, 11, 12, 13, 14, 15, 16, III; pp. 19, 20, 21, and plates I, to Trat. I°, also pl. I, to Trat. II°). *Acosta* (Lib. VII, cap. II, p. 454, and cap. III entire). *Mendieta* (Lib. II. cap. XXXIV, p. 147). *Torquemada* (Lib. I, cap. XXIII, p. 51; cap. XXVI, p. 54; Lib. II, cap. I. p. 78, etc.). *Garcia* ("*Origen*, etc.," Lib. III, cap. I, p. 81; Lib. V, cap. III, p. 321). *Herrera* (Dec. III, Lib. II. cap. X, pp. 59, 60). *Veytia* (Lib. II, cap. VI, p. 39 of 2d Vol.). *Vetancurt* (Vol. I, "*Teatro*," Parte II, Trat. I, cap. IX, pp. 254, 255). *Clavigero* (Lib. II, cap. IV, pp. 146, 147), and others.

[32] The number *seven* (7) is almost generally accepted. Compare "*Tenure of Lands*" (p. 399, and note 21). Besides the authors there mentioned as accepting seven kins, I refer to *Dr. Ad. Bastian* ("*Die Culturlaender des Alten Amerika*," Vol. II, p. 460, note 2). *Cabrera* (in *Minutoli's Palenqué*, p. 77. Rather confused).

[33] I have gathered these names out of the following sources: *Durán* (Cap. III, pp. 20, 21), *Tezozomoc* (Cap. I, p. 6, Kingsborough, Vol. IX), *Veytia* (Lib. II, cap. XII, p. 91 of 2d Vol.). They are stated as follows: —

By Durán.	*By Tezozomoc.*	*By Veytia.*
Yopica.	Yapica.	Yopica.
Tlacochcalca.	Tlacochcalca.	Tlacochcalca.
Vitznagoa.	Huitznahuac.	Huitznahuac.
Cuatecpan.	Cihuatecpaneca.	Cihuatecpaneca.
Chalmeca.	Chalmeca.	Chalmeca.
Tlacatecpaneca.	Tlacatecpaneca.	Tlacatecpaneca.
Yzquiteca.	Yzquiteca.	Itzcuintecatl.

Indian wards, their peculiar organization, and their communal lands, disappeared only after the secession of Mexico from Spain, not more than fifty years ago.[34]

There is, however, a fundamental difference between Durán on one hand, and Veytia and Tezozomoc on the other, inasmuch as the former says that these seven names were those of the *tutelar deities* of the seven kins ("barrios"), whereas the latter two give them as the names of *these kins themselves*. The seven tutelar deities are also named by them, and called as follows: "Quetzalcohuatl, Tlazolteotl, Macuilxochiquetzalli, Chichilticcenteotl, Piltzinteuhtli, Tezcatlipuca, and Mictlanteuhtli" (*Veytia*, as above quoted). *Tezozomoc* (p. 6), calls these gods: "Quetzalcohuatl, Oxomoco, Matlaxochiquetzal, Chichilticzenteutl, Piltzintecutli, Meteutl, Tezcatlipuca, Mictlantecuhtli y Tlamacazqui, y otros dioses con ellas. . . . . ." A discussion of these names is very difficult, and its results appear doubtful. Still, we distinctly recognize: "Tlacochcalca," plural of "Tlacochcalcatl," therefore, "men of the house of darts." (See "*Art of War*," p. 121, note 104). "Huitznahuac," according to *Molina* (IIa, p. 157), "uitztic" is a pointed object, "uitztli" a large thorn, but "uitztlan" is the south. "Nahuac," in this instance, probably (or rather possibly), signifies "among" or "near to," thus perhaps, "people from the south" or "from near the thorns." (Example: "Quauhnahuac"—"por de los arboles," *Molina*, II, p. 63. *Pimentel* "*Cuadro descriptivo*, Vol. I, pp. 170, etc.) "Cihuatecpaneca" from "Cihuatl" woman, and "tecpan" official house. "Tlacatecpaneca" from "Tlacatl" man, and "tecpan." Finally, "Itzcuintecatl" seems to derive from "Itzcuintli" Dog, and "tecatl." The latter again decomposes into: "nitla tequi" to cut (*Molina*, II, p. 105), and "tlacatl" man, therefore the whole would be "dogcutters." "Yzquitecatl" gives a still more curious etymology, which is, however, so improbable, that we refrain from mentioning it even

It will be seen at a glance that none of these seven kins were named after the Mexican days, the last one alone containing, perhaps, the word "Itzcuintli," but even this is very doubtful yet. I shall but refer here to a singular passage in *Durán* (Cap. III, p. 20). "Ya hemos dicho como traian á su principal dios, sin cuyo mandado no se osaban menear: traian empero otros siete dioses, que á contemplacion de los siete cuevas donde auian auitado siete congregaciones de gentes ó siete parcialidades, los reverenciaban con mucha grandeza."

After the capture of Tenochtitlan by Cortés, its site was reserved by him for the erection thereupon of the Spanish city, whereas the site of Tlatilulco became the Indian settlement for a time, or rather was intended for that purpose. *Cortés* ("*Carta.* IV, pp. 110, 111, Vedia I). *Motolinia* (Trat. III, cap. VII, pp. 180, 181). *Oviedo* (Lib. XXXIII, cap. XLIX, pp. 528, 530). *Juan de Torquemada* (Lib. IV, cap. CII, p. 572. Lib. III, cap. XXVI, p. 299). *Herrera* ("*Descripcion de las Indias Occidentales*," Cap. IX, p. 17. "*Historia*," Dec. III, lib. IV, cap. VIII, p. 122). *Vetancurt* ("*Crónica de la Provincia del Santo Evangelio de México*" 4th Part of the "Teatro," pp. 124, 131, 132, 212, and 213).

It is the latter author, *Vetancurt* ("*Crónica*," pp. 131, 132, 212, and 213), who gives us the names and numbers of the Mexican quarters, "barrios," or localized kins who, under the form of "Indian wards," still existed in 1690. I assume this date from the fact that the "Licencia" of the "Comisario general de Indias," is dated 17 April, 1692, (p. 13, Vol. I, "*Teatro*"). Besides mentioning the four great quarters of Mexico (p. 124), of which we shall hereafter speak, he says: "Los barrios son veinte, donde están once ermitas fabricadas que sirven para sacramentar en ellas á los que no tienen casa, decente, sirviendo de oratorios del barrio, donde en las fiestas particulares se suelen decir misas rezadas, y en algunas fiestas de devocion cuando la piden." He also gives us (pp. 212, 213) information about Tlatelulco,—information which proves that the aborigines settled there "en seis parcialidades, que cada cual tiene sus barrios, y veinte ermitas con sus titulares que celebran." This is rather obscure, and I shall

While the seven consanguine clusters above mentioned composed, to all intents and purposes, one tribe as towards outsiders, there still appear among them germs of discord which, at a later date, caused a disruption of mutual ties. The details are too vague and too contradictory to allow any inference even as to the real nature of such dissensions.[35] One fact, however, is ascertained, namely : that the whole group bore in common all the hardships and vicissitudes of a wandering life and the encroachments, aggressions and temptations from outsiders ; that they had sheltered together in a safe retreat, and that only when relative safety from violence was secured, a permanent division took place. These considerations should dispose of the

therefore give the names of the Mexican "barrios" by the side of the "ermitas" of Tlatelulco, leaving the reader to notice coincidences himself.

"Barrios" of Mexico.	*"Ermitas"* of Tlatelulco.
Santo Cristo de Tzapotla.	Santa Ana Atenantitech.
Santa Véronica de Huehuecalco.	Santa Lucia Telpochcaltitlan.
Santa Cruz de Tecpancaltitlan.	La Concepcion de Atenantitlan.
San Pedro de Cihuateocaltitlan.	San Francisco Mecantalinco.
Espiritu Santo de *Yopico.*	La Asuncion de Apazhuacan.
San Felipe de Jesus de Teocaltitlan.	San Martin Atezcapan.
Santiago de Tlaxilpan.	Santa Catalina Cohuatlan.
Los Reyes de Tequicaltitlan.	San Pablo Tolquechiucan.
La Candelaria de Atlampa.	Nuestra Señora de Belen Tlaxoxiuhco.
La Ascension de Tlacacomoco.	Los Reyes de Capoltitlan.
San Diego de Amanalco.	San Simon Iztatla.
El Niño Jesus de Tepetitlan.	Santa Inés Hueipantonco.
El Descendimiento de Atizapan.	San Francisco Izcatla.
San Salvador de Xihuitongo.	Santa Cruz Azococolocan.
La Navidad de Tequixquipan.	San Antonio Tepiton.
San Salvador de Necaltitlan.	La Asuncion de Tlayacaltitlan.
La Concepcion de Xoloco.	San Francisco *Cihuatecpan.*
San Juan de Chichimecapan.	San Juan *Huitznahuac.*
San Antonio de Tezcatzonco.	Sa Asuncion de Izayoc.
San Sebastian Copolco.	Santa Clara Acozac.

I have italicized those names which are also found among those of the seven original kins above enumerated, and thus we find three of them, one in Mexico, and two among the "Ermitas" of Tlatelulco.

[34] *Fernan Gonzalez de Eslava* ("*Coloquios espirituales y Sacramentales, y Poesias Sagradas,*" Second Edition, 1877, by Sr. Icazbalceta.) The learned editor makes the following note, 50. to page 57. "Cuando se reedificó la ciudad de México, despues de la conquista, se colocaron en el Centro las casas de los españoles, y los Indios levantaron las suyas alrededor de aquellas. Esta poblacion india se dividió en cuatro barrios ó *parcialidades,* regidos por caciques de su nacion, sujetos á un gobernador de la misma, Los barrios principales eran San Juan y Santiago." Calling my attention to this note in his letter of 14 Nov., 1878, my esteemed friend adds : "Con el tiempo se confundió la poblacion y desaparecieron esos barrios; pero aun quedó el nombre y los bienes que poseian las 'parcialidades' los cuales desaparecieron tambien en mi tiempo."

[35] The dissensions between what subsequently became the Mexicans and the Tlatelulcans are so variously described by the authorities, that it is hardly worth while to discuss them.

assumption, frequently made, that the Mexicans were divided into two distinct clusters at the outset.

A council of chiefs, representing the seven kins meeting on equal terms, composed the government of the ancient Mexicans at that period of their history. Among these, occasional "old men" of particular ability loom up as leading advisers. But no permanent general office of an executive nature is mentioned; although even occasional braves acquired historical prominence through their deeds of valor and of sagacity.[36]

But, while the organization was thus amply sufficient for the needs of a straggling band, Indian worship or "medicine" (as the native term implies) represented, inside of that organization, the lingering remains of what we have already suggested to be the oldest aboriginal clusters of society. Corresponding to the *four* original kins of the QQuiché, to the *four* leading days of the calendar with the traditions attached to their origin, we find among the ancient Mexicans at that period *four* chief medicine men, or "old men," who at the same time are "carriers of the God."[37]

[36] "*Tenure of Lands*" (P. 398 and 399, Notes 21 and 22). In addition to the authorities quoted there, I refer to: *Gomara* ("*Conquista de Méjico*" Vedia I, p. 431). "y dicen que no trajeron señores, sino capitanes." (Idem p. 433. " De los reyes de Méjico"). *Motolinia* (" Epistola proémial," p. 5). " aunque se sabe que estos Mexicanos fueron los post-reros, y que no tuvieron señores principales, mas de que se gobernaron por capitanes." —*Mendieta* (Lib. II, cap. XXXIV, p. 148). " Dicen que el èjército mexicano trajo por cau-dillos ò capitanes diez principales que los regian, ... Entre estos eligieron, luego como hicieron su asiento, por rey y principal señor á Tenuch." *Torquemada*. (Lib. II, cap. I, p. 78; cap. XII, pp. 94 and 95).

The fact of the election of the *first* so-called " King" of the ancient Mexicans, so generally acknowledged that no evidence of it is needed, is proof enough that, previous to it, the government of the Mexicans was at least, not monarchical. The words of Torquemada, (p. 94, vol. I.) " Dicese, que aviendo pasado veinte y siete años, que se governaban en comun, los unos, y los otros, les tomó gana de eligir Rey, ..." are plain enough.

Aside from the " leaders" (caudillos) of the Kins frequently mentioned, occasional war-chiefs or directing braves turn up during this period of their wandering existence. Thus, a chief whom they called " Mexi" is mentioned by *Acosta* (Lib. VII, cap. IV. p. 460), *Sahagun* (Lib. X, cap. XXIX, p. 138 and 139), *Hererra* (Dec. III, lib. II, cap. X. p. 60); and another very famous warrior, "Humming Bird." (Huitzilihuitl) led the Mexicans during their fray with the valley-tribes at Chapultepec, losing his life in the sally by which they broke through their surrounding enemies. *Durán* (Cap. III, p. 27; IV, 30). *Acosta* (Lib. VII, cap. V, p. 463). *Torquemada* (Lib. II, cap. III, p. 82; IV, p. 84; Lib. III, cap. XXII, p. 289). *Vetancurt* (Parte IIa, Trat. Io, cap. IX, p. 261; cap. X, p. 265 and 266). *Granados y Galvez* (*Tarde Quinta*, p. 151). *Veytia* (Lib. II, cap. XII, p. 97; cap. XIII, p. 110; cap. XIV, p. 116, 124; cap. XV. p. 130 and 131). He affirms that " Humming Bird" was the first " King of the Mexicans," which, however, is expressly disproved by other authors.

[37] *Tezozomoc* ("*Crónica*" cap. I, p. 6), mentions the four old men who carried the so-called sister of Huitzilopochtli, "y á esto dijo Tlamacazqui Huitzilopochtli ǎ los viejos

It seems to indicate, that as relics of four very ancient kins, a kind of superstitious ("standing over") deference was paid to them, implying a voice and vote in the councils of the tribe.[38]

que la solian traer cargada, (que se llamavan Quauhtlonquetzque, y Axoloa el segundo, y el tercero llamado Tlamaca⸱qui Cuauhcoatl, y el cuarto Ococaltzin"). (Cap. III. p. 8), at Chapultepec "y alli les habló Huitzilopochtli ă los sacerdotes, que son nombrados Teomamaques, cargadores del dios, que eran Cuauhtloquetzqui, Axoloa, Tlamacazqui y Aococaltzin, á estos cargadores de este idolo, llamados sacerdotes, les dijo."— *Durán* (Cap. III. p. 21). Llegados a aquel lugar de *Pazcuaro*, viéndole tan apacible y alegre, consultaron ă su dios los sacerdotes y pidiéronle: . . . . . . el dios *Vitzilopochtli* respondió ă sus sacerdotes, en sueños . . . " These words repeat themselves almost, several times in cap. IV, V, and VI. Finally he is very positive, (Cap. VI. p. 46), "con los quátro ayos de *Vitzilopochtli*, los quales le vian visiblemente y lo hablaban, que se llamauan *Cuauhtloquetzqui*, el segundo *Ococatl* el tercero *Chachalaitl* y el cuarto *Axoloua*, los quales eran como ayos, padres, amparo y reparo de aquella gente," *Acosta* (Lib. VII, cap. IV, p. 459), "Con esto salieron lleuando ă su ydolo metido en una arca de juncos, la qual lleuavan quatro Sacerdotes principales, con quien el se communicava, y dezia en secreto los successos de su camino auisandoles lo que les auia de suceder, dandoles leyes, y enseñandolos ritos y ceremonias, y sacrificios. No se mouian un punto sin parecer y mandato deste ydolo." *Herrera* (Dec. III, lib. II, cap. X, p. 60). "Llevaron este Idolo en una Arca de Juncia en hombros de quatro Sacerdotes, los quales enseñaban los Ritos, i Sacrificios, i daban Leies, i sin su parecer no se movian en nada." Besides these specifically and exclusively Mexican sources, to which others will be added hereafter, the fact of these four chief-medicine men "tlamacazqui" from "tlama"— medicine-man, (*Molina* II, p. 125), is proven by authors who rather incline to the tezcucan side. *Torquemada* (Lib. II, cap. I, p. 78), "y ordenó, que quatro de ellos, fuesen sus ministros, para lo qual, fuéron nombrados Quauhcohuatl, Apanecatl, Tezcacohuatl, Chimalman," (Lib. VI, cap. XXI, p. 41, but especially Lib. IX, cap. XIX, p. 205). "De los primeros Mexicanos, que vinieron ă estas Tierras, sabemos, que no traxeron Rei, ni otro Caudillo particular (contra los que tienen, ó afirman lo contrario) sino que venian regidos de los Sacerdotes, y ministros del Demonio; sobre cuios hombros venia la Imagen del Dios Huitzilupuchtli, y ă los consejos, y determinaciones de estos ministros eran obedecientes." The most explicit of all, however, is again *Veytia* (Lib. II, cap. XII, p. 93). At the death of Huitziton, "y aqui fué dondo empezaron las embustes de los viejos y sacerdotes que con mas inmediacion trataban ă Huitziton; porque, ó concebido ya el ambicioso deseo de quedarse con el mando del pueblo, ó para disminiurle ă este el dolor que debia causarle tan gran pérdida, ..." (p. 94). "Esto es el origen de la famosa deidad Huitzilopuchtli," (p. 99), here Veytia is in error in stating that *Tezozomoc* reports that the four priests were left with Malinalxochitl in Malinalco. This author mentions them again at Chapultepec, "*Crónica*," (Cap. III, p. 8). Further on (Cap. XIII, p. 102), "Yo me persuado ă que es distinto, que Ocelopan y sus tres compañeros fueron los cuatro Tlamacazquis que fingieron el embuste del rapto de Huitziton," (p. 109), he says that the "old priests" opposed the election of a head-war-chief ("rey") "por no dejar el mando." (Also Cap XV, p. 131.)

It results from these statements, that the four "Carriers of the God" indeed exercised, or at least claimed some governmental power. In tribal society such power can only come through some *kin*, hence the four "medicine-men" represented four very old clans or relationships, whose names even may have been lost, whereas the former power "stood over," in the form of a participation of "medicine" or worship in the tribal business. I here recall the important utterance of *Boturini* ("*Idea*," pp. 111 and 112 of §XVI), "como fué costumbre de los Indios poner muy pocas Figuras en los mapas, baxo de cuya sombra se hallan numerosos Pueblos, y gentes; y assi dichos siete Tultécos, cuyos nombres refiere el mencionada Don Fernando, se entiende haver sido siete principales Cabezas de dilatados Parentescos, que se escondian baxo los

When the Mexicans, thus constituting a migratory cluster of kins, reached the present central valley of Mexico, they found it occupied by a number of tribes of the same language as their own, though dialectically varied. The arrival of the new-comers was to those who had already settled, a matter of either war or of adoption. Adoption became very difficult, as well on account of the number of the immigrants as of the rivalry between already settled tribes. Therefore the Mexicans were tossed to and fro, until at last the straggling remnant found a shelter on some dry patches protruding from the marsh along which the other tribes had formed their settlements.

This settlement occurred about 196 years previous to the Spanish conquest, and it limits therefore the time, within which the

nombres de sus Conductores." What the unfortunate Italian Cavaliere here says of the Toltecs, is applicable to all the other branches of the Nahuatl stock, and bears also on the four "Carriers of the God," under discussion.

Veytia affirms (Cap. XIII, p. 110. lib. II), that after the election of the Huitzilihuitl mentioned in my note 36, the god Huitzilopochtli "did not dare to claim the government of the people." Is this an indication to the effect that the four "priests" exercised a military command?

Referring to note 29, concerning the four names of the years and leading days in the Mexican and Central American Calendars, and their probable connection with as many very ancient kinships, I beg leave to add here some additional data in regard to the singular part played by the number four, in Central American and Mexican mythology and earliest tradition. In note 27, I have already alluded to the four original pairs, as mentioned by the " *Popol-Vuh* " as well as by *Sahagun.* Previous to the creation of the four men, the " *Popol-Vuh* " has the following remarkable passage: (Part III, cap. I, pp. 195–197), " In Paxil and in Cayalá, as this place is called, there came the ears of yellow and of white corn. These are the names of the barbarians (? Chicop), who went after subsistence: the fox (Yac), the wolf (Utiü) the parrot (Qel), and the raven (Hoh), four barbarians (?) who brought them the news of the ears of yellow corn and of white corn which grew in Paxil, and who showed them the road to Paxil." " There they found at last the nourishment which went into the flesh of man made, of man formed, this was his blood, it became the blood of man, this corn which went into him by the care of him who engenders and of him who gives being." This QQuiché tale of *four* animals or "barbarians" (the latter is an interpretation of Mr. Brasseur, since "chicop" signifies simply a *beast*) carrying the material out of which man was made, also finds an equivalent in Mexican traditions, as reported by *Sahagun* (Lib. X. cap. XXIX, § 12. p. 140), of four wise men who remained in the earthly paradise of "Tamoanchan" inventing there "judicial astrology, and the art of interpreting dreams. They composed the account of the days, of the nights, of the hours, and the differences of time, which were kept while the chiefs of the Toltecs, of the Mexicans, and of the Chichimecs ruled and governed." "Tamoanchan" as paradise, is strictly equivalent to "Paxil in Cayalá" of the QQuiché. The tradition of the four "Tutul-Xiu" among the maya of Yucatan. may also be classed among these tales. " *Séries of Katunes,*" " *Epochs of Maya History.*" " *This is the Series of Katunes in Maya.*" ("*helo lai u Tzolan Katunil Ti Mayab*") in Mr. *Brasseur's* (" *Relation des choses du Yucatan*") also in *J. L. Stephens* (" *Travels in Yucatan,*" Vol. II, p. 465, appendix.) Also *Durán* (Cap. XXVII, pp. 222, 224).

[38] *Tylor* ("*Early History of Mankind,*" Edition of 1878. p. 165), " Super-stitio" or " Standing Over,"—the German "Aberglaube" in the sense of "what has remained."

organization and Institutions of the ancient Mexicans must have reached their ultimate development, to less than two centuries.[39]

"In the midst of canes of reeds" the remains of the Mexican tribe found their future home upon a limited éxpanse of sod, which even their enemies on the mainland seemed to regard but as a spot fit to die upon.[40] Although much reduced in numbers, the kins themselves remained and a settlement necessitated at once their localization. How this took place, can best be told in the words of one of the native chroniclers, the Dominican monk, Fray Diego Durán.

"During the night following, after the Mexicans had finished to improve the abode of their god, and the greatest part of the lagune being filled up and fit for to build thereon, Vitzilopochtli spoke unto his priest or keeper and said to him : "Say unto the Mexican community that the chiefs, each with their relatives, friends and connections, should divide themselves in four principal quarters, with the house which you have built for my resting place in the middle, and that each kin might build within its quarter as best it liked." These quarters are those remaining in Mexico to this day, to wit: the ward of San Pablo, that of San Juan, of Santa Maria la Redonda as it is called, and the ward of San Sebastian. After the Mexicans had divided into these four places their god sent word to them that they should distribute among themselves their gods, and that each quarter should name and designate particular quarters where these gods should be worshipped. Thus each of these quarters divided into many small ones according to the number of idols called by them Calpulteona, which is to say god of the quarter. I shall not recall here their names because they are not of importance to history, but we shall know that these quarters are like unto what in Spain they call a collation of such and such a saint."[41]

This statement we do not hesitate to accept as expressing gen-

[39] My friend, Prof. Ph. Valentini, of New York, has in hand the study of Central American Chronology proper, as well as Mexican. In his latest work " *The Mexican Calendar stone*" (published first in German as a " Lecture," and afterwards in No. 71, of the " *Proceedings of the American Antiquarian Society*"), he has given a general idea of his researches, but not any details yet about their results. If, therefore, I here admit 1325, A. D. as about the date of the so-called " foundation" of Tenuchtitlan-Mexico, it is subject to correction by him.

[40] *Durán* (Cap. IV, p, 32), *Herrera* (Dec. III, lib. II, cap. XI, p. 61).

[41] " *Tenure of Lands* " (p. 400, note 29, and p. 402, notes 32 and 33). In addition to the authorities quoted, I refer to *Herrera* (Dec. III, lib. II, cap. XI, p. 61), and *Samue Purchas* (" *His Pilgrimages*," 1625, Part III, lib. V, cap. IV, p. 1005).

uine aboriginal traditions, notwithstanding the attempt, on the part of Fray Juan de Torquemada, to impugn its truthfulness and consequently its validity,[42] It results from it that while the kins, which for the first time in Mexican history are distinctly identified here with the "calpulli," are settling, "as best they liked ;" the creation of four geographical divisions, composed each of a number of kins, is attributed here to the influence of worship or, as we have already termed it, of "medicine." This connects those, who subsequently became the four "Indian wards" of Mexico, with the four "carriers of the gods" already mentioned, and this perhaps may be considered a reminiscence of the four original relationships. Of these the sections mentioned appear like a shell, geographically enclosing a number of settled kins. The supposition is not, therefore, devoid of interest that they may have represented brotherhoods of kins, for purposes of worship and warfare. If now we substitute for *kin* the term "*gens*" adopted by Mr. Morgan, those *brotherhoods* necessarily appear in the light of as many "*phratries*."[43]

The time of this occurrence seems almost to coincide with a division (already indicated as in progress) of the original Mexican band into *two* sections. It now culminated in the secession of a part of the tribe and its settlement apart from the main body, though not far away from it and within the lagune also. While the "place of the stone and prickly pear" (Tenuchtitlan) remained, virtually, ancient Mexico, the seceding group founded the Pueblo of Tlatilulco as an independent community at the very door of the former. It appears as its rival even until forty-eight years previous to the Spanish conquest.[44]

---

[42] "*Tenure of Lands*" (p. 402, notes 32 and 33).

[43] *Morgan* ("*Ancient Society*," Part II, cap. III, p. 88) "The phratry is a brotherhood, as the term imports, and a natural growth from the organization into gentes. It is an organic union or association of two or more gentes of the same tribe, for certain common objects. These gentes were usually such as had been formed by the segmentation of an original gens." If we recall the manner in which the four "quarters" or Mexico first appeared, it will easily be seen that the analogy with phratries is indeed striking. Compare, "*Art of War*" (p. 101, and note 22, and pp. 120, 121, and notes 97, 99, 100, and 101), In "*Tenure of Lands*" (pp. 400 and (401), I have rather favored the view that these four were "calpulli" which subsequently segregated into minor quarters or "barrios." I now correct this, having become convinced that the so-called minor *quarters already existed at the time of settlement* (*compare notes* 37 *and* 41).

[44] *Motolinia* (Trat. III, cap. VII, p. 180), mentions a division into but two "barrios" in course of time through increase of population. "Despues andando el tiempo y multiplicandose el pueblo y creciendo la vecindad, hizóse esta ciudad dos barrios ó dos ciudades," *Ixtlilxochitl* ("*Hist. des Chichim.*" Cap. p. 72), merely states they were

It is much to be regretted that our information on this point is so meagre and unsatisfactory, as not to enable us to ascertain whether several *entire kins* separated from the rest to form the new tribe, or whether *fragments of kins* only composed the secessionists. In fact even the cause of the division is stated in such a varied and contradictory manner, that we must withhold any expression of positive views on the subject.

Without losing sight altogether of the tribe of Tlatilulco, we still must devote our attention chiefly to the inhabitants of Tenuchtitlan, in which we recognize the ancient Mexicans proper. The number of kins composing the latter at the time of their

divided in two "bands," without saying why and how this division occurred. *Durán* (Cap. V, p. 43), "Hecha esta division y puestos ya en su órden y concierto de barrios, algunos de los viejos y ancianos, entendiendo merecian mas de lo que les daban y que no se les hacia aquella honra que merecian, se amotinaron y determinaron ir a buscar nuevo asiento, y andando por entre aquellos carriçales y espadañales allaron una albarrada pequeña, y dando noticia della á sus aliados y amigos fuéronse á hacer alli asiento, el qual lugar se llamaba Xaltelulli y el qual lugar agora llamamos Tlatilulco, ques el barrio de Santiago. Los viejos y principales que alli se pasauan fuéron quatro; el uno dellos se llamaba Atlaquauitl, el segundo Huicto, el tercero Opocatli, el quarte Atlacol. Estos quatro señores se dividieron y apartaron de los demas y se fuéron á vivir á este lugar del Tlatilulco, y segun opinion tenidos por hombres inquietos y revoltosos y de malas intenciones, porque desde el dia que alli se pasaron nunca tuvieron paz ni se llevaron bien con sus hermanos los mexicanos; la qual inquietud a ido de mano en mano hasta el dia de hoy, pues siempre a auido y ay bandos y rancor entre los unos y los otros." *Acosta* (Lib. VII, cap. VIII, p. 468), and *Herrera* (Dec. III, lib. II, cap. XII, p. 62), both are but concise repetitions of the above. *Torquemada* (Lib. III, cap. XXIV, pp. 294 and 295), opposes both Acosta and Herrera, as well as the "*Codex Ramirez*," and substitutes a story about voluntary settlement of the Tlatilulca on a sandy patch near by, but apart from the others, in consequence of the old grudge or feud already mentioned. There is but little difference between this version and the preceding, the act of secession, in both, being voluntary. One singular fact is mentioned by *Vetancurt* (Part II, trat. I, cap, XI, p. 269), namely: that the Tlatilulca made a market-place for *both* parties. Otherwise (p. 257), he concurs with Torquemada. *Granados y Galvez* (Tarde 6a, p. 174), after saying that both "eran deudos y parientes unos con otros" adds "whether this division proceeded from past quarrels, or out of the incommodities which they suffered among canes and reeds; it is certain that they divided peaceably . . ." *Veytia* (Lib. II, cap. XV, pp. 135 and 142), reporting on all the various traditions about the foundation of Tlatilulco, comes to the conclusion that the "nobles" retired to Tlatilulco, whereas the "common people" remained at Mexico. *Clavigero* (Lib. II, cap. XV, p. 178), agrees with Veytia in regard to the real import of the fables told concerning the ancient feuds among the migratory band, but (Cap. XVII, pp. 187 and 188), he accepts the version that these old dissensions were the causes of the final division.

I have not been able, yet, to find whether the seceding Tlatilulca formed one kin, or one brotherhood of kins, or whether they were discontented fractions of kins removing. Had Vetancurt given us the names of the "barrios" of Tlatilulco, we might possibly infer something from them. As it is, the fact of the four "principals" mentioned by Durán, seems to indicate four kins, or rather (perhaps) fractions from four kins, whom want of space probably caused to remove. They may have been crowded out, and in course of time the feeling of jealousy and rivalry sprung up of which the authorities speak both freely and frequently. See *Veytia* (Lib. II, cap. XV, p. 135).

settlement is not stated, but while some sources mention *twenty* chiefs as composing the original council of the tribe, others speak of but *ten leaders*. This might, according to the view taken, indicate in both instances *ten* kins, or *twenty* in the former and *ten* in the latter. At any rate the number is larger than that originally composing the tribe, thus showing that the segmentation so characteristic of tribal society according to Mr Morgan, had already begun. Of the government of the tribe Clavigero says : "The whole nation was under a senate or college of the most prominent men."[45] No mention is made anywhere of a head-war-chief

[45] *Clavigero* (Lib. III, cap. I, p. 190). *Torquemada* (Lib. II. cap. XII, p. 94. Lib. III, cap. XXII, pp. 289, 290, and 291). *Durán* (Cap. VI, p. 47).

It is difficult to ascertain the actual number of kins composing the Mexican tribe at at that time. The number of chiefs and their names are variously stated. *Durán* (Cap. VI, p. 47), mentions six chiefs and four priests. *Mendieta* (Lib. II, cap. XXXIV, p. 148), mentions ten chiefs. The "*Codex Mendoza*" also says ten chiefs (Tab. I, Vol. I, Kingsborough). *Clavigero* (Lib. III, cap. I, p, 190, note r), mentions twenty. It is interesting to compare the names, also those of the twenty leaders of *Torquemada* (Lib. II, cap, III, p. 83), with those of the twenty " barrios " of Vetancurt.

Durán.	*Mendieta.*	*Torquemada.*	*Clavigero.*	*"Barrios" of Vetancurt.*
Acacitli,	*Acacitli,*	*Acacitli,*	*Acacitli,*	Tzapotla,
Tenoch,	*Tenuch,*	*Tenoca,*	*Tenoch,*	Huehuecalco,
Meci,	Tecineutl,	*Nanacatzin,*	*Nanacatzin,*	Tecpancaltitlan,
Ahuexotl,	*Auexotl,*	*Ahuexotl,*	*Ahuexotl,*	Cihuateocaltilan,
Ocelopan,	*Ocelopan,*	*Ocelopan,*	*Ocelopan,*	Yopico,
Teçacatetl,	Quahpan,	*Teçacatetl,*	*Tezacatl,*	Teocaltitlan,
Quauhtloquetzqui,	*Xomimitl,*	*Xomimitl,*	*Xomimitl,*	Tlaxilpan,
Ococal,	Xocoyal,	*Quentzin,*	*Quentzin,*	Tequicaltitlan,
Chachalaitl,	*Xiuhcaqui.*	*Xiuhcac,*	*Xiuhcac,*	Atlampa,
Axoloua.	Atototl.	*Axolohua,*	*Axolohua,*	Tlacacomoco,
		Tlalala,	Tlalala,	Amanalco,
		Tzontliyayauh,	Tzontligagauti,	Tepetitlan,
		Tuzpan,	Tochpan,	Atizapan,
		Tetepan,	Tetepan,	Xihuitengo,
		Cozca,	Cozcatl,	Tequixquipan,
		Ahatl,	Atzin,	Mecaltitlan,
		Achitomecatl,	Achitomecatl,	Xoloco,
		Acohuatl,	Acohatl,	Chichimecapan,
		Mimich,	Mimich,	Copolco,
		Tezca.	*Tezcatl.*	*Tezcatzonco.*

I have italicized such names as are alike. We see that of the ten chiefs named by Durán and Mendieta, six are also named by the two other authorities. As might be expected, there is hardly any concordance between these names of chiefs and those of the Mexican " barrios."

If it were known to us whether, in this case, each " chief" represented a kin only, or whether Durán, Tezozomoc, and Mendieta alone indicated the true number, we could or might, of course, determine the number of the calpulli. That the chief is used to denote his kinship in the old authors is distinctly stated by *Durán* (Cap. XXVII, p. 224). This chapter relates the mission of sixty " wizards " (" brujos "-" hechiceros,") sent by the chief " Montezuma Ilhuicamina " (the first " stern or wrathy chief " of that name), to an old woman or goddess purported to be " Huitzilopochtli's " mother. Arrived before the old hag (as she is described), she inquires of them for her son and for

as yet; this peculiarly military office was not yet established in permanence. However, there are indications that one executive chieftain for tribal affairs may, at least rudimentarily, have existed namely: the "Snake-woman" (cihuacohuatl). But the attributes of this office did not assign to it any marked prominence.[46]

The position of the Mexican tribe, about the middle of the fourteenth century, was still a very precarious one. With barely sufficient sod to dwell upon, blockaded, so to say, by powerful tribes along the lake shore; with the independent cluster of Tlatilulco, jealous and threatening, within an arrow-shot of its homes, it was forced into a peculiar attitude of military defence. The elements for a warlike organization were contained in the autonomous kins, which were grouped into the still larger cluster of the brotherhood, and all together composing the tribe. The leaders were found in the officers and chiefs of the kins. But the state of insecurity then prevailing required an office whose incumbent should be in constant charge of the military affairs of the tribe. This was plainly within the scope of tribal society; such functions had already been exercised previously, in times of particular need. Now, under the pressure of circumstances, and with a permanent settlement, permanence of the charge became a necessity.[47]

the seven chiefs " which seven went for leaders of each quarter " (p. 222). The wizards reply (among other things): "Great and powerful Lady (?) we have neither seen, nor spoken to, the chiefs of the *calpules:*" Judging from this, the original number of them was *ten*, and it is presumable that if such was the case they were the *war-chiefs*, whereas the others were more properly the administrative officers analogous to the "*sachems*" of the Iroquois. (Compare *Morgan*, " *Ancient Society*." Part II, cap. II, pp. 71, 72, and 73. Cap. IV, p. 114. Cap. V, pp. 129, 130, etc., etc., to 148). We shall have occasion to return to this again in a subsequent note.

[46] The office of " Cihuacohuatl " is very old. *Ixtlilxochitl* (" *Relaciones*" " *Segunda Relacion*," pp. 323 and 324), after speaking of the seven leaders of the Toltecs, mentions "Ziuhcoatl" tambien uno de los cinco capitanes inferiores" as discoverer of Jalisco. Confirmed (the last mention excepted) by *Torquemada* (Lib. I, cap. XIV, p. 37). *Veytia* (Lib. I. cap. XXII, p. 220). The " *Codex Mendoza*" (Plate II in Vol. I of Lord Kingsborough), represents the first regular head-war-chief of the Mexicans, " Handful of Reeds " (Acamapichtli) with a head and face of a woman and snake surmounting his own head or rather the forehead, whereas the " name " proper stands, as usual, behind the occiput. The explanatory note thereto (Vol. VI, p. 8), says: " The first figure probably denotes that Acamapichtli, before he was elected king, possessed the title of Cihuacohuotl, or supreme governor of the Mexicans; when Mexico afterwards became a Monarchy this title was retained."

[47] *Durán* (Cap. V, pp. 43 and 44). *Acosta* (Lib. III, cap. 8, p. 458). *Herrera* (Dec. III, lib. II, cap. XII, p. 62). *Torquemada* (Lib. II, cap. XIII, p. 95). " The cause of his election was the increase in numbers, and their being surrounded by enemies who made war upon them and damaged them." " La causa de su eleccion, fue, aver crecido en numero, y estár mui rodeados de Enemigos, que les hacian guerra, y afligian."

Therefore, near the eighth decade of the fourteenth century, or about thirty years after the settlement of Mexico, the office of "chief of men" (Tlacatecuhtli) appears to have been established.[48] This is commonly heralded as the creation of monarchy, thus abolishing the basis of organization, or tribal society itself. It is however overlooked that only an office was created, and not a hereditary dignity with power to rule.[49] Its first incumbent, "Handful of Reeds" (Acamapichtli), was duly elected, and so were his successors.[50] We have already seen that the Mexican family itself was so imperfectly constituted as to preclude the notion of a dynasty, and it was therefore, as we shall further establish, to the " kin " that the so-called succession, or rather the choice was limited.[51] We do not know, nor would it be safe to guess, *which*

Veytia (Lib. II, cap. XVIII, p. 159; cap. XXI, pp. 186 and 187). *Clavigero* (Lib. III, cap. I, pp. 190 and 191). It was a military measure.

[48] The dates are variously given. *Durán* (Cap. VI, p. 53), says 1364, or rather he states that " Handful of Reeds " died at the age of 60, and that his death occurred 1404. He had been elected when 20 years old, therefore forty years previous to the latter date, or in 1364, A. D. *Vetancurt* (Parte IIa, trat. I, cap. XI, p. 270), says 3d of May, 1361, or 1368. According to *Sahagun*, and from his lists of Mexican "Kings" (Lib. VIII, cap. I, pp. 268–271), it would be about 1369, but (Lib. VIII, cap. V, p. 280), he says he was elected in 1384. *Veytia* (quoting also *Carlos de Siguenza*), says (Lib. II, cap. XXI, pp. 186 and 188), 1361. *Clavigero* (Lib. III, cap. I, p. 190. Appendix to 1st Vol., p. 598. Vol. II, Sec'd Dissertation, Cap. II, p. 327), says 1352. *Mendieta* (Lib. II, cap. XXXIV, p. 148), 1375. In the " *Real Ejecutoria* " (Col. de Doc., Vol. II, p. 9), a date 1384 appears, but this date is of doubtful origin. The " *Codex Telleriano-Remensis* " (Vol. I, Kingsb., Plate I, and Explanation, Vol. VI, p. 134), says in the year 11, cane, (" Acatl ") or 1399. *H. H. Bancroft* (Vol. V, cap. VI, p. 358), 1350. *Prof. Valentini* (" The Mexican Calendar-Stone," p. 108), 13, Acatl, or 1375.

In regard to the title of " Tlacatecuhtli " compare " *Art of War*," (p. 123, note 104). There is a singular analogy between it and the title of " *Great War Soldier*," given by the Iroquois confederacy to its head-war-chiefs (" *Ancient Society*," p. 146). Under " men " the Mexicans also understood " braves." Therefore " chief of the braves " also.

[49] In a general way, the following passages are interesting. *Durán* (Cap. LXIV, p. 498), " because in these times the brothers, sons of the King inherited one another, although from what I have noted of this history, there was no heredity nor succession, but that only those which the electors chose, whether brother or son, nephew or cousin, in the second degree, of him who died, and this order it strikes me they carried (on) in all their elections, and so I believe that many of those who clamor and pray for lordships (" señorios ") because of their fathers having been Kings and Lords at the time of their infidelity do not, as I understand, justly claim (" no piden justicia "). For according to their ancient law there were rather elections than successions and inheritances, in all kinds of lordships." I shall give the full text of this very important passage further on. *Torquemada* (Lib. XI, cap. XXVII, p. 358). " Of the Mexican republic I confess this manner of succession, and that sometimes they were elected without regard to anything save their personal qualification."

[50] *Sahagun* (Lib. VIII, cap. XXX, p. 318).

[51] Compare *Durán* (Cap. LXIV, pp. 498 and 499). *Torquemada* (Lib. XI, cap. XXVII, p. 358). The former says in addition to what is quoted in note 49. " In all the other lordship I only found but elections and the will of the electors, and thus they never could fail to have a King of that lineage, even to the end of the world, because if to-

was the particular "calpulli" of Mexico who furnished the Mexican head-war-chiefs down to 1520 A. D.

Analogous to the New Mexican pueblo, the tribe of Mexico had, from that time on, its supreme council and finally two executive head-chiefs; for with the creation of the military office of "chief of men," the "Snake-woman" rose correspondingly in importance.[52] No change in that organization took place until the Spanish conquest although within the period of nearly one hundred and fifty years (approximately) thus indicated, we find, at three distinct epochs, mention of virtual changes or subversions of the aboriginal institutions of the Mexican tribe.

The first one of these critical dates agrees with the third decade of the fifteenth century, or the time when, through a well executed dash, the Mexicans overthrew the power of the Tecpanecas on the mainland.

This successful move, perhaps originally conceived in self-defence, finally brought about the confederacy of the "nahuatl" tribes of Mexico, Tezcuco, and of Tlacopan. We have nothing to add to our first picture of this military partnership, as drawn in "Tenure of Lands."[53] Still the event deserves special men-

day they elected the brother, to-morrow they elected the "grandson, and the day after the nephew, and thus they went through the whole lineage without any end." This is a plain description of the succession of office in the kin. Torquemada is about equally explicit, and this agreement between two authors who represent antagonistic tribal traditions, is certainly of great weight. To this should be added the statement of *Sahagun* (Vol. II, p. 318), " and (they) selected one of the most noble ones of the lineage ("linea") of the lords post." Even the series of contradictions of *Zurita* (" *Rapport*, etc.," pp. 12–20), contain a plain description (if attentively studied) of succession in the kin, and not in the family.

[52] At the time Francisco Vasquez de Coronado reached and conquered New Mexico, its sedentary Indians were governed by a council of old men, and besides they had governors and captains. This is explicitly stated by *Pedro de Castañeda y Nagera*, (" *Relation du Voyage de Cibola, entrepris en* 1540,"), who went with Coronado in 1540, in the French translation by Mr. Ternaux-Compans, 1838 (Cap. XI, p. 61), about Tuscayan Cibola, although flatly contradicted again by himself (Part. II, cap. III, p. 164), in regard to Cibola. *Torquemada* (Lib. IV, cap. XL. p. 681), mentions the "mandon" (commander) and after him what he calls a "crier" "y despues de èl, es el que pregona, y avisa las cosas, que son de Republica, y que se han de hacer en el Pueblo." The same author is also very explicit (Lib. XI, cap. XVII, p. 337), when he distinctly states: "El Govierno de los del Nuevo-Mexico parece de Senado, ù de Señoria," mentioning also the two other officers.

For the actually prevailing governmental system of the New-Mexican Pueblos the sources are very numerous. I simply refer to *H. H. Bancroft* (Vol. I, pp. 546 and 547), *W. W. H. Davis* (" *The Spanish Conquest of New-Mexico*," 1869, p. 415, note 4), *Oscar Loew* (" *Lieutenant G. M. Wheeler's Zweite Expedition nach Neu-Mexiko und Colorado*, 1874," in Petermann's " *Geographische Mittheilungen*," Vol. 22, p. 212). All the other main sources it would be useless to enumerate.

[53] Pp. 416, 417, and 418, and notes 61 to 70 inclusive. Also note 4 of this paper. In re-

tion here, because of its unveiling, so to say, the full organization of the ancient Mexicans as they preserved it until the time of their downfall.

Upon the occasion of the division of spoils gathered from the defeated Tecpanecas, and of the establishment of regular tribute, there appear the following war captains and leaders of the Mexicans, as representatives of the latter's organization.

The "chief of men."

Four captains of the four principal quarters of Mexico.

Twenty war-chiefs of as many kins composing the tribe.

One chief representing the element of worship, or " medicine."

The " Snake-woman."[54]

gard to the date of its occurrence, *Bancroft* (Vol. V, p. 395), says about, or immediately after, 1431, following Brasseur de Bourbourg, *Clavigero* (Lib. IV, cap. III, p. 251), 1426, *Ixtlilxochitl* ("*Hist. Chichimeca.*" Cap. XXXII, p. 217), also 1431, *Veytia* (Lib. III, cap. III, p. 165) 1431, The "*Codex Telleriano-Remensis*" (Kingsb., Vol. I, p. 7, and Vol. VI, p. 136), has it 7, "Tochtli" or 1404.

[54] *Durán* (Cap. XI, p. 96). Besides distributing land "juntamente con daros y repartiros las tierras que aveis ganado, para que tengais renta para el sustento de vuestros estados y personas segun el mérito dellas," he gave them " ditados" or titles " y (quiere) haceros señores de titulo" (the latter would be to make them noblemen). I must advert here that " ditado o titulo de honra " is expressed in the Mexican language by " tecuyotl" " tlatocazotl" " mauiçotl" (*Molina*, " *Vocabulario*," Part I, p. 46). These words however mean but, respectively " chieftainship," " speakership," and " honor," (the latter see *Molina* II, p. 54), all of them terms which, as we shall hereafter see, apply to *personal merit*, and not to hereditary privilege among the Mexican aborigines. Durán then proceeds (p. 97) to give these titles as follows : —

" Primeramente ă su general dió por ditado					*Tlacochcalcatltecutli.*
A Veue Moteucçuma, Tlacacleltzin dió por ditado					*Tlacatecatl.*
A Tlacauspan,	d.	p.	d.		*Ezuauacatl.*
A Cuatlecoatl,	d.	p.	d.		*Tlillancalqui.*
A Veueçacan,	d.	p.	d.		*Tezcacoacatl.*
A Aztacoatl,	d.	p.	d.		*Tocuiltecatl.*
A Caualtzin,	d.	p.	d.		*Acolnauacatl.*
A Tzonpantzin,	d.	p.	d.		*Hueiteuctli.*
A Epcotiuatzin,	d.	p.	d.		*Temillotzin.*
A Citlalcoatzin,	d.	p.	d.		*Tccpanecatl.*
A Tlaueloc,	d.	p.	d.		*Calmimelolcatl.*
A Ixcuetlatoc,	d.	p.	d.		*Mexicalteuctli.*
A Cuauhtzitzimitl,	d.	p.	d.		*Huitznauatl.*
A Xiconoc,	d.	p.	d.	y renombre,	*Tepanccatlteuctli.*
A Tlazolteotl,	d.	p.	d.		*Quetzaltocatl.*
A Axicyotzin,	d.	p.	d.		*Teuctlamacazqui.*
A Ixauatliloc,	d.	p.	d.		*Tlapaltecatl.*
A Mecantzin,	d.	p.	d.		*Cuauhyauacatl.*
A Tenamaztli,	d.	p.	d.		*Coatecatl.*
A Tzontemoc,	d.	p.	d.		*Pantecatl.*
A Tlacacochtoc,	d.	p.	d.		*Huecamecatl.*

To these he adds (pp. 98 and 99), five more, namely : *Quauhnochtecutli, Cuauhquiauacatl, Yopicatltecutli, Cuitznauatl, and Itcotecatl*. The three last were from Culhuacan. Adding to this the " chief of men " himself, who was " Flint-Snake," or

The existence of *twenty* autonomous consanguine groups is thus revealed, and we find them again at the time of the conquest,

"Obsidian-Snake" (*Itzcohuatl*), we have twenty-five chiefs in all. · Now we cannot fail to notice:—

(1). "Itzcohuatl," the "chief of men" or head-war-chief.

(2). "Tlacochcalcatl," "Tlacatecatl," "Ezhuahuacatl," and "Cuauhnochtli," the four military leaders of the four great quarters ("phratries") of Tenuchtitlan. (See *Art of War*," pp. 120, 121, and 122, also notes 97 to 101 inclusive.)

(3). "Tlillancalqui"—"Man of the black-house," a chief connected with "medicine" or worship, as I shall hereafter show. He was rather a counsellor or advisor, than a captain, as *Acosta* (Lib. VI, cap. XXV, p. 441), and *Herrera* (Dec. III, lib. II. cap. XIX, p. 75) positively state, whereas *Durán* (Cap. XI, p. 103) asserts the religious origin of his office.

(4). "Tlacacllel," who, as Durán and Tezozomoc both repeatedly and plainly assert, was the snake-woman or "Cihuacohuatl." In this intance, however, he is graced with the title of "man of the house of darts" ("Tlacochcalcatl"), and thus made one of the four leaders of the "phratries." This is an evident mistake, as the latter title belonged to Montezuma (the first, or "old one"). Compare *Torquemada* (Lib. II, cap. XXXVI, p. 140; cap. XLIII, p. 150, where he is called "captain-general"), *Vetancurt* (Part II, Trat. I, cap. XV, p. 293), also *Durán* (Lam. 8a, Parte Ia).

(5). Twenty war-chiefs, each one of whom commanded the warriors of one kin or calpulli, hence they were the military leaders of twenty Mexican kins. Besides the indications to that effect furnished by *Durán* (Cap. XXVII, p. 224), "á los señorés de los *calpules* no los vimos ni nos hablaron," said the sorcerers which had been sent to Huitzilopochtli's mother, after she had asked them about the chiefs or captains, seven in number, which had led the Mexicans originally, (see note 33). *Tezozomoc* ("Crónica," Cap. XV, pp. 24 and 25), while corroborating the statements of Durán (with the exception that he omits the chief "Mexicatltecutli," and thus gives only twenty-seven chieftains), inserts the following explanation about these twenty (or twenty-one after Durán) captains: "After these four (the four first ones), go the Tiacanes, called valorous soldiers, surnamed captains." The "Tiacan" or "tiacauh," properly "teachcauhtin," *Elder brother*, was the military chief of each "barrio" or "calpulli," therefore of each *kin* ("*Art of War*," p. 119, notes 91, 92, and 93), consequently these twenty chieftains represent here as many consanguine relationships composing the tribe of the ancient Mexicans.

It will be noticed, however, that Durán has twenty-one chiefs, whereas we assume but twenty, according to Tezozomoc. The latter omits "Mexicatl-tecutli" and, perhaps properly too. This word signifies but "Mexican chief," in general, and cannot therefore well be the title of one particular leader. It recurs occasionally in the course of Mexican history. Still, this is only a suggestion on my part, for the matter is far from being proven. *Torquemada* (Lib. IV, cap. CII, p. 571) mentions "*Mexicatl-achcauhtli*" among the chiefs who went with Quauhtemotzin before Cortés on the day after the resistance of the Mexicans had ended. Again Tezozomoc mentions two chiefs of the same title "Cuauhquiauacatl," as also does Durán. Now this would be impossible, since Tezozomoc calls the second one of that name, a son of "Cuauhnochtli." It may be now that the latter author has omitted the "Mexicatl-tecutli," and that "Cuauhquiauacatl" is to be counted but once. It results from the statements of Vetancurt already alluded to, that there were twenty Mexican "calpulli," consequently there were but twenty leaders of kins. The analogy between these "barrios" and the chiefs of Durán and Tezozomoc is greatly increased by the fact that for the three chiefs of Culhuacan mentioned by the latter, we have also three barrios of "Otomites," therefore, in each case but seventeen original kins of Mexicans proper (*Vetancurt* "*Crónica*," Vol. III, p. 132).

while their last vestiges were perpetuated until after 1690, when Fray Augustin de Vetancurt mentions four chief quarters with their original Indian names, comprising and subdivided into *twenty* " barrios." Now the Spanish word " Barrio " is equivalent to the Mexican term " calpulli." Both indicate the kin, localized and settled with the view to permanence.[55]

What is often conceived as the establishment of a vast feudal monarchy at the time just treated of, resolves itself therefore into two very plain features. One of these consists in the establishment of the confederacy, the other is but the appearance in broad daylight of the peculiar organization of aboriginal society among the Mexicans. Thus we have no sudden change of base, no revolution in the institutions of the tribe ; the only progress achieved consisted in the extension of inter-tribal relations and in their assuming the shape of a military partnership.

The year 1473 witnessed another event which seemed to affect

All these titles were permanent, though not hereditary, as it is plainly seen in the case of the four leaders of the four "phratries" about which *Sahagun* says: (Lib. VIII, cap. XXX, p. 318) " The chief elected, forthwith they elected others four which were like senators that always had to be by his side . . . . (these four had different names in different places) . . . . " *Durán* (Cap. XI. p. 103). " To these four lords and titularies, alter they were elected princes, they made them of the royal council, like presidents and members (" oydores ") of the supreme council, without whose opinion nothing should be done. When the king died, his successor had to be taken from those, neither could any others but brothers or sons of kings be clothed with these dignities. Thus if one of these was elected, they put another in his place. We must know that they never put a son of him who had been elected (" King ") or of the deceased, since, as it has been said, the sons never succeeded (in office) by inheritance, to the titles or lordships, but through election. Therefore, whether son, brother, or cousin, if elected by the king and those of his council, to that dignity, it was given to him,— it being sufficient his being of that lineage and near relative, and so the sons and brothers went on inheriting gradually, little by little . . . . and the title and lordship never went outside of that descendancy (" generation " also kin), being filled by election, little by little."

The other titles are frequently met with up to the time of the conquest, as a few instances will abundantly prove. Assuming, with the majority of authors, the date of 1431, for that of the formation of the confederacy, we meet, during the unlucky foray of the confederates against Michhuacan, about fifty years later, with the following war-chiefs of the Mexicans. Tezcacoatl, Huitznahuacatl, and Quetzaltocatl (*Tezozomoc,* Cap. LII, pp. 84 and 85), also Coatecatl (Cuauhtecatl). At the time of Cortés' first arrival off the coast (1518) we meet in the council of Mexico with Huitznahuacatl, Hueycamecatl (*Torquemada,* Lib. IV, cap. XIII, p. 379). Finally when, after the resistance of the Mexicans had ceased, Cortés assembled all the chiefs in his presence, we again meet with Huitznahuatl, Mexicatltecuhtli, Teuctlamacazqui (*Torquemada,* Lib. IV, cap. CII, p. 571). Evidence of this kind could be produced in profusion, but it would only increase unnecessarily the size of this annotation. Compare the titles of the Iroquois sachemships in *Morgan* ("*Ancient Society*," Part II, Cap. V, pp. 130 and 131).

[55] Compare note 33. Also *Molina* (Part I, p. 18), and others.

the Mexican tribe in a more direct manner. It was the overthrow
and capture, after a short but bloody struggle, of the pueblo of
Tlatilúlco.[56] Owing to the close connection of the latter with the
Mexicans both had remained on a non-hostile footing; for the
suspicious watchfulness with which each viewed the other did not
comport with any more intimate relations, those of trade and exchange excepted. When the confederacy came into existence,
Tlatilulco was counted in as a part of Mexico, since its people
acknowledged themselves to be Mexicans ; but there is no evidence
authorizing the conclusion that the Tlatilulca played any other role,
beyond that of auxiliaries to their kindred of Tenuchtitlan.[57] The
rash attempt of the former at the organization of a conspiracy to
become "Mexico alone" terminated fatally ; their place was taken
and barbarously sacked, their leaders were killed in the fray or
sacrificed afterwards, and the Mexicans, exasperated at the conduct
of their treacherous kinsmen treated them in an unusually severe
manner. We have seen already that, in any conquest, the conquered tribe, if not exterminated, was only subjected to more or
less heavy tribute. But the Tlatilulca were dealt with far worse :
they were degraded to the rank of "*women,*" their public market
was ordered closed, their council-house left to decay and their
young men, expressly debarred from the privilege of carrying
arms in aid of the Mexicans, were required to become the carriers
of supplies to their captors. Such a punishment was unknown in
the annals of Indian conquest, and appears even to militate
against our views of aboriginal society in Mexico ; still it was
in perfect harmony with the institutions of the latter. The
Tlatilulca were, as we should never forget, not only a tribe

[56] The "*Codex Telleriano-Remensis*" (Plate XIV, also explanation Vol. VI, p. 138),
concurs in this date. or the year seven "calli" which is indeed 1473.

[57] This acknowledgment—"to be Mexicans"—on the part of the inhabitants of
Tlatilulco, was in the nature of a *claim*, and with a spirit of jealousy and envy. Although *Durán* says (Cap. XXXII, p. 257), "auiendo estado hasta entonces sujetos á
la corona real de Méjico." this affirmation is utterly disproven, not only by all the
other sources, but by his own statements (Cap. V, pp. 43 and 46). The confused and
contradictory tales about the state of war preceding the formation of the confederacy
still make the Tlatilulca always appear as assisting their neighbors of Tenuchtitlan,
more or less. Sometimes they were neutral only, and at times they may have felt in-
clined to foster attempts at destruction of their rivals by outsiders, but they still were
afraid of the consequences of it for their own independence. *Durán* (Cap. V, p. 46).
The singular statement that the Tlatilulca even attempted, though fruitlessly, to with-
draw the Tezcucans and Tlacopans from Tenuchtitlan, inducing them to become their
associates in the work of its overthrew, is significant. See *Torquemada* (Lib. II, cap.
LVIII, p. 176) "Quisose aliar con los de Tlacupa, y Tetzcuco, los quales no le acudie-
ron."

connected, through stock-language or even dialect, with the Mexicans, but they were actually "kin of their own kin." Their punishment therefore was that of a crime committed against kinship and tribe. As we shall hereafter attempt to show, such delicts entailed death. Instead of exterminating a whole settlement however, the Mexicans treated the survivors as *outcasts from the bond of kinship*, degrading them to manual, therefore female labor.[58]

[58] The descriptions of the capture of Tlatilulco by the Mexicans, while "Face in the Water" (Axayacatl) was the latter's head war-chief, are so numerous, and in their features as far as the subject of this paper is concerned, so generally concordant, that I may be permitted to forego quotations. I simply refer to the best known authors on ancient Mexico in general. Still, these authors seem to report but the "Tenuchcan" side of the story. Although *Boturini* ("*Idea*" " *Catalogo del Museo Indiano*," p. 23), mentions the copy of " Un Mapa en papel Européo, donde estan pintados los Reyes de Tlatilulco, y de México" as the only specifically "Tlatilulcan " document of which he knows, there still is preserved to us a tale of the overthrow of the pueblo of Tlatilulco, which bears distinctly the stamp of a genuine Tlatilulcan version. We owe it to *Oviedo y Valdés* ("*Historia general y nat. de Indias*," Lib. XXXIII, cap. XLVI, pp. 504 and 505). " Avia dos parcialidades ó bandos en aquella república, la una se decia Mexicanos, é la otra Tlatebulcos, como se dice en Castilla Oneçinos í Gamboinos, ó Giles é Negretes. Y estos dos apellidos teuvieron grandes diferencias: é Monteçuma, como era mañoso, fingió grande amistad con el señor principal del bando Tlatebulco, que se decia por sus nombre proprio Samalce, é tomóle por yerno, é dióle una su hija, por le asegurar. Con este debdo, en cierta fiesta é convite ă este Samalce, é á todos sus capitanes é parientes é hombres principales, hizolos embeodar: é desque estuvieron bien tomados del vino, hiçolos atar é sacrificarlos ă todos, sacándoles los coraçones vivos, como lo tienen por costumbre. E los que padescieron esta crueldad passaban de mil hombres, señores principales; é tomóles las casas é quanto tenian, é poblólas de sus amigos é de los de la otra parçialidad Mexicana. É á todos los que tuvo por sospechosos, desterrólos de la ciudad, que fuéron mas de quatro mil hombres; y en los bienes é moradas destos hiço que viviessen los quel quiso enriquesar con bienes agenos. É aquellos que desterró, hiço que poblassen quatro leguas de alli, en un pueblo que de aquella gente se hiço, que se llama Mezquique, é que le sirvirssen de perpétuos esclavos. É assi como la cibdad se deçia, y es su proprio nombre Temistitan, se llamó é llama por muchos México dende aquella maldad cometida por Monteçuma." This story is repeated by him with less detail (Cap. I, p. 533). Although manifestly incorrect, it is still interesting to compare with the current version.

The punishment which the Tlatilulca received, is also mentioned by a number of authors. The prominent sources, however, are: *Durán* (Cap. XXXIV, pp. 270 and 271), *Tezozomoc* (Cap. XLVI, pp. 74 and 75). Both of these relate that, besides, the great market place of Tlatilulco about which the latter says: "that the tianguis (market) was esteemed beyond, as if they had gained five tribes." The Tlatilulca were, as we shall hereafter see, mostly traders and, as one of their old men is made to say to " Face in the Water," by *Tezozomoc* (p. 74): " We are traders, merchants, and will give you (follows a long list of articles promised) . . . . . since by force of arms this tianguis has been gained." *Durán*, (p. 270): "After this was done, the King commanded that this place and market which they had gained should be distributed among the lords, since the Tlatilulca had no other soil." Compare also the statements in regard to trading and bartering in aboriginal Mexico, and to the beginning of the traders at Tlatiluco, in *Sahagun* (Lib. IX, cap. 1, pp. 335 and 336).

" Kin of their own kin." In regard to this statement I beg to refer to one made by *Veytia* (Lib. II, cap. XV, p. 135): " Some modern national writers say that this separation did not occur precisely as between nobles and plebeyans, but that eight families

Still, this low condition did not remain forever. The Tlatilulca were in a measure " re-adopted " into the tribe. After this, they formed a fifth quarter, or " phratry," which Father Vetancurt (in 1690) mentions as containing six " parcialidades." But this re-habilitation never extinguished the fire of revenge kindled once among the Tlatilulca towards the Mexicans. The latter treated the former therefore, not as a tribe subject to tribute, but as a suspicious group, to which the rights and privileges resulting from consanguinity could not well be denied, but to which voice and vote in the leading councils should not be accorded. In this singular position, not strictly inferior, but evidently more " distant," we find the Tlatilulca at Mexico at the time of the conquest.[59]

or tribes, in which there were of both kinds, were those who divided themselves from the rest." (See note 44.) It is much to be regretted that the eminent Mexican scholar has not given us the names of these "Algunos escritores nacionales modernos."

[59] According to *Durán* (Cap. XXXIV, p. 271), they remained in a degraded condition for 160 days at least, or eight aboriginal months: " y que les turase esta penitencia y castigo hasta los ochenta dias del segundo tributo." But they were, according to him, relieved of it but conditionally : " y asi les quitauan aquellos entiedichos que e contado, los quales, en faltándoles, eran tornados á poner." In order to comply with the demands of the Mexicans for slaves, the Tlatilulca were forced to carry arms again, so as to take part in the wars. *Tezozomoc* (Cap. XLVI, p. 75) confirms, but implies previously (p. 75) that the Tlatilulca were specially obligated to be the traders for Mexico : " y haveis de ser nuestros tratantos y mercadres en los tianguis de Huexotzinco, Tlaxcalan, Tlilinquitepec, Zacatlan, y Cholula." A similar punishment was meted out to them by " Stern chief" the younger (the last Montezuma), after an unsuccessful campaign against Huexotzinco, Cholula, and Atlixco. *Durán* (Cap. LIX, pp. 468, 469), *Tezozomoc* (Cap. XCVI, p. 170). It is, besides, positively asserted by the former (p. 271) that the "medicine lodge," or temple of Tlatilulco, was closed thereafter, abandoned and left to ruin and decay ("y asi dice la ystoria questuvo hasta entonces lleno de yerba y de vasura y caidas las paredes y dormitorios del "). It is, of course, confirmed by *Tezozomoc* (p. 75. cap. XLVI): " y asi fué que lo estiuvo muchos años hasta la venida que hizo Don Fernando Cortés, Marquis del Valle, en esta nueva España, como adelante se dirá, á que me refiere." It is somewhat difficult to reconcile these statements with those of *Bernal Diez de Castillo* (Cap. XCII, pp. 88, 89, 90, 91, Vedia, Vol. II), and of *Sr. Icazbalceta* in *Cervantes-Salazar* ("*Tres Dialogos*," note 40 to 2d Dial., p. 201) to the effect that Cortes visited that temple of Tlatilulco and found " Stern chief" worshipping in it, and still more difficult is it to reconcile the relation of Bernal Diez with that of *Andrés de Tapia* ("*Relacion, etc., etc.*," pp. 582-586, Col. de Doc. II), who, as an eye-witness too, deserves similar credit.

Tlatilulco formed a quarter, a fifth great one, of Mexico at the time of the conquest. This is distinctly stated by *Motolinia* (*Historia, etc.*, Trat. III, cap. VII, pp. 180 and 181), *Torquemada* (Lib. II, cap. XI, p. 93) confirms Motolinia in general, (Lib. III, cap. XXIV, p. 295), *Mendieta* (Lib. III, cap. II, p. 182), " en el barrio llamado Tlatelulco;" (Lib. IV, cap. XV, p. 414), " y el barrio se dice Tlatelulco," adding (p. 418) " que son del mismo pueblo de Tlatelulco;" (Cap. XVII, p. 423), " El convento de Santiago de Tlatelulco que es como barrio de Mexico;" (Cap. XXVIII, p. 466), " pueblo de Tlatelulco;" (Id., p. 483, Cap. XXIX). That this fifth great quarter was again divided into six smaller ones, is proven by *Vetancurt* ("*Crónica, etc.*," pp. 207 and 212): " Tiene cuatro religiosos que con el ministro colado administran á más de mil quinientas personas en

This incident in Mexican history does not exhibit any features different from those found at the basis of tribal society, and it is not until the first decade of the sixteenth century that we are referred to the period when aboriginal institutions of ancient Mexico emerged from their former condition into that of political society proper and exhibited the features of rule as despotic as any on the three eastern continents. Even Robertson has so far yielded to this preconceived idea as to write, "This appearance of inconsistency has arisen from inattention to the innovations of Montezuma upon the Mexican policy. His aspiring ambition subverted the original system of government, and introduced a pure despotism. He disregarded the ancient laws, violated the privileges held most sacred, and reduced his subjects of every order to the level of slaves."[60] In general, many deeds, creditable and disreputable, are charged to that ill-starred "chief of men" of the Mexican tribe, whose tragical death has furnished a welcome topic to the most brilliant writers. "Wrathy chief" (Motecuzumah or Montezuma) was however innocent of many or of the most, if

seis parcialidades. que cada cual tiene sus barrios." This is indefinite and vague, and we are still left in doubt as to whether there were only six or whether there were more. The words "each of which has its quarters" would indicate that each of these "parcialidades" was divided into smaller ones. Still, "parcialidad" and "barrio" are regarded as equivalent terms, and both signify *kins*. The history of the capture of the Mexican pueblo has, in some details of the siege, preserved to us the names of some aboriginal "barrios" of Tlatilulco. *Vetancurt* (Vol. II, Part. III, Trat. II, cap. VII, p. 194) mentions two of them: "Yocacolco" (with the ermita of Santa-Ana) and "Amazac" (ermita of Santa Lucia), the latter of which is again named (Cap. X. p. 206) by him, and by Torquemada also. *Torquemada* gives a number of names even: Nonohualco (Lib. IV, cap. XCIII, pp. 551, 552), Yacocalco (p. 552). Tlacuchcalco (p. 552), Amazac, Coyonacazco (p. 552). This gives the names of five barrios of Tlatilulco. If to this we add "el Barrio, que se llama Xocotitlan, que es agora San Francisco. que por otro nombre se llama Cihuatecpan," (p. 552), we would have the sixth quarter also.

That the administration of Tlatilulco remained separate from that of Tenuchtitlan is proven by the fact that Montezuma was assisted by twenty chiefs corresponding to the twenty kins of the *Tenuchca only*, and without representation for the Tlatilulca. See *Bernal Diez de Castillo* (Cap. XCV, p. 95. Vedia II). But the war-chief of Tlatilulco was present at the council. Thus "Itzquauhtin" is frequently mentioned as the companion of Montezuma. *Sahagun* (Lib. XII. cap. XVI. p. 24; cap. XVII, p. 25; cap. XXI, p. 28; cap. XXIII, p. 31). *Torquemada* (Lib. IV, cap. LXX. pp. 498, 499). *Vetancurt* (Vol. II, cap. XV, Parte III, p. 132). *Clavigero* (Vol. II, Lib. IX. cap. XIX, p. 153).

Of the hatred between Mexicans proper and Tlatilulca the last days of the siege of Mexico furnish numerous instances. Both *Torquemada* (Lib. IV, cap. XCII, p. 550) and *Vetancurt* (Parte III, cap. VI of 2d Trat., p. 193) mention the flight of the former into Tlatilulco as taking refuge among enemies. Finally the following passage is sufficiently plain: *Durán* (Cap. XXXIV, p. 271), "E fué tanta la pertinacia de los Mexicanos, que hasta que los españoles vinieron à la tierra no les dejaron tornar à libertad ninguna, ni à tener templo particular."

[60] "*History of America,*" (9th Edition, 1800, Vol. III, Book VII, p. 291).

not all, of these good or bad actions, and this simply for the reason that he had not the power to commit them. Thus he is charged with remodelling his household, removing certain assistants, and filling the vacancies with "scions of noble stock," creating, at the same time, hereditary charges. It may be that, in the case of simple runners for instance, the "chief of men" held ample authority to select his men, consequently to remove them ; but it is certain that for any office of permanence with the kin or tribe, he had not the least discretionary power. How insignificant his influence even was, when severed from organized tribal government, is amply shown by his utter helplessness from the very moment that the Spaniards had *once* treated him as a fettered captive.[61]

[61] The name is variously written "Mutizuma," " Muteczuma," " Moctezuma," " Montezuma," " Moctheuzoma," " Motecuhzoma ;" and " Señor severo," is the most current interpretation. On the tables of *Durán* (Trat. I, Lam. 7, 8, 9, 21, 22, 23, 26) and in general, the "name" is painted as the head-dress (" Xiuhhuitzolli ") of a chieftain, transpierced by an arrow. The etymology may be: " mo "—" thine," " tecuhtli "—" chief," and " çumale "—"furious and wrathy " (*Molina*, II, p. 28), therefore " wrathy chief," or " stern chief." Aside from the charges prefered against him by Ixtlilxochitl and his " school " of subverting gradually the basis of the confederacy, Mexican authors accuse him of having revolutionized the institutions of his own tribe. These reports have been beautifully remodelled into classical English by *Mr. Prescott* ("*Conquest of Mexico,*" Book II, cap. VI, pp. 309 and 310). *Mr. H. H. Bancroft* (Vol. V, pp. 457, 473, 474, 475, etc.), is equally careful in reproducing all such tales, or a résumé thereof, in a shape more palatable to refined and impressionable readers.

The substance of these accusations becomes, however, reduced to the following statements, as expressed by *Tezozomoc* (Cap. LXXXIII, pp. 145 and 146): " He said once to Zihuacoatl Tilpotonqui : I have thought it might be well to change the manner in which the chiefs and messengers should be selected and to establish a different way from that introduced under my uncle Ahuitzotl. Let those serving within their life-time, be dismissed and others put in their places, elected from the four quarters of Moyotlan, Teopan, Aztacualco, and Cuepopan,—which shall be children of chiefs, and shall stay at the huehuecalli, or houses of the community, with the chief-steward dwelling near by. Some of the principals of this tribe now have sons, begotten from slaves, now — these are principals, and let them become delegates (ambassadors, messengers, "embajadores"), and not be cast aside for a miserable macehual who because he is Tequihua, Cacauhtli, or Cuachic, Otomies, should therefore be set over the principal Mexican chiefs, and the sons of head-chiefs (Kings, "reyes") . . . . . . What I want is to bring forth those children of chieftains, which have been forgotten so long, and that such as held the office under the chief Ahuitzotl and your father Zihuacoatl may return to rest. . . . . . Zihuacoatl then called together the council : " al palacio comun," and submitted to them this suggestion, " of which they were all satisfied." With this resolution Zihuacoatl went to the chief and said : I do not want them to be of age now, but only ten or twelve years old, that they may be instructed properly, and become skilled in speaking, well disposed, like unto pages to the chieftain. When they had come before Zihuacoatl, as second person of the chief, he made a long speech to them concerning their line of conduct : Every day you shall attend to Huitzilopochtli and to the chief, rising early for orations, and doing the same at nightfall, to become expert in the ways of penitence and sacrifice. Then you shall cleanse the temple, and the chief-house, afterwards have it swept before he comes

It is therefore vain to look for any important change in the institutions of the ancient Mexicans even at this third and latest date, which was the last chance, so to say, if any at all, for such

out. Keep your dresses clean and in order, also his own dress and ornaments; his tress, medal, and chain; also every five days his blow-tube and bow, that he may recreate himself with it. Attend to him at meal-time, morning and evening. serving him with cacao, roses, perfumes, with much humility and respect, never looking into his face under pain of death. Take care that the cooking be well done, and that the stewards provide for everything. But, while there you stay, beware, for many women of worth are seen there, and to whose needs you have also to attend,—watch your behavior, for should you attempt anything against them, you and your relations will be driven off, and if you commit any bad action with any of these women, your fathers houses will be razed, salt strewn over their ruins, and you and your lineage must perish." At the close of this and other (less important) talk it is said : "and in course of time they became so well bred, refined, and instructed, and skilful, that they were of the most prominent chieftains and leading men in this house and court." *Durán* (Cap. LII, pp. 416–422) does not fail to confirm the statements of Tezozomoc, extending, however, the removals to nearly all the offices : " asi en el servicio de sus casa y per-sona, como en el régimen de la provincia y reyno" (p. 417); also excluding illegitimate offspring (" nengun bastardo "), and giving a number of more or less pertinent details. He even asserts that the officers of the kins were removed. In short, he represents it as the introduction of absolute despotism, surrounding at the same time the throne by a powerful nobility. *Acosta* (Lib. VII, cap. 21. p. 505) and *Herrera* (Dec. III, lib. II, cap. XIV, p. 66), "porqué mandó, que no le sirviesen sino nobles, i que la Gente Ilustre estuviese en su Palacio, i exercitase oficios de su Casa, i Corte." *Torquemada* (Lib. II, cap. LIX, p. 196). *Vetancurt* (Part II, Trat. I, cap. XIX. p. 328). and others, confirm, although in a more concise style than the first named authors. It is evident that all these authors must have gathered from the same source, which cannot be *Sahagun*, nor *Motolinia*, neither *Mendieta*. nor any of the known conquerors. The story, as told and detailed by Durán. presupposes a class of hereditary nobles, already formed and in full vigor, but excluded in part from tenure of office or rather sharing such right of tenure equally with those of the common class. This is distinctly acknowledged by Tezozomoc, and more particularly yet by Durán himself: " y mudar todos los que su tio Auitzotl auia puesto y de los que se auia servido, porque munchas dellos eran de baxa suerte y hijos de hombres baxos," p. 417, etc. Now I have proven (*"Tenure of Lands*, pp. 419. 420, 421, etc., to p. 448) that there was no privileged class based on tenure of the soil. The revolution assumed presupposes that there was, up to the last "wrathy chief," no class of nobles in exclusive possession of the offices, consequently, even if the " chief of men " in question had any inclination or desire to oust the "com-mon people" from their official positions, the main desideratum, namely, the "uncom-mon " ones wherewith to replace them, and for whose benefit the whole affair was planned, were not on hand. For nobility not based on hereditary ownership, or heredi-tary command of some kind, is no nobility at all. As far as heredity of office is con-cerned, Durán himself is one of the most powerful witnesses against it (*e. g.*, Cap. LXIV, pp. 498 and 499). If, therefore, "wrathy chief" created a class of privileged office-holders about the year 1503, it must have been very short-lived, for it was cer-tainly out of existence sixteen years later, at the beginning of the Spanish conquest.

The version of Tezozomoc is evidently the correct one, and thus the whole story dwindles down to the selection of certain boys. probably of his own kin, for the special service of the tribal house of government, which took place *with the knowledge and consent of the council only*. Whether this act, if converted into a custom, might have gradually merged into prevalence of a certain kin over the rest, is another question, which the intervening conquest of Mexico by the Spaniards, has left without decisive answer. About the helplessness of Montezuma while a captive, see authors on the Conquest in general.

a revolution before the advent of Europeans. We are consequently, by this investigation of the history of aboriginal Mexico, justified in claiming the state of its society to be as yet
exclusively tribal.

Tribal society presupposes equality of rights among all members
of the kins composing the tribe. Hence it follows that "caste"
and hereditary rank could not exist, that there could not be any
division, among the ancient Mexicans, into higher and lower
classes, into "nobles" and "common people," or into hereditary
professions or vocations like "priests," "warriors," "merchants,"
"artisans," and "tillers of the soil." In vindication however of
our assertion, which might otherwise appear as too sweeping, we
may be permitted here to dwell at some greater length on this
particular question.

Nobility is based upon hereditary privilege of some kind. Either
it consists in landed property with hereditability of title and (at
least originally) office, or in a hereditary charge alone, or privilege
or power over others transmitted with the blood. While the former
has become more usually known and is therefore regarded as
characteristic, the latter, always accompanied by "loose wealth"
at least, is still found among pastoral nations.[62] It may even
have been the incipient form of the other. Now, among the
ancient Mexicans, we have seen that :—

1. The notion of abstract ownership of the soil, in any shape,
had not yet arisen.

2. Individuals, whatever might be their position or office, without any exception, had but a right to use certain tracts, and no
possessory rights, even, to land were attached to any office or
dignity.

3. No office itself, whether of the kin or tribe, was hereditary
in any family, since the Mexican family, as such, was yet in but
a nascent state.[63]

4. Futhermore loose property was subject to such diminutions
occasioned by the mode of worship,[64] and especially of burial,[65]

---

[62] The Arabs for instance. See *Kremer* (" *Geschichte der herrschenden Ideen des
Islam*").

[63] For these three points see " *Tenure of Lands*" in general, and pp. 447–48 in particular.

[64] *Motolinia* (Trat. I, cap. IV, p. 31). " Otros trabajaban y adquirian dos ó tres años
cuanto podian, para hacer una fiesta al demonio, y en ella no solo gastaban cuanto
tenian, mas aun se adeudaban, de manera que tenian que servir y trabajar otro año y
aun otros dos para salir de deuda; . . ."

that it could not accumulate so as to exert any influence in the hands and in behalf of any individual or of his immediate relatives.

Consequently, aboriginal Mexico could have neither nobility nor patriciate, and when such a privileged class does not exist, it is useless to seek for another to which the term "unprivileged" or "common" can be applied.

In a future essay we shall attempt to prove that the Mexicans had no hereditary caste of "medicine men" or priests. We have elsewhere shown that there was no caste of warriors.[66] The mode of Tenure and distribution of the soil precludes all possibility of the existence of a permanent class of "tillers." It yet remains to cast a glance at the so-called artisans, and at the traders or "merchants."

Neither of these two professions were held to personal improvement of their garden lots ("tlalmilli") but, like officers, they could have them improved by others under their names and for their benefit.[67] The statement of Zurita "that a quarter was composed of all kinds of people" [68] disposes of the opinion, that such quarters contained each but members *practising a single trade*. Thus there was no geographical agglomeration by professions.[69] Again, no rule existed enforcing or establishing hereditament in kind of work, or manner of sustenance. The son might embrace, at his choice, his father's occupation, but *nothing*

[65] Compare the burial rites of the Mexicans as reported by the majority of old sources.

[66] *"Art of War"* (p. 98, notes 8, 9, 40). *Zurita "Rapport,"* (p. 48), "Ils étaient tenus seulement au service militaire, pour lequel aucune excuse n'était admise."

[67] "*Tenure of Lands*" (p. 426, note 98). Consult the authorities therein quoted.

[68] "*Rapport*" (p. 224).

[69] It is mostly on the authority of *Sahagun* (Lib. IX, vol. II), that the settlement by professional clusters is admitted. *Ixtlilxochitl* ("*Histoire des Chichimèques*," Cap. XXXVIII, pp. 262 and 263, "*Duodécima Relacion*," p. 388, Kingsborough, Vol. IX) also says that, at Tezcuco, each profession had its own quarter in the pueblo. But an attentive reading of the first author named (Cap. XVIII, p. 392), where he treats of the featherworkers "De los oficiales que labran pluma, que hacen plumajes, y otras cosas de la misma," satisfies us at once of the fact, that the venerable author only refers to worship of certain idols in a certain quarter, and not to compulsory residence therein, of certain kinds of working men. Nowhere does he say that the "Amantecas" wer *all* featherworkers. He mentions a barrio "Amatlan" or "Amantla." Might it be the "Amanalco" of Vetancurt? Compare also *Torquemada* (Lib. VI. cap. XXX, pp. 59 and 60), *Motolinia* (Trat. I, cap. XII, pp. 67 and 68). "*El conquistador Anónimo*" (Col. de Doc. Vol. I). "Le piazze de i mercati," (pp. 392 and 393), although concerning the markets exclusively. *Herrera* (Dec. III. lib. IV, p. 138, cap. 138), "i estos andaban por los Barrios, porque en ellos havia de todo género de gentes." Copied after Zurita *Vetancurt* (Part II, Trat. I, cap. IV), *Clavigero* (Lib. VII, cap. LI, p. 561).

compelled him to do it.[70]   It is true, that such as formed gold or silver into pleasing or (as viewed from eastern notions of taste) rather striking shapes, enjoyed some particular consideration; but this was not so much in deference to their skill, as to the *material* upon which they exerted it.   Gold ("teo-cuitlatl") and silver ("Iztac-teo-cuitlatl") were regarded as "offal of gods." Thus they became objects of " medicine," and those who wrought them into useful or decorative articles, were near to the "medicine-men" themselves.[71]   Furthermore, the manner and method of working was so slow, it relied so exclusively upon that patient disregard of time which characterizes even the manufacture of a simple arrowhead, that no accumulation of wealth could result from it.[72]   Besides, the artisan had, like any other member of the kin, to furnish his share towards the requirements of public

[70] *Zurita* (" Rapport, etc ," p. 129). " Les chefs inférieurs et les personnes du peuple élevaient aussi leurs enfants avec beaucoup de soin, leur inspiraient l'horreur du vice, leur recommandaient le respect des dieux, les conduisaient aux temples et les faisaient travailler suivañt leurs dispositions; cependant, en général, le fils embrassait la profession de son père." *Gomara* (" *Conquista,* etc.," Vedia, Vol. I, p. 438). " Los pobres enseñaban á sus hijos sus oficios, no porque no tuviesen libertad para mostralles otro, sino porque los aprendiesen sin gastar con ellos," *Carlos Maria de Bustamante. Tezcoco en los ultimos Tiempos de sus antiguos Reyes,*" 1826. Parte tercera, (Cap. III, p. 212). "Enseñaban ademas los oficios á que tenian aficion." *Clavigero* (Lib. VII, cap. V, p. 462). "The sons generally learned the trade of their fathers," but they were not bound to do it, and therefore no " caste."

[71] The words are composed of: "Iztac," white object (*Molina* II, p. 49), "Teotl" god (II, p. 101), "Cuitlatl" filth, therefore gold was " offal of God," and silver, " white offal of God."

The working of gold and silver was regarded, by the Mexicans, as an invention of "Quetzalcohuatl." *Sahagun* (Lib. III, cap. III, p. 243). " y los vasallos que tenia eran todos oficiales de artes mecánicas, y diestros para labrar las piedras verdes, que se llaman chalchivites, y tambien para fundir plata, y hacer otras cosas; y estas artes todos tuviéron principio y origen de l dicho *Quetzalcoatl* " (Also Lib. X, cap. XXIX, p. 113, etc.) Theft of gold or precious stones was punished by death through sacrifice. *Clavigero* (Lib. VII, cap. XVII, p. 487). *Vetancurt* (Parte IIa, Trat. 1°, p. 484. " Leyes do los Mexicanos ").

[72] A very remarkable way of manufacturing their most admired works — those made of feathers — is reported by *Mendieta* (Lib. IV, cap. XII, pp. 405 and 406): "And there is, besides, something else to notice of this featherwork, namely: that if there are twenty artisans, they will undertake jointly the manufacture of one piece (" imágen"), for, dividing among themselves the figure of the image in as many parts as there are of their number, each one takes his piece home and finishes it there. Afterwards they all meet again and put their pieces together, thus finishing the figure in as perfect a manner as if one alone had made the whole." (Copied by *Torquemada,* Lib. XIII, cap. XXXIV, p. 489, and, with slight variations, also by *Vetancurt,* Vol. I, p. 389.) In regard to the manner of working, *Torquemada* (Lib. XIII, cap. XXXIV, p. 487), makes the pertinent remark: "All this they worked (as we have said) with other stones, and with flint; and according to the subtlety of the work, I think they must have spent long time in finishing it." See in general *E. B. Tylor* (" *Researches into the Early History of Mankind,*" Cap. VII, pp. 187 and 188), also *Motolinia* (Trat. I, cap. IV, pp. 31 and 32).

life :[73] hence little was left to him beyond his legitimate wants. We see thus, that hardly any chance was given for the formation of a class which, resting upon the kind of occupation, might assume the position of "caste" in the organization of aboriginal Mexican society.

It is repeatedly asserted, and on high authority, that the merchants or traders of Mexico enjoyed particular privileges. We must premise here that merchants, in the sense of venders of other people's manufactures or products (thus living off of the difference between cost and proceeds) were known only in one way.[74] The name for merchant was "man who exchanges one

[73] That the artisans or mechanics contributed a portion of their wares in the shape of tribute, is amply proven. See for instance, *Oviedo* (Lib. XXXIII, cap LI, p. 530. Easily misunderstood!) This passage of Oviedo explains the action of "wrathy chief" towards the "jewellers" and "goldsmiths" at the arrival of Cortés, as related by Tezozomoc, Durán, and by Sahagun. See also: *Zurita* ("Rapport, etc.," p. 223). *Bustamante* ("Tezcoco, etc.," Parte III, cap. V, p. 232). *Herrera* (Dec. III, lib. IV, cap. XVII, p. 138). *Clavigero* (Lib. VII, cap. XV, p. 480). *Bancroft* (Vol. III, cap. VI, pp. 231 and 232).

[74] The existence of currency, or of money, in the shape of grains of cacao, T shapen pieces of tin or copper, and quills filled with gold dust is generally admitted. See for instance, *Prescott* ("Conquest of Mexico," Book IV, cap. II. p. 140). *H. H. Bancroft* (Vol. II, cap. XII, pp. 381, 382. and 383). Cacao played, among the ancient Mexicans, the same role as "wampum" did among the northern Indians, for purposes of exchange, but did not go beyond it. In regard to the so-called copper or tin coins, or rather marks or checks, it is well to examine the matter more closely. *Cortés* ("Carta Quarta" in Vedia I, p. 111), says very positively that at Tachco, he obtained sundry small pieces of tin like very thin money ("á manera de moneda muy delgada"), which he indeed found to have been used as currency by the natives, ("halló que en dicha provincia, aun en otras, se trataba por moneda"). *Bernal Diez* (Cap, XCII, p. 89, Vedia II) mentions axes of "brass, copper, and tin" ("hachas de laton y cobre y estaño"), bartered at the market place of Tlatelulco, "and before we left this square ("plaza") we met with other traders, who from what they said, sold gold in grains as they obtained it from the mines, and enclosed in quills of the geese of the land, and so thin ("asi blaucos" so white) that the gold might be seen, and by the length and size of the quills they determined how many mantles or "jiquipiles" (bags of 8000 grains) of cacao they were worth, or slaves, or any other things for which they bartered it," ("ó otra qualquier cosa á que lo trocaban"). *Gomara* ("Conquista, etc.," pp. 348 and 349). "But the chief one is cacahuatl, which serves as coin. . . ." "Their buying and selling consists in exchanging one thing for another. . . ." (Id., p. 451). "No tenian moneda, teniendo mucha plata, oro y cobre, y sabiéndolo hundir y labrar, y contratando mucho en ferias y mercados. Su moneda usual y corriente es cacauatl ó cacao." *Oviedo* (Lib. VIII, cap. XXX, pp. 316, 317. Lib. XXXIII, cap. LI, p. 536) mentions only cacao as currency. *Torquemada* (Lib. XIV, cap. XIV, p. 260). "It was customary at these marts ('en estos mercados') to exchange ('trocar') one thing for another, and even nowadays this is sometimes practised; but everywhere cacao is most commonly used. In other parts they used, besides, some small mantles which they call Patol-quachtli. . . . . . Elsewhere they used plentifully some copper coins, almost like unto ("de hechura") a Tau T, two or three fingers wide and made of thin plates ("plan-chuela") some thicker, other less thick. Where there was much gold ("donde avia mucho Oro"), small quills filled with it, circulated among the Indians," ("traian unos Canutillos de ello, y andaba entre los Indios mucho de esto"). *Alonzo Zuazo* ("Carta

thing for another" ("tlanamacani"),[75] and such was every artisan, since, in the market place of aboriginal Mexico, every artisan bartered his own manufactures for whatever he needed for sub-

al Padre Fray Luis de Figueroa." Santiago de Cuba, 14 Nov., 1521. Col. de Doc. Vol. I, p. 361). "Hay una moneda entre ellos con que venden y compran, que se llama cacahuate, . . ." *Anonymous Conqueror* (p. 380, etc.) mentions Cacao, "e é moneta la piu comune, ma molto incomoda dopo l'oro é l'argento . . . . *Acosta* (Lib. IV, cap. 3, p. 198) " No se halla. que los Indios usassen oro, ni plata, ni metal para moneda, ni para precio de la cosas, usauanlo para ornato, como esta dicho." The statement of Torquemada is plain. While it explains the gradual ascent and development of the notion that the Mexicans had an equivalent to money, it clearly proves that only barter and exchange, and no actual buying. took place. The copper-plates which, as Mr. Bancroft justly remarks, "constituted perhaps the nearest approach to coined money," still were not intended even for such a purpose, since they were of varying size and thickness. But the story of the *copper* or *golden "Eagles"* given to the Mexican traders as money wherewith to buy, as faithfully reported and gravely discussed by Mr. Bancroft also, deserves some special ventilation. This story is taken from *Sahagun* (Lib. IX, cap. II, p. 342) " y dábales 1600 toldillos, que ellos llaman quauhtli para rescatar." These toldillos they divided into two parts of 800 each. Now Sahagun's editor, Sr. C. M. de Bustamante, very confidently asserts in note a, (p. 342): " Era una moneda que consistia en unos pedazos de cobre cortados en figura de T.— Clavigero, tom. I, pág. 349." The reference to *Clavigero* is for Lib. VII, cap. XXXVI. Now "Toldillo" is derived from " toldár" that is, to shroud or cover, and means merely a *cover*, and not a piece of metal. Used also for a covered litter or portable chair. Besides, "quauhtli" indeed signifies Eagle, but it is an evident misprint and should read " quachtli," which signifies a *mantle* or *sheet*, thus perfectly agreeing both with the "toldillo" and with the "patolquachtli" of Torquemada. The "golden eagles" of Mr. Brasseur are therefore rendered utterly useless.

Anyone reading *Tezozomoc* will see at a glance what a conspicuous part these mantles "Quachtli," (*Molina.* II, p. 84) played in intercourse and barter. According to *Ramirez de Fuenleal* (Letter, etc., Col. de Doc's conc. le Méxique, I, p. 251) they formed to a certain extent the basis of tribute. These cotton-sheets are well described by *Peter Martyr* (" *De nouo Orbe.*" Dec. V., cap. X, p. 230): "Concerning the shape and fashion of their garments, it is ridiculous to behold: they call it a garmente, because they couer themselves therewith. but it hath no resemblance with any other garment, of any fashion: it is only a square couering like unto that, which your holiness cast on your shoulders, sometimes in my presence, when you are about to kimbe your heade, to preserve your garments. least haire, or any other filth should fal upon them. That couering they cast about their necke, and then knitting two of the four corners under their throate. they lette the couering hang downe, which scarce couereth the bodie as lowe as the legges. Having seen these garments I ceased to wonder, that so great a number of garments was sent to Cortes, as we mentioned before: for they are all of small moment, and many of them take uppe but little roome."

With the absence of money the profession of merchant as one who lives from the profits of his sales, becomes limited almost to what he can gather from outside of his own community. in other words, to what he can *import*. Their main and almost exclusive business consisted in effecting intercourse between the tribes. At home, every artisan sold or rather exchanged his own wares in the public markets. See *Cortés* ("*Carta Segunda,*" Vedia I, pp. 32 and 33), *Bernal Diez* ("*Hist. verdad.,*" etc., Vedia II, p. 89, cap. XCII), *Gomara* ("*Conquista.*" p. 348, Vedia I), " Cada oficio y cada mercaderia tiene su lugar señalado . . . .", *Sahagun* (Lib. X, cap. XVI, p. 41), "El que vende piedras preciosas, ó lapidario es de esta propriedad. que sabe labrar sutilmente las piedras preciosas y pulirlas. . . ." He mentions as manufacturers of their own goods the following: "plateros de oro" (41), "Tratantes en mantas" (Cap. XVII, 42), "que venden mantas," "que venden cotaras" (Cap. XX, pp. 48, 49 and 51), "olleros," "que

sistance. Another name for the same profession was "man who takes more than he gives" "tiamicqui,"[76] a surname or slur. Lastly they were called "puchtecatl."[77] It is with this title that traders appear, among the ancient Mexicans, as privileged people. But such they became always only under peculiar circumstances. At certain intervals of time a number of men gathered, forming a company for the purpose of visiting the market places of other tribes and exchanging their home products for those of distant regions. Such an enterprise was always a great venture, and required a peculiar organization. The participants were to be numerous enough to resist the assaults of straggling bands, but they should not appear so numerous as to arouse suspicion. They should be well armed, but at the same time anxious to avoid collision. They needed a certain number of carriers, not only for the wares which they took along, but for their supplies, still the number of these carriers could not be too great. Such an expedition was in reality not a private, but a tribal undertaking. Its members not only carried into distant countries the industry of their tribe, but they also had to observe the customs, manners, and resources of the people whom they visited. Clothed with diplomatic attributes, they often were less traders than *spies*. Thus they cautiously felt their way from tribe to tribe, from Indian fair to Indian fair, exchanging their stuff for articles not produced at home, all the while carefully noting what might be important to their own tribe. It was a highly dangerous mission. Frequently they never returned, being waylaid, or treacherously butchered even while enjoying the hospitality of a pueblo in which they had been bartering.

The safe return however of such a party to the pueblo of Mexico was always an important and joyful event. The reception was sometimes, in solemnity of exercises and in barbarous

venden comales," "que venden cestos," "que vende petacas" (Cap. XXIII, p. 56, etc.), "oficial de navajas," "Los que hacen esteras" (Cap. XXIV, p. 69). In general, nearly all the aboriginal manufacturers are mentioned by him also as selling the products of their industry, and vice versa. *H. H. Bancroft* (Vol. II, pp. 383 and 384, cap. XII).

[75] *Molina* ("*Vocabulario*" Parte Ia, p. 84). "Tlanamacac," "tendero," "á vendedor de algo," Parte IIa, p. 127; "nite-tlanamictia," "dar o trocar una cosa por otra, o recompensar" (p. 127, II). Exchange and sale appear almost synonymous.

[76] *Molina* (Parte Ia, p. 84). From "nite-tiamicaquitia," "mohatrar" (II, p. 112).

[77] *Molina* (I, 84), also (II, 83, 84). *Sahagun* (Lib. IX, cap. III, p. 348, cap. V, pp. 354, 355, cap. X, p. 372, etc.), calls them also: "naoaloztomeca," literally "peddlars of the Nahuatl." *Molina* (II, p. 78). The derivation of both words I am unable to give.

pomp, second only to that of the tribal forces returning from a successful campaign or foray. The traders went first to the central place of worship, there to stoop before the idols in token of adoration. From the great "medicine-lodge" the band repaired to the "tecpan," where they met the council of the tribe and its leading officers. Sometimes in presence of a concourse of people, and again if required, in "secret session" the traders communicated, for the benefit of the tribe, any results of their explorations. After this their particular quarters gave them appropriate receptions also, and in some instances even the whole tribe celebrated their return with solemn dances, and a distribution of victuals corresponding to what in our time would be called a popular feast.

In order to realize the substantial results of such expeditions we must bear in mind, that whatever they brought back had to be carried by men. As already intimated, the number of these men was limited. They could not, without jeopardizing the object of their mission or enterprise, take large bodies of assistants along. Besides, as these assistants also had to carry their own food, providing for many journeys through uncultivated ("neutral") wastes, this also restricted the amount of material brought home. However precious that material might be to the Mexican tribe, it was certainly limited in quantity. Finally, custom demanded that the most highly priced articles should be offered up to worship, to the stores of the tribe and of the kins. Little material gain therefore, remained to the courageous travellers themselves. The proceeds of their enterprise were largely for the benefit of the community and the reward bestowed upon them by that community rather than the profits derived from any traffic, composed the personal gain of the participants. This reward consisted of presents out of the public stores, and especially in the marks of distinction bestowed upon them.

Thus the so-called "merchants" of ancient Mexico became equivalent to distinguished braves, and their deeds entitled them frequently to the rank of chiefs. But if, on one hand, they had no opportunity to secure anything like personal wealth, on the other the rewards of merit did not attach to their offspring. No *class* of traders, no *caste* of merchants, can therefore have existed, and if a certain well-earned consideration attached itself to the person of those who embraced occasionally such a hazardous

and important occupation, this consideration did not go beyond
the persons themselves, and was in proportion to the value of the
achievements.[78]

[78] *Prescott* ("*Conquest,*" Book I, cap. V, p. 147). *Bancroft* (Vol. II, cap. XII, p. 387,
etc.). *Bastian* ("Culturlaender," Vol. II, pp. 697 and 698) and others like *Brasseur de
Bourbourg* ("*Histoire des Nations civilisées du Méxique et de l'Amérique Centrale,*" 1857–
1859, Paris, Vol. III, p. 612, etc.), have given more or less detailed descriptions of the
Mexican mode of traffic and commerce. Among the older sources, and those which
necessarily formed the basis of my imperfect sketch, the leading position is occupied
by *Father Sahagun* (Lib. IX, Vol. II, "*Historia general de la Cosas de Nueva-España*).
From these statements we gather, what has already been said (note 58), that the Tlatilulca were the leading traders (Cap. I, pp. 335, 336), and that they were organized and
directed by particular chiefs of their own. The venerable father is not very clear in
the matter of these particular officers, as (Cap. I) he names first two (p. 335), then five
(p. 337, cap. II), and lastly (Lib. X, cap. XVI, p. 40), one: "Señor ó Principal entre
ellos," whom he calls: "puchtecatlailotlac, ó acxôtecatl, que es tanto, como si
dijésemos que es gobernador de los mercaderes, y estos dos nombres y otros muchos
que están puestos en la letra, se atribuyen al que es mayor principal gobernador ó señor
ó que es casi padre y madre de todos los mercaderes." (Lib. IX, cap. III, pp. 348 and
349), he speaks of " the principals," "los mercaderes viejos" as " speakers of the
traders " " pochtecatlatoque." Further on (Cap. X, p. 372), he speaks of the "poch-
tecatlailotlac " as the principals. We must infer from this that there were a *number of
these leading traders,* and not one chief of the " caste." This evidence or rather indication of a possible separate organization is not noticed by *Torquemada* (Lib. XIV,
cap. XXVII, p. 586), who simply speaks of the "old traders who remained at the
pueblo." *Clavigero* (Lib. VII, cap. XXXVIII, pp. 526 and 527) merely mentions the
older and the younger traders, but says nothing of a peculiar organization. It is
singular, besides, that those authors or more properly chroniclers, in whose annals of
Mexican warfare the Mexican traders play a very conspicuous part, make no mention
at all of this peculiar caste-like organization which Sahagun seems to imply. Those
authors are *Durán* and *Tezozomoc.* (In this instance I need not resort to detailed quotations, since the references in their works are far too numerous). Furthermore,
Zurita, who is very detailed in his " *Rapport,*" or rather as the full title has it " *Breve
y Sumaria Relacion de los Señores, y maneras y diferencias que habia de ellas en la Nueva
España,*" while enumerating carefully the different kinds of chiefs and officers, is rather
reticent about any such organization of the merchants. Compare for instance, p.
223, where he distinctly says that, they had a chief to treat with the "Lords and governors" in their name, and p. 240, where he incidentally mentions a "chief of the
merchants" only. *Sahagun* goes further yet, however, in stating (Lib. IX, cap. V, pp.
356 and 357), that the merchants had their own jurisdiction over themselves, apart
from that of the tribe or kin : 'y los señores mercaderes que regian á los otros, tenian
por su jurisdicion y judicatoria, y si alguno de estos hacian algun delito, no los llevaban
delante de los senadores á que ellos los juzgasen; sino que estos mismos que eran
señores de los otros mercaderes juzgaban las causas de todos por si; si alguno incurria
en pena de muerte ellos le sentenciaban, y mataban ó en la carcèl, ó en su casa, ó en
otra parte segun que lo tenian de costumbre." This he distinctly applies to the
" pochtecas " of Tlatilulco, and to the time when " wrathy chief" (Montezuma the last),
was at the head of the Mexicans. Not content with this he relates (Cap. II, pp. 339–342),
how the merchants of Tlatilulco alone conquered several tribes, subjecting them to
tribute for the benefit of the Mexicans. In all these statements Father Sahagun stands
quite alone, and, if not directly contradicted, he is, at least so unsupported as to make his
reports rather doubtful so far as they concern the organization and power of these
traders as a distinct class. The story has a suspiciously Tlatilulcan coloring. Compare note 58. It is interesting to note, in connection with this, that Sahagun derived
the information, the which he laid down in his " Historia general," almost exclusively

After this review of the question of stratification, so to say, among the ancient Mexicans, it may appear strange on our part

from *Tlatilulcan sources* ("Prologo," pp. 4 and 5, Vol. I). This diminishes necessarily in this instance, the value of his otherwise very full and highly important testimony.

The existence of such a body, powerful through wealth as well as through mental and intellectual faculties would, even as much as nobility, at once have destroyed the tribe as such, by breaking up the kins. The inconsistency of such a picture with the historical facts is glaring, and is shown even by the statements of modern writers. Compare for instance, Mr. H. H. Bancroft's statement of the condition of Tlatilulco after its capture by the Mexicans (Vol. V, p. 431), "heavy tributes were imposed, including many special taxes and menial duties of a humiliating nature" with his description of the state of its "merchant princes" (Vol. II, pp. 380 and 381). One fact is evident: if the traders formed occasionally, lor certain purposes, clusters of their own, they selected their own leaders or directors and this was the case with trading expeditions as well as with feasts. See on feasts: *Sahagun*, Lib. IX, cap. III to XIV inclusive, Lib. I. cap. XIX, pp. 29 to 32. *Motolinia*, Trat. I. cap. VIII, p. 47. *Acosta*, Lib. V, cap. XXIX, p. 389, etc. *Torquemada*, Lib. VI, cap. XXVIII, pp. 57 and 58. Lib. XIV, cap. XXVII, pp. 586 and 587. *Clavigero*, Lib. VI, cap. VII, p. 360. Lib. VII, cap. XXXVIII, p. 526, etc., and others. But as to any separate, permanent government of their own, this rests exclusively upon the authority of Sahagun, whereas it is amply proven, on the other hand, that any crime committed in trade or barter, was summarily disposed of by the regular officers of the kin or tribe without regard to the traders or merchants. We shall furnish the evidence in regard to this point in another note.

That the "pochtecas" occupied but one calpulli, that of Pochtlan, is also disproved, and even by *Sahagun* himself (Lib. I. cap. XIX, p. 31). "En este calpulli donde se contaba el mercader." (Lib. IX, cap. III, p. 347): "respondiante los mercaderes principales de los barrios que son uno que se llama Pochtlan, otro Aoachtlan, y otro Atlauhco como está en la letra"). (Cap. III, p. 349) "convidaban á solos los mercaderes de su barrio; pues el que habia de ir por capitan de la compañia de los que iban, no solamente convidaba á los de su barrio, sino tambien á los que habian de ir con él." Also by *Zurita* ("Rapport," etc., pp. 223 and 224).

Lastly the question of wealth amassed in such quantities as to become an influential power in the merchants' hands, is also summarily disposed of by *Sahagun*. However often he speaks of riches gathered by them, the following quotations show how it must be understood: (Lib. IX, cap. II, p. 338, Speech of one of the traders) "Cuando lleguemos á nuestro tierra, será tiempo de usar los barbotes de ambar, y las oregeras que se llaman quetzalcoyolnacohtli, y los aventaderos y ojeadores de moscas, las mantas ricas que hemos de traer, y los maxtles preciados, solo esto será nuestra paga, y la señal de nuestra valentia," (p. 341) "y que las otras presias que les dió que arriba se dijéron, solo ellos las usasen en las grandes fiestas . . . ." It thus appears that hoarding of any actual wealth was not to be expected. The lack of currency alone made it almost impossible for want of space, and gold and silver being only used for ornamental purposes and as a part of "medicine," we should mistake in expecting anything like "treasures." Here, as anywhere else, the supply was regulated by the demand, and this demand was in turn created by the numbers of the population, and by the use made of the metal. Since the latter was used only in a few ways, this had its effect on the amount also. Another cause, which is not sufficiently estimated, is found in the fact that carriers had to be used for everything, including food. Now, even if thousands went along (of which there is hardly any proof), the load of each hardly exceeded sixty pounds: "y daban á cado uno de estos que tenian alquilados, para que llevasen acuestas la carga que tenian señalada, y de tal manera las comparaban que no eran muy pesadas" (Cap. III, p. 350, Lib. IX). *Don Antonio de Mendoza* ("*Avis sur les prestations personnelles et les Tamemes*, ler Recueil of Ternaux-Compans), says in 1550, "They must not carry any loads heavier than two arrobas," or about fifty pounds. *Bartolomé de las Casas* ("*Brevissima relacion de la destruycion de las Yndias*," Venetia, 1643, Italian and Spanish, p. 101), complains of three to four arobas or

to concede, that nevertheless there were two very distinct classes within the area occupied by the tribe enjoying each a very different quality of rights. Now equality of rights is the fundamental principle of kinship;[79] if therefore there was a body connected with the tribe whose rights and privileges were inferior, it follows that the members of this body must have stood outside

seventy-five to one hundred pounds, as an excessive load. *Clavigero* (Lib. VII, cap. XL, p. 529), sixty pounds.

To conclude, I advert to the fact that the traders were held to tribute and especially to offerings for worship, as strictly as any other members of the tribe. I merely refer to *Herrera* (Dec. III, Lib. IV, cap. XVII, p. 138), who embodies in a few words the statements of other writers. *Motolinia* (Trat. I, cap. IV, p. 76), "No se desvelan en adquirir riquezas," and further on to p. 77; also (Trat. I, cap. IV, p. 31), "otros trabajaban y adquirian dos ó tres años cuanto podian, para hacer una fiesta al demonio, y en ella no solo gastaban cuanto tenian, mas aun se adeudaban". The picture of the trading expedition is mainly taken from *Sahagun* (Lib. IX, cap. II, III, IV) and *Torquemada* (Lib. XIV, cap. XXVII). The reception only applies to cases of great importance. But every departure of a merchant as well as his return was feasted by the traders of his " barrios," sometimes with the concurrence of other barrios and of the chiefs and officers.

That, in consequence of their deeds, the merchants and traders were treated with distinction and created chiefs, follows from *Sahagun* (Lib. I, cap. XIX, pp. 30 and 31), " para que fuese honrado en el pueblo, y tenido per valiente: poniante un barbote de ámbar, que es una piedra larga amarilla trasparente, que cuelga del beso bajo, ahujerado, en señal de que era valiente y era noble, y esto se tenia en mucho." But especially (Lib. IX, cap. II, pp. 338–341), " Estos mercaderes eran ya como caballeros, y tenian divisas particulares por sus hazañas "). "*Des Cérémonies observérs autrefois par les Indiens lorsqu'ils faisaient un tecle*" (Ternaux, 1er Recueil, pp. 233 and 234). The custom of giving the rank of chief (" tecuhtli") to traders remained after the conquest when the chief became transformed into the Spanish *hidalgo* in consequence of a misconception of the former dignity. This is shown plainly by the arch-bishop, *Fray Alonzo de Montufar* ("*Supplique à Charles V en faveur des Macéuales*, Mexico, 30 Nov. 1551, French translation by Mr. Ternaux, Appendix to his "*Cruautés horribles des Conquérants du Méxique*," p. 257). It was done to evade taxation.

The true position of the Mexican traders in their tribe and society is also stated plainly by *Sahagun* (Lib. I, cap. XIX, p. 30): " Son estos mercaderes sufridores de muchos trabajos, y osados para entrar en todas las tierras (aunque sean las de enemigos) y muy astutos para tratar con los estraños, asi aprendiendo sus lenguas, como tratando con ellos con benevolencia para atraerlos asi con su familiaridad." (Lib. IX, cap. II, p. 339) "pues que aunque nos llamamos mercaderes y lo parecemos, somos soldados que disimuladamente andamos á conquistar." (Id., p. 341) "Los dichos mercaderes del Tlaltelolco se llaman tambien capitanes y soldados disimulados en hábito de mercaderes que andaban por todas partes." (p. 342) "Cuando quiera que el señor de Mexico queria enviar á los mercaderes, que eran capitanes y soldados disimulados á alguna provincia para que la atalayasen." *Zurita* ("*Rapport*," etc., p. 223) "Ils jouissaient de certains privilèges, parceque leur profession était utile à l'état." This is textually copied by *Bustamante* ("*Tezcoco*," Parte IIIa, cap. V, p. 232). They were frequently but official spies and used as such, not only *by* the Mexicans, but *against* the Mexicans by foreign tribes. *Mendieta* (Lib. II, cap. XXVII, p. 130) copied by *Torquemada* (Lib. XIV, cap. II, p. 538).

[79] *L. H. Morgan* ("*Ancient Society*," Part II, cap. II, p. 85, in relation to Iroquois more particularly). Among the ancient Germans or Teutons, see *Heinrich Luden* (" *Geschichte des teutschen Volkes*," 1825, Vol. I, Lib. III, cap. V, on the " *Gau*," pp. 492 and 493).

of any connection by kin. This presupposes *a class of outcasts from the bond of kinship.*

There is no evidence of the formation of such a cluster prior to the permanent settlement of the tribe. Neither can we trace its gradual increase from a given time. But a glance at some of the rules of kinship, and at the practical working of these rules finally crystallizing into an equivalent for laws, will enable us to discern its origin.

The relation of sexes being at the bottom of society based upon kin, it follows that sexual intercourse gradually assumed a regulated shape, proportionate to the progress in institutions. The ancient Mexicans had, as we have already established, advanced into descent in the male line, and had secured a nascent state of the modern family. Marriage was well known to them as a *rule*. But so powerful was the influence exercised by the kin, as unit of public life that, once the ritual union of a couple acknowledged as a necessity for future joint life, it exacted of its male members the obligation to marry for the purpose of propagating and increasing the kin. Only such as were naturally helpless, and such as in view of " medicine" made vows of permanent chastity, were excused. Any other youth therefore, who refused to take a wife at the proper age, was treated with contempt and consequently expelled from the kin.[80]

Woman, among the aboriginal Mexicans, was in a singular predicament. Through the establishment of descent in the male line she lost her hold on public life, (which she latterly regained through the establishment of the family proper) and thus remained little else than a *chattel* in the power of man. Still, the ritual act of marriage being once adopted, the same obligation to marry, which we have already found incumbent upon the male, also devolved upon the female, and any girl therefore, who did not " take vows" for "medicine," or who was physically not mis-

[80] *Clavigero* (Lib. VII, cap. V, p. 461). *Zurita* (" Rapport, etc.," pp 133 and 134) "s'ils ne voulaient pas prendre des femmes, on les congédiait." *Mendieta* (Lib. II, cap. XXIV, p. 125), "Llegados á la edad de casarse, ... Si pasando la edad se descuidaban, y veian que no se querian casar, tresquilábanlos, y despedianlos de la compañia de los mancebos." This meant exclusion from the kin since, as soon as they were married, " they were classified, since, according to their custom, they were divided into sections each of which had a chief or captain, as well for the collection of taxes as for other reasons." These " chiefs or captains " were those of the calpulli. *Zurita*, (p. 135), also *Bustamante*, (" Tezcoco," Part III. cap. III, p. 213), "Cuando se casaban los empadronaban. . . . ." *Torquemada* (Lib. IX, cap. XII, p. 186, almost a copy of Mendieta).

shapen, if she did not join a husband at the proper age, was also regarded as a reprobate.[81]

To these two kinds of outcasts others should be added. It is a known fact that, if any member of a calpulli failed to cultivate his garden lot for two years, or if he failed to have it cultivated under his name, then he lost every and all rights thereto. This implied expulsion from the calpulli, consequently again, *expulsion from the bond of kinship*. Any one who removed from the quarter or calpulli to which he belonged, lost his rights thereby; in other words he became an outcast.[82]

The lot of such people, thrust, as they were, outside of the pale of regular society, was an unenviable one. Removal to foreign tribes was not only dangerous, but even impracticable in the earlier times, when the class came into existence. Still they had to *live*. Therefore the males bargained their services to such members of the kins, as could afford to nourish them in return for manual labor.[83] No other remuneration but subsistence could be thought of. For the sake of subsistence therefore the outcast became, what the majority of authorities have called a *slave*.

Fray Juan de Torquemada writes as follows; — "The manner, in which these Indians made slaves, was very different from that of the nations of Europe and other parts of the world. It was very difficult at the outset of their conversion to understand it properly, but to make it clear (especially as the customs of Mexico, and Tetzcuco had it, since other Provinces not subject to these king-

---

[81] *Anonymous Conqueror* (Vol. I, Col. de Doc., p. 397) " & gente che stima meno le donne di quanti nationi sono al mondo, perchi non gli comunichereble mai i fatti loro, anchora che conoscuse che il farlo gli potesse melter conto." *Oviedo* (Lib. XXXIII, cap. LI, p. 536). See *Torquemada* (Lib. XII, cap. III. p. 366), on " mancebas " in general in regard to women who refused to marry, though living a dissolute life. Also *Sahagun* (Lib. X. cap. XV, p. 37); *Zurita* (p. 129). If a girl abandoned her house, she might finally be disposed of as a slave, or be abandoned (" on les abandonnait ").

[82] *Zurita* (p. 56). " Le propriétaire qui ne cultivait pas pendant deux années, par sa faute ou par négligence, sans juste cause, ... était averti de les cultiver; et s'il ne le faisait pas, l'année d'ensuite on les donnait à un autre." (Id. p.54.) " Si, par hazard, le membre d'un calpulli le quittait pour aller demeurer dans un autre, on lui retirait les terres qui lui avaient été assignées. . . . . Adopted also by *Herrera* (Dec. III, lib. IV, cap. XV, p. 135). Compare " *Tenure of Lands* " (p 426).

[83] *Gomara* (" *Conquista*," Vedia I, p. 441). "Los hombres necesitados y haraganes se vendian. . . ." *Cortés* (" *Carta Segunda*," Vedia I, p. 34). "Hay en todos los mercados y lugares públicos de la dicha ciudad, todos los dias, muchas personas trabajadores y maestros de todos oficios, esperando quien los alquile por sus jornales." *Torquemada* (Lib. XIV, cap. XVI, pp. 564 and 565; and Cap. XVII, pp. 565 and 566). *Clavigero* (Lib. VII, cap. XVIII, p. 489).

doms, had other ways to make slaves) we say : that many conditions were lacking, to create them actual slaves. For of these slaves of this New-Spain, some had means, might own and possess them of their own, and they could not be sold again except under the conditions mentioned hereafter. The service rendered to their master was limited, not for always, nor ordinary. Some, upon marrying, became released, their relatives or brothers taking their place. There were also skilful slaves who, besides serving their masters, still kept house, with wife and children, purchasing and holding slaves themselves. The children of slaves were born free."[84]

The Mexican term for slave was, literally a "purchased man" ("tlacotli.") He was in fact but a " bondsman." Through a special contract, made before authorized witnesses, his services, the proceeds of his labor, *and not his person*, became pledged to another. The member of a kin had no direct ownership in him whom he employed, he could not sell him again without that employer's consent, nor could he take his life in punishment of crime. If the latter broke his contract through repeated evasion he might finally be "collared," that is, his neck was enclosed in a wooden yoke, by means of which he was fastened to a wall at night. If the man still contrived to escape, then he was turned over to worship and sacrificed ; but in case he succeeded in secreting himself in the official house without being intercepted by his master or one of that master's people, then he was spared, and even liberated from his bonds.[85] In addition to the supply furnished to the class of outcasts in the manner above indicated, there were accessions to it from outside. Fugitives were of rare occurrence, since such, if from a tribe against which war was waged, were regarded as precious additions, too important to be ranged among the outcasts.[86] But we have several instances, in the ancient history of Mexico, of destructive drouths as well as of disastrous inundations, depriving the inhabi-

---

[84] "*Monarchia Indiana*" (Lib. XIV, cap. XVI, p. 564).

[85] I have gathered these details mostly from *Torquemada* (Vol. II, pp. 564–566). Compare besides others, *Vetancurt* (Vol. I, pp. 483, 484, and 485) and nearly all modern writers.

[86] *Mendieta* (Lib. II, cap. XXVI. p. 130) : " Y si de la parte contraria salia alguno á descubrir y dar aviso cómo su señor ó su gente venian sobre ellos, al tal dábanle mantas y pagábanle bien." Copied by *Torquemada* (Lib. XIV, cap. II, p. 538), and *Vetancurt* (Parte II, Trat. II, cap. III, p. 384).

tants of the valley of their annual crops. In order to escape threatened famine, fathers bartered their services and those of their children for food, to such tribes as possessed sufficient stores.[87]

If the consequence of expulsion from the bond of kinship or of voluntary abandonment of the rights as members, were, for the male, a degradation to work for others, it was altogether different for the female. The position of women was, as we have already intimated, little better than that of a costly animal, and protection was awarded them only in so far as they represented a part of their husbands' property. This the kin itself was obligated to defend and protect. The wife, however, had no other right than that. She could not complain if her lord and master increased his "family-stock" by the addition of one or more concubines, nor if he strayed about to satisfy his desires with other females. Such acts were even subservient to the kins' interest, since they led to an increase of numbers. But the women themselves who gave their persons away for such purposes could only belong to the class of outcasts; for illicit intercourse with wives and daughters of the kins was, as we shall hereafter see, severely punished. Through the formation of the class of outcasts, or at least along with it, prostitution became tolerated among the ancient Mexicans, while polygamy in the shape of concubinage was introduced as a legitimate custom.[88]

---

[87] Besides the famines recorded since the conquest, the older authors and sources in general notice several (at least two) previous to 1520. It is not to our purpose to discuss their dates. They are given with the usual variation and discordance. Thus for instance, the "*Codex Telleriano Remensis*" (Kingsborough, Vol. I, plate VII, and Vol. VI, p. 136) mentions one in 1404 (1 Tochtli), which is evidently incorrect, since 1 Tochtli would be 1402. The Ce-Tochtli thus mentioned, is 1454, In that year, *Durán* (Cap. XXX, p. 245) places the beginning of the great drouth which, after three years duration, so completely exhausted the Mexican stores and supplies that "wrathy chief" the older, ("Huehue Motecuzuma") told the people "que cada uno vaya á buscar su remedio" (p. 247). In consequence of it, it is reported that many people "sold their sons and daughters to the merchants and principals (señores) of the tribes that had wherewith to give them to eat, and they gave for a baby (or boy rather, "niño") a small basket of corn (maiz) to the father or mother, obligating themselves to sustain the child as long as the famine might last, for that if afterwards the father or mother might wish to redeem it, they should be obligated to pay these aliments." This is, as usual, also stated by *Tezozomoc* (Cap. XL, p. 64), though with less details. *Torquemada* (Lib. II, cap. LXXIII, p. 203) reports the same, but placing it fifty years later, under the last "wrathy chief" (Cap. CX, p. 235) in 1505, A. D. *Sahagun* (Lib. VIII, cap I, p. 269), agrees with Durán and Tezozomoc, so does *Clavigero* (Lib. IV, cap. XII, p. 263): "Many sold themselves for food." This date is also 1451-1454. It is singular that *Torquemada* (Lib. II, cap. XLVII, p. 158) also relates the famine under the older "wrathy chief," and his words are almost textually copied by Clavigero.

[88] The possession of more than one woman, or rather the enjoyment of more than

We thus witness, among the ancient Mexicans and beneath the kins composing the tribe, a lower class of society, a floating

one, was a mere matter of subsistence. As already remarked by *Peter Martyr* (Dec. V, cap..X, p. 232): "He further saith, that the common sort of people content themselves with one wife; but that every Prince may maintayne harlotts at his pleasure." *Gomara* ("*Conquista*, etc.," Vedia I, p. 438): "Cuatro causas dan para tener tantas mujeres: la primera es el vicio de la carne, en que mucho se deleitan; ls segunda es por tener muchos hijos; la tercera por reputacion y servicio; la cuarta es por granjèria; y esta postrera usan mas que otros, los hombres de guerra, los de palacio, los holgazanes y tahures; hacènlas trabajar como esclavas, etc." The same author adds: "Aunque toman muchas mugeres, á unas tienen per légitimas, á otras por amigas, y á otras por mancebas. Amiga llaman à la que despues de casados demandaban, y manceba á la que ellos se tomaban." According to this statement, a husband could entertain three classes of women: one legitimate wife, concubines which he obtained with permission of their parents and prostitutes or mistresses. *Varietas delectat!* *Torquemada*, however (Lib. XII, cap. III, p. 376), says: "Otra especie de mancebas havia, y se permitia, que era la que los Señores principales, ó las tomaban ellos, ó las pedian despues de iá casados, con la Señora, y muger legitima, que llamaban cihuapilli." This reduces the "stock" to two kinds, at least. *Motolinia* (Trat. II, cap. VII, pp. 124-128) mentions polygamy as a rule, and describes the infinite trouble of the priests to find out the legitimate wife, assuming it to be "aquella con quien estando en su gentilidad primero habian contraido matrimonio" (p. 127). According to him the first legitimate marriage took place 14 October, 1526 (p. 124), but nevertheless for three or four years afterwards: "no se velaban, . . sino que todos se estaban con las mujeres que querian, y habia algunos que tenian hasta doscientas mujeres, y de alli abajo cada uno tenia las que queria" (p. 125). In defence of this state of polygamy the Indians alleged "tambien las tenian par manera de granjéria, porque las hacian à todos tejer y hacer mantas y otros oficios de esta manera" (p. 125). *Mendieta* (Lib. III, cap. XLVII and XLVIII, pp. 300-306) is very explicit on the same question. He asserts that the early missionaries found: "Por otra parte se hallaba que el comun de la gente vulgar y pobre no tenian ni habian tomado sino sola una mujer . . . . . sino que los señores y principales, como poderosos, excederian los limites del uso matrimonial, tomando despues otras, las que se les antojaba" (p. 301). The final result of these troublesome disputes and investigations is expressed as follows (p. 305): "y que sabiendose cual era la primera mujer, era cierta cosa ser aquella la legitima, y viviendo aquella, otra cualquiera habia de ser manceba." The question is as to whether a daughter of any member of the kin could ever lawfully become a concubine, or whether this was only the case with female outcasts? The stories about "Handful of Reeds," who, his first wife being sterile, was subsequently married to a number of daughters of chieftains (see *Durán*, Cap. VI, pp. 48 and 49, *Torquemada*, Lib. II, cap. XIII, p. 96, *Vetancurt*, Parte II, Trat. I, cap. XI, p. 270, *Clavigero*, Lib. III, cap. III, p. 194) is manifestly untrue. The object of these subsequent marriages is given as in order to obtain heirs to the throne. Now it is well known that there was no "succession," but only an "election," consequently there was no such object as the one claimed. The chief certainly had concubines, but there is no evidence to show that he obtained them from the kins. Again we are treated to long descriptions of the dazzling polygamy of the chiefs of Tezcuco. For instance, *Ixtlilxochitl* ("*Hist. des Chichimèques*," Cap. XLIII, pp. 305 and 306) relates of "Fasting wolf" "nezahualcoyotl," from "nezaualitztli," "*ayuno*," etc., (*Molina*, II. 64), and "coyotl" how he had a number of concubines previous to his marriage with an Indian girl of Coatlichan. Further on he relates the well known "Uriah and Bathsheba" story (pp. 509-313), attributed to the same chief, and which has been so often recopied. His successor in office, "Fasting boy" (Nezahualpilli," compare the picture of this name in *Durán, Lam.* 23 and 24, Trat. 1o), is reported by him to have had 2000 concubines, "But, besides the queen, he had intercourse with forty" (Cap. LVII, p. 35 of 2d Vol.). His marriage with that only legitimate spouse is described (Cap. LXIV, p. 66, Vol. II). He is, of course, supported by *Torquemada*

population of " hangers-on to the tribe." This class was yet not very numerous ; still it grew slowly and steadily. Prohibited from carrying arms, and therefore from taking any part in warfare other than that of carriers and, perhaps, runners, the heavy drudgery of work was at their charge.[89] Even the tillage of lots appears to have been frequently assigned to them, and it may be that what is commonly termed the class of " macehuales " consisted of the outcasts who improved " tlalmilpa " for the benefit of members of the kin.[90] Besides, it is distinctly implied, if not stated,

(Lib. II, cap. XLV, pp. 154-156; cap. LXII, p. 184; Lib. XIII, cap. XII, p. 436). *H. H. Bancroft* (Vol. II. p. 265) admits two classes of concubines for married people, one of which he calls " the less legitimate wives." Among other authorities, he adduces in evidence *Oviedo* (Lib. XXXIII, cap. I, p. 260): " Tenia esto Olintech treynta mugeres dentro de su casa, con quien el dormia, á las quales servian mas de ciento otras." The same statement is also found in *Gomara* ("*Conquista*," etc., Vedia I. p. 326) and others. (The name for the mistress ("manceba") of a *married* man is " teichtacamecauh " (*Molina*, I, p. 81), which means literally " thy secret tie," from " Tchuatl "—" thou, " ichtaca "— secretly (II, p. 32), and "mecatl"— rope or cord (II, 56). See in a further note.

The most significant statements, however, are those already reported, of Motolinia and of Gomara, that the Indians explained their polygamy by the fact that *they kept these women for their work.* In other words, they were purchased hands. This is indicated by the following authorities: *Gomara* ("*Conquista*," etc., Vedia I, p. 441), "Las malas mujeres de su cuerpo, que lo daban de balde si no las querian pagar, se vendian par esclavas por traerse bien, ó cuando ninguno las queria. por viejas ó feas ó enfermas; que nadie pide por las puertas." *Torquemada* (Lib. XIV, cap. XVI, p. 563): " Havia tambien mugeres, que se daban á vivir suelta, y libertadamente; y para proseguir este mal Estado, que tomaban, tenian necesidad de vestir curiosa, y galanamente, y por la necesidad, que pasaban, porque no trabajaban . . . . llegaban à necesitarse mucho, y hacianse Esclavas; " and the same authority adds (Cap. XVII, p. 566): " y muchas veces los Amos se casaban, con Esclavas suias," without any closer definition however. Finally, the *Anónimo* says (p. 397): " Nelle nozze di questa patrona principale fanno alcune cirimonie, il che non si osserva nelle nozze dell' altre."

There is no evidence that a married man could increase the number of his women even with the consent of the parents, in other words, marry a girl. But if the latter had, through her own lewd conduct, become abandoned and cast off, then he could associate with her as his mistress without regard to his wife proper. Also he might purchase (or rather barter for) a female and afterwards make a concubine of her, even if she was of a foreign tribe. Prisoners of war (females) *may* occasionally have been spared also, but this suggestion rests on very slight evidence (compare "*Anónimo*," p. 373), and may apply only to prisoners of war purchased from other tribes (*Sahagun*, Lib. I, cap. XIX, p. 32).

[89] They were the " tamenes," carriers. The Mexican word is " tlamama," from "tlacatl"—man, and "nitla-mama"—to carry a load (*Molina*, II, p. 51). *Don Antonio de Mendoza* ("*Avis sur les Prestations personelles*," etc., p. 358, Ternaux, Recueil). *Zurita* (pp. 250, 251, and 280) "*Lettre des auditeurs Salmeron, Maldonado, Ceynos et Quiroga a l'Imperatrice.*" (Mexico, 30 March, 1531, in 2d Recueil, etc., pp. 143 and 144): " Les Indiens ont de tout temps porté des fadeaux, ils y sont accontumés . . . "

[90] This is a mere suggestion. The majority of descriptions, however, are such that the " mazehual " may have been, and probably was, a member of the kin. Still, in such cases, when that member could not improve his lots himself, families of " bondsmen " may have done the work for him, and thus become included in the general picture. Quotations are superfluous, since the information is not, as yet, positive enough.

that for actions of merit such people might be re-adopted, and thus restored to their original rights. The anonymous conqueror asserts that the performer of any valorous deed was highly rewarded and made a chieftain, "even if he was the vilest slave."[91] But without such formal re-adoption, no outcast could emerge from his inferior and unprotected condition. The overwhelming majority of Mexico's aboriginal people, however, consisted of members of the twenty kins shown to have composed the tribe. These all enjoyed equal rights; consequently all had the same duty. Both right and obligation were governed by the organization of kinship. While it is impossible for us to follow here strictly the order of enumeration of these rights and obligations, established in the admirable researches of Mr. Morgan, we still can distinctly trace all of them in ancient Mexican society, operating with more or less unimpaired vitality.

The kin claimed the right to name its members.[92] A family name was unknown to the ancient Mexicans,[93] and thus our assertion that the modern family was not yet established among them, acquires further support. Within a few days after the child's birth, its mother in presence of all the neighbors (consequently of the "calpulli" or kin) gave the child a name through the medium of the women assisting her delivery. This name, generally taken from that of the day of birth, had a superstitious bearing, and was to accompany the child during the period of its utter helplessness.[94] A second "naming" took place several

---

[91] *"Relatione di alcune Cose della Nuova Spagna"* (Col. de Doc., I, p. 371). *Torquemada* (Lib. XIV, cap. XVII, p. 566): "y Esclavos havia que regian, y mandaban la casa de su Señor, como hacen los Maiordomos."

[92] *Morgan ("Ancient Society,"* pp. 71 and 78).

[93] *Motolinia* (Trat. I, cap. V, p. 37): "Todos los Niños cuando nacian tomaban nombre del dia en que nacian." *Torquemada* (Lib. XIII, cap. XXII, pp. 454 and 455). The family name was introduced by the Spaniards, who gave other names at the time of baptism.

[94] *Motolinia* (Trat. I, cap. V, p. 37). *Sahagun* (Lib. IV, cap. I, pp. 283 and 284, in general the entire fourth Book, which gives a very full idea of all the superstitions connected with birthdays; more especially Cap. XXXV and XXXVI and Lib. VI, cap. XXXVII, pp. 217–221). All the children of the quarter were invited to the festival: "En este tiempo que estas cosas se hacian, juntabanse los mosuelos de todo aquel barrio, y acabadas todas estas ceremonias, entran en la casa del y toman la comida que alli les tenian aparejada, ..." The naming took place in presence of "todos los parientas y parientos del niño, viejos y viejas" (p. 218). *Mendieta* (Lib. II, cap. XIX, p. 107): "Estos nombres tomaban de los idolos ó de las fiestas que en aquellas signos caian, y á veces de aves y animales y de otras cosas insensatas, como se .es antojaba." (Lib. XIII, cap. XXXV, p. 267). *Torquemada* (Lib. XIII, cap. XX, p. 450: "Luego hacian convocacion de todos los Deudos, y Parientes, de los Padres, y de todos los Amigos, y

months later, which was performed by the medicine-man of the kin.[95] Both of these names were preserved, but if the full-grown man ever performed some action of merit in the service of the whole tribe, then the tribe bestowed upon him a third name as an honorable title attached to his person in reward for his deeds.[96]

It was the duty of the kin to educate or train its members to every branch of public life. For all public purposes, *man* only must be taken into account. This appears obvious from what was said already concerning the position of women in general. Now each calpulli, or localized kin, among the ancient Mexicans had, as we have shown in "Art of War,"[97] its "House of the Youth" ("telpuch-calli") joined to its "medicine-lodge" or temple. Thither the boys were brought at an early age, to be instructed in whatever was needed for after-life. In order to train their bodies they were held to manual labor, and to the ordinary duties of worship. The use of weapons was made a prominent object of teaching; so was the dance and song, the latter coupled with ordinary Indian rhetorics.[98] These houses of education were under the

Vecinos, que para este acto se juntavan . . . y entonces le ponian el nombre." Also (Cap. XXII, p. 455; cap. XXIII, p. 456): " De la misma manera, que quando alguna de estas Indias paria, se usaba juntarse toda la Parentela, y las vecinas, y amigas, ... De esta misma manera lo acostumbraban hacer para el fingido Bantismo." *Gomara* ("*Conquista*," Vedia I, p. 438): " En este lavatorio les ponian nombre, no como querian, sino el del mismo dia en que nacieron.' *Vetancurt* (Parte II, Trat. III, cap. VIII, p. 462).

[95] This is stated by *Gomara* (Vedia I, p. 438): " y dende á tres meses, que son de los nuestros dos, los llevaban al templo, donde un sacerdote que tenia la cuenta y ciencia del calendario y signos, les daba otro sobrenombre, haciendo muchas ceremonias, y declaraba las gracias y virtudes del idolo cuyo nombre les ponia, pronosticándoles buenos hados." *Motolinia* (Trat. I, cap. V, p. 37): " Despues desde á tres meses presentaban aquella criatura en el templo del demonio, y dabanle su nombre, no dejando el que tenia, y tambien entonces comian de regocijo, . . . "

[96] *Gomara* (Vedia, p. 438). *Motolinia* (Trat. I, cap. V, p. 37). *Torquemada* (Lib. XIII, cap. XXII, p. 456). *Clavigero* (Lib. VI, cap. XXXVII, pp. 437, 438). *Durán* (Cap. XI, pp. 96, 97, and 98).

[97] "*Art of War*," p. 101. Relying on Humboldt, I assumed fifteen years to be the age when military instruction began, but the general instruction began much sooner. See note 98.

[98] *Gomara* (Vedia, p. 438). *Sahagun* (Lib. III, cap. IV, cap. V, p. 268): " Habiendo entrado en la casa del Telpuchcali el niño, dábanle cargo de barrer, limpiar la casa, poner lumbre, y hacer los servicios de penitencia á que se obligaba. Era costumbre que á la puesta del sol, todos los mancebos iban á bailar, y danzar à la casa que se llamaba Cuicacalco cada noche, y el muchacho tambien bailaba con los otros mancebos; llegando á los quince años, y siendo ya mancebillo, llevábanle consigo los mancebos mayores al monte á traer la leña, que era necesaria para la casa del Telpuchcali, y Cuicacalco, y cargabànle las rodelas para que las llevase acuestas;" (p.269): "La vida que tenian era muy áspera . . . " (Cap. VI, pp. 270 and 271; Lib. VI, cap. XXXIX, p. 224), and other incidental notices. *Mendieta* (Lib. II, cap. XXIV, pp. 124, 125). *Torque-*

special direction of experienced men, called therefore " Speakers
of the Youth" ("telpuchtlatoca") and "elder brothers" ("teachcauhtin,") in another capacity. They had not only to provide
for the physical training of their pupils, but also for their intellectual development, as far as the state of knowledge permitted.[99]
Such places of training were called also "the place where I
grow" ("nezcaltiloyan"), or "the place where I learn" ("nem-
achtiloyan.")[100] It is not 'true that the youth were constrained
to a permanent, almost monastic residence in such houses ; but
while there they improved in common certain special plots of land,
in all likelihood the so-called "temple-tracts," out of which the
daily wants of worship were supplied.[101] In connection with this
mode of education, we have to consider here an objection which
cannot fail to be raised against our views.

It is frequently given out as a fact, that besides the " Houses
of the Youth" mentioned, there was a *special* place of education
for the children of "*noblemen*" and this is adduced as a proof of

mada (Lib. IX, cap. XII, pp. 185 and 186; Lib. XIII, cap. XXVIII, XXIX and XXX)
and others.

[99] "*Art of War*" (pp. 101, 119 and 120). *Mendieta* (Lib. II, cap. XXIV, pp. 124 and
125): " Los otros se criaban como en capitanias, porque en cada barrio habia un capitan
de ellos, llamado telpuchtlato, que quiere decir, guarda ó capitan de los mancebos."
Torquemada (Lib. IX, cap. XII, p. 185): "y tenian un Rector, que los regia, y governaba,
que se llamaba Telpochtlato, que quiere decir, Guarda, ó Caudillo de los Mancebos, el
qual Telpochtlato tenia gran cuidado de doctrinarlos. y enseñarles, en buenas costumbres." *Sahagun* (Lib. III, cap. V, p. 269): "y si era ya hombre valiente y diestro,
elegianle para regir á todos los mancebos, y para castigarlos, y entonces se llamba Telpuchtlato." (Lib. VIII, cap. XIII, p. 301): "Tambien daban de comer ă los que criaban
los mancebos que se llaman telpuchtlatos, . . ." (Cap. XVII, p. 305): "en este lugar se
juntaban los maestros de los mancebos que se llamaban tiachcauan. y telpuchtlato-
ques . . ." (Also Cap. XXXVIII, p. 331). *Vetancurt* (Part II, Trat. III, cap. VI, p. 451):
" y un rector que llamaban Telpochtlato, el que habla y gobierna ă los mancebos."
Codex Mendoza (Vol. I of Kingsborough plates 62 and 63).

Sahagun usually calls the "achcauhtli," "alguaziles," or executors of justice. But
above we see that he calls the "tiachcaoan," also "masters of the youth." Both names
are corruptions of "teachcauhtlin." *Tezozomoc* (Cap. XXXVIII, p. 60) calls the "Achcacauhtin, mayorales de armas y de doctrina y de ejemplo." (Cap. LVII, p. 95): "Tras
ellos vinieron los que llaman Achcauhtin, señores de los varrios, y maestros de mancebos." (Cap. LXXI, p. 121): "mayorales y ministros, y los hicieron juntar como escu-
elas en cada un varrio que llamaban telpochcalli." (Cap. LXXXVIII, p. 134): "Los
mancebos iban cada dia á los varrios al egercicio de las armas ă la escuela de armas
telpochcalco, adonde los enseñaban con valerosos ánimos, y las maneras de combatir."
Finally *Clavigero* (Lib. VII, cap. II, p. 452) refers also to the 53d picture of the Mendoza
Codex, representing a boy of fifteen years, who is turned over to an "achcauhtli, or
officer," to be instructed in the art of war.

[100] *Molina* (*Vocabularia* II, pp. 66 and 72). *P. Ignacio de Paredes* ("*Doctrina Breve
sacada del Catecismo Mexicano,*" Reprint of 1809).

[101] *Sahagun* (Lib. III, cap. V, p. 269) says that, whereas they slept at home, that is, at
the "house of youth," they ate with their families ("aunque comian en sus casas pro-

the existence of a privileged class of nobles.[102] Besides the other evidence which we have mentioned, as against the existence of nobility in ancient Mexico, we shall state here that the place called "calmecac" which is the name given to that supposed "school for the nobles," was in reality something quite different.

Fray Bernardino Sahagun, in his description of the central medicine-lodge or great temple of the Mexican tribe, says that in the house called calmecac those who devoted themselves to "medicine," or to the priesthood were trained for that office and lived in said house along with the medicine-men themselves.[103] There were several buildings or rooms bearing that name, all within the square occupied by what is commonly termed "the great temple of Mexico," and these were the places where the medicine-men and whoever was attached to them and to their offices, actually dwelt.[104] Consequently these places were also

pias"). *Zurita* (pp. 131–133) asserts that "certain fixed days, the children of land-tillers had permission to share their father's labor." That the "temple tracts" were probably identical with those worked by the young men is made evident by *Sahagun* (Cap. V, Lib. III, p. 269; cap. VIII, p. 275). *Zurita* (p. 131): "Ils étaient obligés de travailler aux terres affectées â ces établissements." *Torquemada* (Lib. IX, cap. XII, p. 185): "Tenian sus Tierras, y Heredados para su sustento (que debian de ser de las dedicadas al uso, y gasto de los Templos) en ellas sembraban, y cogian Pan para su sustento." *Mendieta* (Lib. II, cap. XXIV, pp. 124 and 125). *Gomara* (Vedia, p. 438). The latter is very plain, connecting all the "schools" and their lands with the temples.

[102] *H. H. Bancroft* (Vol. II, pp. 243 and 244). Nearly all the older writers call it a higher school, but I shall hereafter discuss their statements. See also Prescott ("*Mexico*," Book I, ch. III, p. 69).

[103] "*Historia general de las Cosas de Nueva España,*" (Lib. III, cap. VII, p. 271): "Los señores, ó principales, ó ancianos, ofrecian á sus hijos á la casa que se llamaba Calmecac, era su intencion que alli se criasen para que fuesen ministros de los idolos." Id., (Cap. IV, p. 266): "y lo ofrecian á la casa de los idolos que se llama Calmecac, para que fuese ministro de ellos, viniendo á edad perfecta." But especially (Lib. VI, cap. XXXIX, p. 223): "si le prometian ã la casa Calmecac, era para que hiciese penitencia, sirviese á los dioses, viviese en limpieza, en humildad y castidad, y para que del todo se guardase de los vicios carnales."

[104] The description furnished by *Sahagun* (Lib. VI, Appendix, "Relacion de los Edificios del gran Templo de México," pp. 197 to 211) mentions seventy-eight parts or edifices, among which were the following, with the name "Calmecac:"

The 12th edifice "Tlilancalmecac," a shrine to the goddess Civocoatl and inhabited by three priests, medicine-men (p. 201).

13th edifice "Mexicocalmecac," called by him "a monastery wherein the priests dwelt who served daily in the Cu of Tlaloc" (p. 201).

24th edifice, "Vitznaoac Calmecac," inhabited by the priests of the idol Vitznaoac, (p. 203).

27th edifice, "Tetlanmancalmecac," where the priests of the temple dedicated to the goddess Chantico lived, as in a "monastery," (p. 203).

35th edifice, "Tlamatzinco Calmecac," "a monastery," inhabited by the priests of the god Tlamatzincatl, (p. 204).

54th edifice, "Yopico Calmecac, "monasterio ú oratorio," (p. 207).

61st edifice, "Tzommolco-calmecac," "a monastery where dwelt priests of the god Xiuhtecutli," (p. 207).

ritual details themselves, but we must lay particular stress on the fact, that the wife became the *property* of her husband and that she was, as such, placed under the direct protection of his kinsmen. Such marriages could be annulled by mutual consent, provided the kin gave its approbation. In such a case the woman was at liberty to marry again, and also to return to the calpulli from which she issued.[110]

We might now be expected to cast a glance at the funeral rites of the ancient Mexicans since it was *one of the attributes of the kin to enjoy common burial.*[111] But this question is so intimately connected with that of creed and belief that we refrain from trespassing too much on that field. The Mexicans practised cremation and, in the case of warriors slain in battle, at least, it is known that the exercises were conducted by the officers and leaders of each kin, *all its members*, and not the special relatives and friends only of the deceased, attending the ceremony.[112] Our knowledge of the burial places of aboriginal Mexico is still very indefi-

was given by their hand, out of which there arise great discomforts, and marriage among free persons is not as free as it should be, therefore, we ordain and command: that no Indian principal of whichever condition or rank (" estado,") shall of his own accord or authority give away any wife to anybody whatsoever, nor shall he prevent any Macegual from marrying freely the woman whom he may wish, and who may like him,— under penalty of thirty days of imprisonment, and other penalties which the Judge may determine upon."

(" *Concilios Provinciales, Primero y Segundo, celebrados por la muy noble, y muy Leal ciudad de México etc., etc. Dalos á Luz el Ill'mo Sr. D. Francisco Antonio Lorenzana Arzobispo de esta Santa Metropolitana Iglesia* Año de 1769). The "principales Indios" are the officers of the " Kins," and thus we have, thirty five years after the conquest, a formal recognition of the custom among the Mexican Indians that marriage was controlled by the Kin. How the "encomenderos" subsequently interfered with that custom, in order to conceal their own criminal doings, is plainly told by *Fray Antonio de Remesal* " *Historia de la Provincia de San Vicente de Chyapa y Guatemala, etc., etc.*" Madrid, 1619 (Lib. VII, cap. XV, p. 327).

[110] It is singular that some of the earliest ecclesiastical writers imply that there was no rule of repudiation or divorce among the ancient Mexicans. *Mendieta* (Lib. III, cap. XLVIII, p. 303). The same authority, however, attributes this to the baneful effects of contact with the Spaniards, in consequence of which the customs of the natives grew more or less dissolute and immoral (p. 304). *Zurita* (p. 97) confirms, and *Torquemada* (Lib. XVI, cap. XXIV, p. 196), copies Mendieta literally. For the customs of divorce see *Zurita* (p. 97), *Mendieta* (Lib. III, cap. XLVIII, p. 304), *Torquemada* (Lib. XIII. cap. XV, pp. 441 and 442), *Gomara* (Vedia I, p. 440), *Herrera* (Dec. III, Lib. II, cap. C, XVII, pp. 72 and 73), *Bustamante* (" *Tezcoco*," p. 196), and others. The division of property mentioned as accompanying the divorce, applies only to personal effects, since the wife brought nothing else. See " *Tenure of Lands* " (p. 429, and note 107).

The matrimonial customs of the ancient Mexicans will be more thoroughly discussed by me in another monograph, subsequent to one on "Religious Beliefs."

[111] " *Ancient Society* " (pp. 71 and 83).

[112] Compare *Durán* (Cap. XVIII, pp. 154 and 156), and *Tezozomoc* (Cap. XXV, pp. 37 and 38).

nite, owing, in part, to the treasure-seeking propensities of the Spanish immigrants as well as to the diligence of the clergy in obliterating all objects to which the aborigines attached superstitious notions.

For the same reason we refrain here from entering into a detailed account of the customs of worship. Still we feel obliged to state that the feature of " separate religious rites "[113] so characteristic of society based upon kin, is plainly visible among the ancient Mexicans. There are some very remarkable evidences of this, to which we must allude.

It has already been established at the outset, that each calpulli had "its particular god," which was worshipped, as a tutelar deity, within the territory of that calpulli. Consequently each kin had its particular medicine-lodge or temple.[114] Besides, the last one of the seventy-eight places into which Father Sahagun subdivides the great central " teo-calli " of the tribe, is described by him as follows :

" The seventy-eighth edifice was named *calpulli*, these were small buildings enclosing the inside of the square, these little houses they called *calpulli*, and there the principals and officials of the republic gathered, to do penance for four days preceding each festival occurring at twenty days interval. Their vigils thus lasted four days, during which time some of them ate at midnight and others at noon."[115]

This statement, which is confirmed (according to the learned Jesuit John Eusebius Nieremberg)[116] by the celebrated physician and naturalist Francisco Hernandez, is followed by another one, not less important, also of Sahagun :

" They offered up many things in the houses which they called " calpulli," which were like churches of the quarters, where those of the same gathered, as well for to sacrifice, as for other ceremonies they were wont to perform."[117]

Thus the right of the kin to "separate worship" appears not

<hr>

[113] " *Ancient Society* " (p. 71).

[114] Besides the positive assertions of *Sahagun* (Lib. II, Appendix, p. 211. Lib. I, cap. XIX, p. 31): " se ponian en una de las casas de oracion que tenian en los barrios que ellos llamaban calpulli. que quiere decir iglesia del barrio ó parroquia" and (Lib. II, cap. XXXVII, etc.), we have also the testimony of *Durán* (Cap. V, pp. 42 and 43, and Cap. IX, pp. 79 and 80), and *Oviedo* (Lib. XXXIII, cap. X, p. 302).

[115] " *Historia general*," (Lib. II, Appendix, p. 211).

[116] " *Historia naturae*," (Lib. VIII, cap. XXII, p. 146).

[117] " *Historia general*," (Lib. II, Appendix, p. 211. See note 114).

only established within that kin's territory, but it is also recognized even at the central medicine-lodge of the tribe.

A further evidence of it is found in the manner of distribution of the captives, upon the return of a successful war-party. It is known that prisoners were always offered up to the idols. Such a person, therefore, as soon as secured, became an object of "medicine;" he was so to say a sacred object. Well treated as long as he was not needed for the slaughter-block, nothing could in the end save him from sacrifice. But this sacrifice itself was not made in behalf of his captor, but on behalf and for the *kin* to whom the captor belonged. Therefore upon arrival at the pueblo, the prisoners of war were turned over to the respective calpulli as their share thus furnishing another illustration of "Separate Rites of Worship" of the kins composing the ancient Mexicans.[118]

Having already discussed, in a former paper, the *tenure of Lands and customs of Inheritance*[119] we now pass on to one of the most essential features of tribal society, and one which involves some of the vital points of organization and customs.

The kin was obligated to protect and defend the persons and property of its members, and to resent and punish any injury done to them, as if it were a crime committed against the kin itself.[120]

The impression justly prevails, that the so-called "penal code" of the Mexicans was simple but severe, death being, in most instances, the punishment of offenders. This resulted, in a great measure, from the fact that any offence against an individual

---

[118] *Mendieta* (Lib. II, cap. XXVII, p. 132), rather contradicts himself when he says first: that the captive belonged to his captor, but at the same time, that this captor was even killed if he *gave* away his prisoner to another man. Second: that each one had to watch his own prisoners, and at the same time they were guarded in common, and at the risk of the "barrio" or kin, which was responsible for their safe keeping. *Torquemada* (Lib. XIV, cap. III, p. 540) copies this almost literally. Much more positive and clear is *Durán* (Cap. XIX, pp. 172 and 173): "mandó Tlacaellel repartir los cautivos, porque eran muchos, por todos los barrios y que cada barrio se encargase de guardar y sustentar tantos . . . . . Los mandones de los barrios repartieron los presos á cada barrio, á como les cauia." (Cap. XXI, p. 186): "Monteçcuma los mandaua vestir y adereçar y llamauava â los Calpixques, que son los mandoncillos de los barrios, y entregauanlas, para que tuviesen cuidado dellos, diciendo que eran la merced del sol, Señor de la tierra, que los daua para el sacrificio." (Id., cap. XXII, p. 192. Cap. XXVIII, p. 237): "luego fuéron repartidos entre los barrios y encomendados á los mandoncillos." (Cap. XLII, p. 343, etc.). *Tezozomoc* ("*Cronica*," cap. XXIX, p. 45; XXXII, p. 51; XXXIII, p. 53; XXXVIII, p. 61; XLIX, p. 80, etc.), confirms Durán as might be expected.

[119] "*Tenure of Lands and Customs of Inheritance*," 11*th Report of Peabody Museum*, 1878.

[120] "*Ancient Society*," (pp. 76 and 77). Compare *H. Luden* ("*Geschichte des teutschen Volkes*," pp. 501 and 502), among the ancient Germans.

became, according to rules of kinship, one against the social group to which he belonged. This presupposes again a general division of crimes into two classes, one of which includes such as were committed by members of the kin against other members thereof or against institutions of the same group to which they belonged. The other comprises offenses committed by inhabitants of one calpulli against those of another. It is only the first class which we take under consideration here, the second we reserve for our discussion of the mode of government. Crimes committed within the kin can be classified as against persons, against property, and against medicine.

The aborigines of Mexico are generally represented as being, in their every-day's intercourse, of a quiet, peaceable, inoffensive disposition, contrasting strongly with their savage ferocity in warfare. This was not however due to any innate gentleness and mildness of nature, but only to the peculiar restraint enforced upon them by the law of retaliation or revenge.[121] Brawls resulting in bodily injury were therefore of extremely rare occurrence, and then it was left to the parties to settle it among themselves. In such cases, as in the event of mutual jealousy, a challenge often passed between them, and this challenge brought about an encounter at *the next campaign* when, while the warriors were engaged with the enemies of the tribe, the contestants fought as if they had belonged to opposite camps, until one of them

[121] The character of the Mexican Aborigines is variously depicted by older writers. It appears as a mixture of childlike docility and fierce passions. *Cortés* ("*Carta Segunda*," p. 18. Vedia, Vol. I). speaks of them according to the reports of the Tlaxcaltecans. *Bernal Diez* ("*Historia* etc.," pp. 309 and 310. Cap. CCVIII. Vedia II). specially dwells on their vices and their cruelty, as evidenced in their sacrifices. "*El Conquista dor Anónimo*' (Col. de Docum., I, pp. 371, 383, 387, and 397), places great stress on their ferocity, although he also says that they are very obedient. The missionaries generally exalt their good sides — their docility and faithfulness. Compare *Motolinia* (Trat. I, cap. XIV, pp. 76 and 77). The same (Trat. I, cap. II, pp. 22 and 23), mentions, however, their vices also, attributing nearly all of them (idolatry excepted), to their inclination towards intemperance. (Trat. II, cap. IV, p. 113): "Lo que de esta generacion se puede decir es, que son muy extranos de nuestra condicion . . . ." *Zurita* (p. 197—207), is very bitter against such as treat the Indians as barbarians. (Id., 42 and 45). *Mendieta* (Lib. III, cap. XLIII. p. 290), says that they were very willing to forgive and ask to be forgiven, the latter taking place. before going to confess themselves, sometimes before all the relationship and the neighbors: "suelen algunos juntar (al tiempo que se quieren confesar) toda su parentela y vecinos con quien communican, y pedirles perdon en la manera dicha." Against this, it is reported by *Torquemada* (Lib. XIV, cap. I, p. 535), that "these people were naturally more vindictive, than all the rest of the world." Compare also the descriptions of the character of the Mexicans in *Clavigero* (Lib. I, cap. XV).

was disabled or until he voluntarily withdrew.[122] Slanderers, however, were punished by the kin, having their lips cut off or publicly sliced.[123] Homicide, and murder, were invariably punished by death.[124]

Intemperance in public was free to people more than seventy years old, while if grown men below that age appeared in a drunken state (festivities excepted), their heads were shorn clean in punishment. But whenever the delinquent was a chief he was publicly degraded; and any officer was forthwith removed and relieved of his duties.[125] Women who attempted to act as

[122] *Gomara* (Vedia I, p. 440): "no traen armas sino en la guerra, y alli averiguan sus pendencias por desafios." *Bartolomé de las Casas* ("*Historia apologética de Indias*," cap. 213 and 214. Vol. VIII of Lord Kingsborough, note XLV, p. 124). Bystanders interfered, separating the parties, if they came to blows. *Motolinia* (Trat. I, cap. II, p. 23), says that such strife and quarrels only occurred when they were drunk: "Y fuera de estar beodos son tan pacificos, que cuando riñen mucho se empujan uno á otro, y apenas nunca dan voces, si no es las mugeres que algunos veces riñendo dan gritos." (Cap. XIV, p. 76): "Sin rencillos ni enemistades pasan su vida." *Torquemada* (Lib. XII, cap. XV, pp. 398 and 399). *Herrera* (Dec. III, Lib. IV, cap. XVI, p. 136).

[123] *Zurita* ("Rapport," etc., pp. 129 and 130) speaks only of children, punished by splitting the lips for lying. This is copied by *Herrera* (Dec. III, Lib. IV, cap. XVI, p. 136) and *Torquemada* (Lib. XIII, cap. XXX, p. 478). *Vetancurt* (Part II, Trat. III, p. 482), however, declares this punishment to have been meted out to adults, adding: "to-day there would be many without lips, so much do they lie." *Gomara* ("*Conquista*," p. 438, Vedia I) speaks of this punishment as having been instituted by Quetzalcohuatl, and for adults as well as for children. This, attributing it to Quetzalcohuatl, is an evident error. Compare *Sahagun*, (Lib. III, cap. III, p. 244). *Clavigero* (Lib. VII, cap. XVII, p. 489) is positive about adults. *Bustamante* ("*Tezcoco*," p. 195) says that slanderers were killed.

[124] *Las Casas* ("*Historia Apologética*," cap. 213, Kingsb: Vol. VIII, p. 123): Destos era el que mataba à otro, el cual moria por ello." *Gomara* (Vedia I, p. 442): "Matan al matador sin excepcion ninguna." *Mendieta* (Lib. II, cap. XXIX, p. 136): "Sentenciaban á muerte à los que cometian enormes y graves delitos, asi como á los homicidos. El que mataba á otro, moria por ello." *Torquemada* (Lib. XII, cap. VIII, p. 387), almost copies the preceding. Nearly all the authors agree on this point, except, according to *Mr. Bancroft* ("*Native Races*," Vol II. p. 459. note 59), Durán, who is said to assert: "that the murderer did not suffer death, but became the slave for life of the wife or relatives of the deceased." In this Durán agrees with th "Codice Ramirez." *Vetancurt* ("*Teatro*," Vol. I, p. 485) says that even for murder committed in a drunken state, the culprit was killed (hung). *Clavigero* (Lib. VII, cap. XVII, p. 484) briefly states that all homicide was punished with death. As to the manner of execution, it is variously stated. It would be unsafe to attempt going into details.

[125] It is well known that there was an idol for the drunkards. *Sahagun* (Lib. I, cap. XXII. p. 40) even gives the names of thirteen "dioses del vino." According to *Gregorio Garcia* ("*Origen de los Indios*," etc. Lib. III, cap. II, §VI, p. 92, who mentions as authority *Fray Esteran de Salazar*, "*Historia, i Relacion de la Teologia de los Indios Mexicanos*" lost in a shipwreck, 1564), they had three hundred gods of the drunkards "que de solos los borrachos tiener 300 Dioses." See also *Torquemada* (Lib. VI, cap. XXIX, p. 58) and others. The punishments are given by me after *Mendieta* (Lib. II, cap. XXX, pp. 139 and 140). Copied textually by *Torquemada* (Lib. XIV, cap. X. p. 550). Besides these, *Zurita* (pp. 110–112) asserts the same, even more explicitly, and he is followed by *Herrera* (Dec. III, lib, IV, cap. XVI, p. 136). *Vetancurt* (Vol. I, p. 485). *Clavigero* (Lib.

procuresses were severely punished, though not with loss of life.[126]

While clandestine relations between young men and girls were known to exist and, if not sanctioned, still were not punished,[127] it was different if a married man attempted to seduce a maiden who was not an outcast. The seducer was invariably punished.[128] Intercourse between unmarried people was tolerated, as a preliminary to marriage and the consequent increase of kinship, but if a husband, in contravention of the obligation "not to marry in the kin," endeavored to satisfy his lusts upon one of that kin's wards, as the daughters of members all were, then he committed

VII, cap. XVII, p. 488), all affirm, besides, that young people, while yet in care of the "houses of training," if intoxicated, were killed. This is also confirmed by *Sahagun* (Lib. III, appendix, cap. VI, pp. 270 and 271). Except by *Motolinia* (Trat. I, cap. II, pp. 22 and 23), it is generally conceded that drunkenness was well controlled in aboriginal Mexico.

[126] Although prostitution was tolerated, still, houses of ill-fame did not exist. *Torquemada* (Lib. XII, cap. II, p. 376): "Esto parece, porque permitieron, que huviese Mugeres, que se daban à los que querian, y se andaba á esta vida suelta, y gananciosa, como las de nuestra España, y otros Reinos; puesto que no tenian casa señalada, ni publica para la execucion de su mal oficio, sino que cada qual moraba donde le parecia, y el acto deshonesto, en que se ocupaba, servia de lugar publico, y en el mismo vicio se hacia publica y se manifestaba." *Vetancurt* (Vol. I, p. 480): "Permitian los mexicanos, mujeres que ganasen con sus cuerpos, aunque no tenian lugares señalados." It is, therefore, not quite clear what may be meant by the term "alcahueta." In the sense of the French word "entremetteuse," alone, they were amenable to punishment, since it was the duty of the man to hunt his "female," although he sometimes employed women called "cihuatlanqui" for that purpose. I suppose that such women were punished, not for the *immorality* of their conduct, but for their *unauthorized forwardness* in addressing themselves to men, and thus trespassing upon the dignity of that superior being. In regard to authorities on the mode of punishment, I but refer to those quoted by *Mr. H. H. Bancroft* (Vol. II, p. 469, note 101).

[127] I have already shown that young people held intimate relations with each other before the formalities of marriage were arranged. Thus, while he was yet at the "Telpuchcalli," the youth had his female friend, "amiga" or "manceba," outside. This is positively stated by *Sahagun* (Lib. III, appendix, cap. VI, p. 271): "y estos mancebos tenian sus amigas cada uno dos ó tres, la una tenian en su casa, y las otras estaban en las de sus familias," and *Torquemada* (Lib. XII, cap. III, p. 376). That these female "friends" were regarded with more than a feeling of platonic love, is dryly expressed by *Sahagun* (Id: cap. V, p. 270): "y los que eran amancebados ibanse á dormir con sus amigas." It is also asserted by *Torquemada* (see above): "que despues que aquel mancebo havia un Hijo, en la dicha manceba, luego le era forcoso, ó dejarla, ó recibirla por muger legitima." *Vetancurt* (Vol. I, p. 480): "los mancebos antes de casarse tenian sus mancebas, y solian pedirlas á las madres." This almost establishes promiscuity among the ancient Mexicans, as a preliminary to formal marriage.

[128] *Clavigero* (Lib. VII, cap. XVII, p. 485) says that the punishment was not like that of the adulterer, "because the husband was not required to the same amount of conjugal fidelity as the wife." With "slaves" concubinage was permitted, and the result of childbirth was freedom to the child. Death was invariably the punishment of those who held, or attempted to hold, intercourse with girls in care of the house of worship. *Zurita* (p. 106, etc.). *Mendieta* (Lib. II, cap. XXIX, p. 136): "El que hazia fuerza à virgen, ora fuese en el campo, ora en casa del padre moria por ello."

a crime which the calpulli was bound to punish in the most exemplary manner.

While we are not at all surprised at such severity in the cases above stated, it cannot fail to astonish us, that such apparently harmless acts as those of a *man wearing female dress* and of a *woman appearing in male attire* were visited upon the offenders with death.[129] Still, the ancient Mexicans could assign from their peculiar point of departure good cause for such cruel punishments. The position of woman was so inferior, they were regarded as so far beneath the male, that the most degrading epithet that could be applied to any Mexican, aside from calling him a dog, was that of " woman." It was more injurious than coward. Now, for a man to assume the garb of such an inferior being became almost equivalent to a crime against nature. It was an act of wilful degradation which was a deadly insult to his own kin. On the other hand, if a woman presumed to don the dress of her lord and master, it again was a crime of an equally heinous nature. In both cases the dignity of the whole consanguine group became deeply affected, and death alone could satisfy its honor. After this, it is needless to say how the actual crimes against nature were regarded and punished.[130]

It was also a capital crime for any man, to assume the dress or ornaments peculiar to an office, without being himself that office's lawful incumbent. Besides being a grave insult to the rightful officer, it was a dangerous offence towards the kin, especially in case of war, when it amounted to actual treason.[131]

Since it was the kin's duty to protect, not only the persons, but also the property of its members, it follows that adultery committed with a married woman entailed deadly punishment upon the male, whether he was married or not. His crime was that of stealing the most precious chattel of one member of the calpulli.

[129] This is so generally mentioned by all authors, that special references are superfluous.

[130] All authors insist that incest was punished with death. *Torquemada* (Lib. XII, cap. IV, p. 380): " Todos los que cometian incesto en el primer grado de consanguinidad, tenian pena de muerte, si no eran cuñados, y cuñadas." *Mendieta* (Lib. II, cap. XXIX, p. 137). *Vetancurt* (Vol. 1, p. 481). All these authors appear to have gathered their information from the same source, or rather Torquemada is frequently Mendieta's plagiary, while Vetancurt often copies Torquemada. To avoid superfluous quotation, I beg to refer, on the subject of " unnatural crimes," to *Bancroft* (Vol. II, pp. 466, 467 and 468, " *Native Races* ").

[131] *Mendieta* (Lib. II, cap. XXVII, p. 132), copied by *Torquemada* (Lib. XIV, cap. III, p. 540), *Durán* (Cap. XXVI, pp. 214, 215 and 216), and others.

The woman, as participant in the offence, was also killed. Both were executed in public.[132] Theft of objects was variously punished. If the article was of small value and could be returned, its restitution settled the matter;[133] but if it were of greater value and could not be returned, then the thief became "bondsman" to the injured owner or even suffered death for his crime.[134] The

[132] If, however, the husband killed the wife himself, even if he caught her *flagrante delicto*. he lost his own life. This shows clearly, that the crime was considered as one not so much against the man, as against the cluster of kindred to which he belonged, and they were consequently not only bound but *entitled* to avenge it. Evidence of this punishment of the injured husband in case he avenged himself, is found in many authors. See *Mendieta* (Lib. II. cap. XXIX, p. 136). *Torquemada* (Lib. XII, cap. IV, p. 378), *Clavigero* (Lib. VII, cap. XVII, p. 484), and *H. H. Bancroft* (Vol. II, p. 465).

In strange contrast with the frequent assertions of the high-handed manner in which the chiefs are said to have used, at their will and good pleasure, the women of the land, as for instance in *Gomara* (Vedia I. pp. 438 and 439), *Motolinia* (Trat. II, cap. VII, p. 125) and others, we find it positively stated that adultery and rape were severely punished even in the case of the highest officers and chieftains. Thus, the case of the chief of Tlaxcallan. who was executed for adultery, is related with full details by *Las Casas* ("*Hist. apologética,*" Cap. 213, in Vol. VIII, of Kingsborough, p. 123), *Zurita* (pp. 107 and 108) *Torquemada* (Lib. XII, cap. XV. p. 399). Another story of a son of the chief of Tezcuco. killed for intercourse with girls then in the houses of worship, is also fully given. *Ixtlilxochitl* ("*Hist. des Chichiměques,*" Cap XLIV. pp. 315–320). *Torquemada* (Lib. II, cap. LXV. p. 189). etc. These are strange contradictions and are, sometimes, found even between fact and fact as told by the same author.

[133] *Gomara* (Vedia I, p. 442). says: "El ladron era esclavo por el primer hurto," but this is not sustained by others. in the case of small thefts. For instance. *Mendieta* (Lib. II. cap. XXIX, p. 138): "El ladron que hurtaba hurto notable, ... por la primera vez era hecho esclavo." *Torquemada* (Lib. XII. cap. V, p. 381). but especially (Lib. XIV, cap. XXI, p. 564): "Al que hurtaba pequeños hurtos, si no eran muy frequentados, con pagar lo que hurtaba hacia pago." *Clavigero* (Lib. VII, cap. XVII).

[134] The statements are positive to that effect. *Mendieta* (Lib. II, cap. XXIX, p. 138), *Torquemada* (Lib. XII, cap. V. p. 381), *Vetancurt* (Vol I, p. 485). "*Anónimo*" (Col de Doc: I, p. 383) exaggerates. "*De l'ordre de Succession observé par les Indiens*" Mr. Ternaux Compans' translation of a Simancas MSS., (1st Recueil, p. 228) confirms the "anonymous." *Fray Francisco de Bologna* ("*Lettre au R. P Clément de Mondia,*" 1st Recueil. p. 211): "Ils n'étaient pas tres cruels dans les punitions qu'ils infligeaient aux coupables." *Gabriel de Chaves* ("*Rapport sur la province de Meztillan,*' French translation by Mr. Ternaux, 2d Recueil, p. 312,—original held by Sr Icazbalceta). *Herrera* (Dec. III, lib. IV, cap. VII. p. 121), about Nicaragua: "Cortaban los Cabellos al Ladron, i quedaba Esclavo del Dueño de lo hurtado, hasta que pagase." (Lib. III. cap. XV, p. 101). at Izcatlan: "con los bienes del Ladron. despues de justiciado, satisfacian al agraviado. *Ixtlilxochitl* ("*Histoire des Chichiměques,*" Cap. XXXVIII, p. 266): "Celui qui volait dans les villages ou dans les maisons devenait l'esclave du volé, quand il n'avait pas commis d'effraction. et que le vol était de peu d'importance; dans le cas contraire il était pendu." *C. Ortega* (Appendix to Veytia, Vol. III, p. 225): "Casi siempre se castigaba con pena de muerte, á menos de que la parte ofendida conviniese en ser indemnizada por el ladron. Tambien tenia el ladron la pena de ser esclavo del dueño de lo que robaba; y si este no lo queria, era vendido por los juezes, y con su precio se pagaba el robo." *Bustamante* ("*Tezcoco,*" Parte IIIa, cap. I. p. 197).

Several of the authors above quoted, relate the well known tale about "wrathy chief" (Montezuma) picking some ears of corn in a gardenplot, for which he was ap-

duration of this bond, whether for certain time or for life, is not stated. If any one changed the limits (lines) of the individual lots ("talmilpa"), or of the official tracts, he lost his life. His offence was not so much against the occupant as against the kin, who had fixed the destination of each particular plot of land, and determined its boundaries.[135] It is also mentioned that "he who squandered the property of minors left to his care" suffered death for it. The case could only be that of an oldest son, or of a father's brother, in whose care the "tlalmilli" improved by the deceased was left, to be improved for the benefit of the latter's children. If now this warden failed to have that lot tilled for two years, it became lost to his wards, who were thereby left without means of subsistence. There was no restitution possible, therefore the negligent administrator paid with his life for the neglect.[136]

In general, we discern the ruling principle: that for theft there were but two ways of atonement. One consisted in the return of the stolen property, and if that was no longer possible, then the person of the thief had to suffer for it. Wherever no bodily labor could replace the value of the loss (as in the last case mentioned) the life of the criminal became forfeited to the kin, since the sufferers looked to that cluster for redress.[137] This carries us

prehended by its owner or at least occupant. This story shows, that no chief was exempt from punishment even for slight misdemeanors.

I refer to *Torquemada* (Lib. XIV, cap. XXI. p. 564), *Vetancurt* ("*Teatro*," Vol. I, p. 483), *Bustamante* ("*Tezcoco*," p. 197) for the assertion that the *kin* of the thief assisted him in discharging the penalty for his crime. The former says: " y si no tenia de que pagar, una, y dos veces, los parientes se juntaban, y repartian entre si el valor del hurto, y pagaban por el, diez. y doce mantas, y desde arriba: ni es de créer, que hacian Esclavo por quarenta, ni cinquenta mazorcas de maiz, ni por otra cosa de mas precio, si él tenia de que pagar, ó los Parientes." On this important point—the *solidarity of the kindred* in the case of the crime of one of their number, see, further on, note 137.

[135] To the authorities so frequently quoted on other subjects, I will add here *Ixtlilxochitl* (" *Relaciones históricas*," Vol. IX, Lord Kingsborough, p. 387).

[136] *Torquemada* (Lib. XII, cap. VII. p. 385) calls this an "extravagant law." Further quotations useless.

[137] It is stated by *A. de Vetancurt* ("*Teatro Mexicano*, Vol. I, p. 483): "En los hurtos-era ley general que siendo cosa de valor tenian pena de muerte; y si la parte se convenia, pagaba en mantas la cantidad al dueño, y otra mas para el fisco real; á esto acudian los parientes." This "obligation to help" on the part of the kin we have already met with in the case of marriage, where the kin assisted the newly married couple. (See *Zurita*, "*Rapport*," p. 132): "Si le jeune homme était pauvre, la communauté oú il avait été élevé l'aidait." We find it subsisting after the conquest, as when an Indian died, leaving debts, his kinship paid them for his estate (which in most cases was insolvent), or "worked it out for him." This is asserted as follows by *Fray Augustin Davila Padilla* ("*Historia de la Fundacion y Discurso de la Provincia de*

to a class of thefts and other similar offenses, committed against worship or " medicine."

Any attempt at seduction of a female who had taken the pledge of chastity in behalf of medicine, was most cruelly punished, both in the persons of the seducer and the female ; and if a medicine-man broke his vows, he suffered a horrible death.[138]

We have already mentioned that it was a capital crime on the part of a warrior to take for himself a prisoner of war secured by another.[139] Such cases occurred only during an engagement or immediately after it. Why an action of that kind should entail so rigorous a punishment can be easily inferred, if we recollect that a captive of that kind became at once sacred — an object of medicine. No return could atone for the offence, since it had been committed against the " rites of worship," one of the kin's most sacred and important attributes. Under the same head must be placed the capital punishment of such as wrongfully appropriated to themselves gold or silver. Both of these metals were regarded as objects of medicine, and whoever seized them unlawfully, committed a crime against worship also.[140]

Santiago de México," 2d Edition, 1625, Lib. I, cap. XXVI, p. 83): "Si muere alguno dellos con deudas, como si los deudos las heredassen por parecerse deudas y deudas en el nombre, procuran luego entre los parientes pagarlas, porque el anima de su difunto no dilate la entrada en el cielo. Y si no tienen caudal para pagar, procuran que se perdone la deuda, y sino salen con esta traça, se dan luego todos en servicio al acreedor hasta que del todo se pague lo que el difunto devia. Viviendo yo en el colegio de San Luys de predicadores el año de 1586, sucedió morir un Indio que trabajaua en aquel sumptuoso edificio, y era muy diestro cantero; auia recibido dineros adelantados, y quando murió quedava deviendo veynte pesos, ó reales de á ocho. Viniéron luego al colegio los parientes reconocienda la deuda, y pidiendo que los ocupasen en servicio del colegio, para que se descontasse lo que su defunto deuia. No se les daua mucho a los padres del colegio por cobrar estos dineros; porque demas de ser pocos no parecia que auia modo para cobrarlos; y mas por acudir á la devocion de los deudos, le dixéron á uno, que viniesse á trabajar en la huerta. Era marauilloso el cuydado del Indio, ansi en venir cada dia, como en venir muy de mañana; y preguntandole un religioso la causa de su cuydado, dixo, que le tenia porque su pariente se fuesse al cielo, y desde alla le ayudasse con Dios, y no estuviesse en el infierno chiquito, que los predicadores llaman purgatorio."

My friend Col. F. Hecker, to whom I communicated the above, at once recognized in it an analogue to the ancient Teutonic "*Gesammt-Burgschaft.*" He called my attention to the remarkable organization of the Germans. Compare *Luden* ("*Geschichte,*" etc., Vol. I, p. 502), which valuable source I also owe to the kindness of the distinguished German jurist.

[138] In regard to " priests " it is also stated that they were merely degraded and cast away; but this is hardly probable since, the higher the position of the culprit, the severer was his punishment.

[139] Compare also *H. H. Bancroft* (Vol. II, p. 419). *Prescott* ("*Conquest,*" Book I, chapter II, p. 47).

[140] *Mendieta* (Lib. II, cap. XXIX, p. 138). *Vetancurt* (Vol. I, p. 481): "Al que hurtaba

In the above review of those offences and their punishments, immediately connected with that rule of tribal society which places the persons and property of the members of a kin under that kin's special protection, we cannot pretend to have furnished more than illustrations, and not at all a full catalogue. Still, enough has been told, we believe, to explain what is frequently styled the "penal code" of the ancient Mexicans. It is well known, that no actual written laws existed, but on the other hand, at the time of the Spanish conquest, the natives still had a large number of paintings which represented their own manners and customs. Since a considerable proportion of these picture-leaves bore on the same subjects, the inference could be easily drawn that they indicated forms for the guidance of the people, or in other words, that they were a substitute for a written code. This was not at all their object. They were simply efforts of native art intended to represent scenes of everyday life, since these were the most handy subjects for such purposes. Therefore such pictures are to be regarded as convenient remains of aboriginal art, out of which many details concerning aboriginal customs may be gathered, but not as "official" sources, from which to seek information as to the "law of the land."[141]

plata y oro lo desollaban vivo y sacrificaban al dios de los plateros, que llamaban Xipe, y lo sacaban por las calles para escarmiento de otros, por ser el delito contra el dios fingido." This sacrifice to one particular Idol, however, is neither mentioned by Torquemada nor by his predecessor and main source, Mendieta. *Clavigero* (Lib. VII, cap. XVII. p. 487) copies Vetancurt almost textually. So does *Ortega* (Vol. III, p. 225, Appendix to *Veytia's "Hist. Antigua"*). *Bustamante* ("*Tezcoco*," p. 196) copies the former again. Still it is singular that the older the source, that is, the nearer in date to the time of the conquest, the less positive it is on the point of sacrifice. It will be safe to admit that the criminal was killed for a crime committed against worship, without insisting upon a particular place or mode of punishment.

[141] Elsewhere ("*On the Sources for Aboriginal History of Spanish America*," in Vol. XXVII of the "*Proceedings of the American Association for Advancement of Science*," 1878) I have attempted a discussion of the nature of Mexican paintings, and of their value as sources of history. I will add here but two positive declarations, on the subjects of the paintings, which I had not noticed at the time the above paper was read at St. Louis, Missouri, Aug., 1878. *Juan de Solorzano-Pereyra* ("*Disputationem de Indiarum Jure*," 1629, Vol. I, Lib. II, cap. VIII, p. 331. § 96): "Quod de Phœnicibus t adit etiam Lucanus, et in Mexicanis nostris experti fuimus, qui si non litteris, imaginibus tamen, et figuris ea omnia, quæ sibi memoranda videbantur, significabant, et conservabant." The other is of recent date, being taken from a discourse delivered before the "Académia Mexicana." by my friend Señor *D. J. G. Icazbalceta* ("*Las Bibliotecas de Eguiara y de Beristain*," p. 353 of No. 4, Vol. I, of "*Memorias de la Academia*"): "El antiguo pueblo que ocupaba este suelo no conocia las letras, y con eso está dicho que no podia tener escritores ni literatura. Su imperfectisimo sistema de representar los objetos é ideas, tenia que limitarse á satisfacer, hasta donde podia, las necesidades más urgentes de la sociedad, sin aspirar á otra cosa. Asi es que no se empleaba sino en registrar los tributos de los pueblos, en señalar los limites de las

In this rapid sketch, we have failed to find, among aboriginal modes of punishment, two which were common to almost every nation of the old world, namely: whipping, and imprisonment.

Whipping, beating, or lashing was, among the Mexicans as well as amongst all American natives, known only as a *deadly insult*. It is nevertheless true that the Mendoza Codex contains pictures representing a Mexican father who applies to a son the rod of punishment.[142] Again, the candidate for the office of chief had to endure beating[143] along with the other sufferings incident to his time of trial. But no "bondsman" was ever whipped or flogged, neither was a criminal subjected to this degrading penalty, for which death would have been a thousand times preferable.[144]

The Mexicans had places of confinement—dark and gloomy recesses with entrances compared to "pigeon-holes."[145] Every official building, and also the places of worship contained them. They were called: "place of the taken one," "teilpiloyan;"[146] "place of entombment or confinement," "Tecaltzaqualoyan,"[147] and "house of wood," Quauhcalli."[148] The latter, which is particularly described as a wooden cage placed within a dark chamber, was reserved for those whose doom was sealed, whether they were criminals sentenced to immediate execution, or captives to

heredades, en recordar las ceremonias de la religion, y en contribuir á conservar la memoria de los sucesos más notables, que aun con ese auxilio habria perecido, á no perpetuarse en las tradiciones recogidas por los primeros predicadores del Evangelio."

[142] "*Mendoza Codex*" (Kingsborough, Vol. I, plates LX, part 3), the boy being nine years old.

[143] *Mendieta* (Lib. II. cap. XXXVIII. p. 157). *Torquemada* (Lib. XI, cap. XXIX, p. 362). *Clavigero* (Lib. VII, cap. XIII. p. 472), etc., etc.

[144] It was no dishonor to suffer tortures, but whipping was a deadly insult, as among other Indians.

[145] *Mendieta* (Lib. II, cap. XXIX, p. 138): "Tenian las cárceles dentro de una casa oscura y de poca claridad, y en ella hacian su jaula ó jaulas; y la puerta de la casa que era pequeña como puerto de palomar, cerrada por defuera con tablas, y arrimadas grandes piedras." *Torquemada* (Lib. XI. cap. XXV, p. 353).

[146] *Molina* (II, p. 94), "teilpi"—el que prende o encarcela a otro"—"teilpiliztli" "prendimiento tal." (Id. I, p. 98). "prender" "niteylpia." Among the 78 edifices of the great central place of worship, *Sahagun* (Lib. II, Appendix. p. 210) mentions one place "Acatlayiacapan Veicalpulli" "esta era una casa donde juntaban los esclavos que habian de matar á honra de los Tlaloques." (Id., Lib. VIII, cap. XV, p. 304. Cap. XXI, p. 309) mentions "jails" in connection with the official house or "tecpan." That the different calpulli or "barrios" had each its places of confinement is noticed by *Durán* (Cap. XXI, p. 187): "Los calpixques los receuian y los ponian en las casas de sus comunidades ó del sacerdote de tal barrio."

[147] *Molina* (II. p. 91): "Tecalli" a vault, "casa de bóveda." Since the Mexicans had no arches, it meant actually a tomb.

[148] *Molina* (II, p. 85): "Jaula grande de palo, adonde estauan los presos por sus delictos."

be sacrificed forthwith.[149]   The two former kinds of prisons were used for lighter degrees of offenders.   At any rate they were but temporary places of detention, for any prisoner left there for any length of time invariably died of hunger, filth, and bad air.   Permanent confinement simply meant death.[150]

The execution of all these penalties necessarily presupposed for the kin a regulated administration.   It therefore leads us to the governmental machinery proper of the calpulli.   The nature of this government is expressed by the following rule of kinship, already found in vigor among more northern Indians.

The kin had the right to elect its officers, as well as the right to remove or depose them for misbehavior.[151]

This at once establishes the calpulli, as we have already stated in several places, to be an autonomous body, enjoying self-government, consequently a DEMOCRATIC ORGANIZATION.   The truth of this we intend to show by an investigation of the different offices to which the care of the kin's business was committed.

A *council*, consisting of a number of old men, formed the highest authority of the calpulli.   How many they were is not stated, but it is probable that their number varied according to that of the members of the kin.   Medicine men may, also, have been members of this body, which held its meetings at intervals in the official house of the " quarter."   It exercised criminal jurisdiction as well as civil, and attended to all grave questions affecting the kinship.   It is also stated that, on certain occasions, a general meeting of all the members of the calpulli was convened.[152]

---

[149] No better illustration of the " Quauhcalli " can be found than that given by *H. H. Bancroft* (" Native Races," cap. XIV, p. 453.   Volume II).

[150] The cruel and unwholesome nature of aboriginal places of detention previous to the conquest is amply stated.   As it is very justly remarked by *Mr. Bancroft* (Vol. II, p. 453): " They had prisons, it is true, and very cruel ones, according to all accounts. but it appears that they were more for the purpose of confining prisoners previous to their trial, or between their condemnation and execution, than permanently, for punishment."   To the authorities quoted by the celebrated Californian. I will add here in further support of his views (and mine). *Gomara* (Vedia I, p. 442): " Las cárceles eran bajas, húmedas y escuras, para que temiesen de entrar alli."   *Vetancurt* (Vol. I. Part II.   Trat. II, cap. I. p. 370).   *Tezozomoc* (" *Crónica* " cap. XCIX, p. 176): " mandóles llevar á la carcel á todos, que llamaban cuaucalco, que era á manera de una caja, como cuando entapian ahora alguna persona, que les dan de cómer por onzas."

[15] " *Ancient Society* " (Part. II, chapter II, pp. 71, 72, and 73.   Chap. VIII, p. 225, Cap. XI. pp. 285 and 297).

[152] It is singular that this council of the kin or " gens," while some parts of its functions are preserved in nearly every author. has as a body been so generally overlooked Zurita (pp. 55 and 56) says: " the chief does nothing without consulting the other old men of the calpulli."   Indirect evidence of it is given by *Sahagun* (Lib. II, cap.

This council however, while it thus united both the highest administrative and judiciary powers, required other officers for

XXXVII, p. 185), in his description of the feast of the month " Izcalli." These "old men" reappear again in connection with celebrations affecting the calpulli, at least occasionally. This council however, still existed at a recent date (1871) among the natives of Guatemala. *Sr. D. Juan Gavarrete* of the City of Guatemala (La Nueva) writes to me under date of 14th March, 1879: " Cuando en el pueblo hay varias parcialidades ó calpules, ... cada una de ellas tiene su calpul ó consejo de cierto número de Ancianos y estos reunides eligen las Autoridades comunes del pueblo, nombrando tambien alcaldes subalternos para las diversas parcialidades." In his Introduction to the "*Real Ejecutoria*" (Col. de Doc. II. pp. XII and XIII), the late *Sr. José F. Ramirez* attributes the creation of an elective municipal council to an act of policy of the Spanish government. It is clear, however, from the authors of the XVIth century, especially from Zurita, that this "democratic element" ("el elemento democrático" as Sr. Ramirez calls it), was an *aboriginal* one. Therefore the council still subsisting in Guatemala is an original feature, with changes in names and functions, made to suit the laws of Spain. *Ramirez de Fuenleal* (Letter of 3d Nov., 1532, 1st Recueil, p. 249), mentions "other officers called *riejos* (old men)" in "each quarter or as they were now called, parishes." The following quotation from *Juan de Solorzano* ("*De Indiarum Jure*," Vol. II, lib. I, cap. XXIII, pp. 210, § 21), is of interest upon the question raised by Sr. Ramirez: "In Nova quoque Hispania, cum hae reductiones, quas ibi *Aggregationes* vocant, i praestanti illo, et prudenti Duce Ferdinando Cortesio stab'lit io, et constituite fuissent, et postea, temporam, et Hispanorum iniuriae, valde collapsae, ac subversae; alias deuo fieri et factas instaurari curavit Excellentissimus ille, et Pijissimus Prorex Canes de Monte Regio, schedulis etiam, et provisionibus Regijis sibe ad hoc demandatis, morem gerere cupiens: in quibus tamen exequendis, magnae dificultates, et Indorum strages expertae sunt, quia eorum aliqui voluntario suspendio vitam finire maluerunt, quan in designata sibi municipia reduci." This was published in 1639."

In all likelihood there was no regular time of meeting of these "old men." They met as emergency required, and as they were called together. There is even a trace of a general meeting of the inhabitants of a calpulli, in *Zurita* (p. 62): " Dans ces circonstances, les habitants du calpulli se réunissent pour traiter les intérets communs, et règler la répartition des impôts, etc." We thus witness in the calpulli the following methods of exercising authority: through the joint meeting of all its members for the discussion of matters affecting the whole community, through the "old men" controlling the regular business, and, through what the older authorities called "chiefs" or executive officers, of whom I shall treat hereafter. An important question remains to be examined here namely: whether the calpulli really had, as I have asserted, criminal jurisdiction over its members, or whether this pertained to higher officers or so-called "tribunals."

Against the assumption, that questions of life and death could be decided by the "quarters," "barrios," or "calpulli," there is we confess it, apparently weighty evidence. In order to examine this vital question critically, I am compelled to take each author by himself, comparing his various statements (if there are more than one) on the same subject with each other. I must premise, however, that neither *Cortés*, nor *Andrés de Tápia*, nor *Bernal Diez de Castilo* mentions having seen any one judged and condemned by the head-war-chief of the Mexican tribe. This, however, may be a simple omission on their part.

Sahagun (Lib. VIII, cap. XXV, p. 314): "y los casos muy dificultuosos y graves, llevábanlos al señor para que los sentenciase, juntamente con trece principales muy calificados, que con el andaban, y residian. Estos tales eran los mayores jueces, que ellos llamaban tecutlatoque: estos ecsaminaban con gran diligencia las causas que iban á sus manos; y cuando quiera que esta audiencia que era la mayor, sentenciaba alguno á muerte, luego lo entregaban á los ejecutores de la justicia." Thus far the jurisdiction of the tribal officers only comes into play. But the same author also mentions the

everyday business, who should at the same time be the executors of its decrees. Of these officers there were two, both strictly

power of certain officers of the kin to kill in punishment of certain crimes, (Lib. III, Appendix, cap. VI, p. 271). If a young man was caught drunk : "castigábanle dandole de palos hasta matarle, ò le daban garrote delante de todos réunidos." This being done in the case of a youth committed to the "telpuchcalli," it necessarily follows that the power to punish by death, was vested in the kin to which the particular "telpuchcalli" belonged.

Zurita (p. 101 and 106) intimates rather than asserts, that all grave matters, including life and death had to be submitted to the highest "court of appeals," "les douze juges d'appel" over which the king presided. But he does not state that this body had *exclusive* jurisdiction.

Gomara (Vedia I, p. 442, " *Conquista* ") evidently mistakes in confounding the gatherers of tributes with judicial officers and says nothing in regard to criminal jurisdiction. His statements will be examined elsewhere.

Mendieta (Lib. II, cap. XXVIII, pp. 134–136) says that all the "Judges" remained in the official house of each tribe : "cada uno de ellos en su propio palacio tenia sus audiencias de oidores que determinaban las causas y negocios que se ofrecian, asi civiles como criminales, repartidos por sus salas, y de unas habia apelacion para otras." Further on he says that every eighty days " se sentenciaban todos los casos criminales, y duraba esta consulta diez ó doce dias." *Torquemada* (Lib. XI, cap. XXV, pp. 352 and 353) is remarkably indefinite on the point. To him, the tribal officers alone appear prominent in the case. (Cap. XXVI, pp. 354 and 355), however, wherein he fully treats of the judicial organization of *Tezcuco*, enables us to discern the separate jurisdiction of each calpulli. The textual rendering of the whole chapter would be too lengthy, and I must therefore confine myself to abstracts. He begins by saying that, while Tezcuco had fifteen " provinces" subject to it (" sujetas á su Señoria "), " not all of them had supreme Judges " (" pero no en todas havia Jueces de estos inmediatos, y Supremos "). Therefore it was ordained, " that there should be six courts (" audiencias "), like chancery-offices (" como chancillerias ") in six particular pueblos, to which all the other said Provinces were reduced, and to them they applied from all over the kingdom." He further states that at each of these houses (which he subsequently calls " tecpans ") were stored the " royal tributes : " " se recogian todos los Tributos Reales, por los mismos Jueces." Besides, there were " four Judges " at the " palace," and at each of these six " courts," two " Judges " and one " executive officer " (alguazil).

From further details given, it follows that these six " pueblos " were so near to the official house of the tribe, as to make it more than likely that they were the six *Calpulli* of Tezcuco, mentioned by *Ixtlilxochitl* (12th " *Relacion* " or " *Pintura de México*," Vol. IX of Kingsborough, p. 387) as having been established by " Fasting wolf " (Nezahualcoyotl), which story he repeats in the " *Histoire des Chichimèques* " (Cap. XXXVIII, pp. 263 and 264).

The description of Tezcuco by *Torquemada* (Lib. III, cap. XXVII, p. 304) : " pero no se ha de entender, que toda esta Caseria estaba recogida, y junta ; porque aunque en su maior parte lo estaba, otra mucha estaba repartida, como en Familias, y Barrios ; y de tal manera corria esta Poblacion, desde el corazon de ella (que era la Morada, y Palacios del Rei) que se iba dilatando, por tres ò quatro Leguas," shows that the calpulli of that ancient pueblo were scattered over a great expanse. At the close of the 17th century (1680, about) it is stated by *Vetancurt* (" *Crónica de la Provincia del Santo Evangelio de México*," pp. 159 and 160), that, besides the " city," there were " 29 pueblos de visita, en cinco parcialidades repartidos." All this corroborates our assumption : that the six " pueblos " of Torquemada were in fact but the six " barrios " or kins, each of which exercised, for itself and through its officers, *criminal jurisdiction over its members*.

There is no need of proving the fact that the several tribes of the valley had identical customs, and that their Institutions had reached about the same degree of development. It is even asserted by some (*Prescott*, Book I, cap. II, p. 30) that " In Tezcuco

elective and therefore liable to be deposed, one of whom represented more properly the administrative, the other the executive (consequently military) authority. The first one of these was the "calpullec" or "chinancallec;"[153] the second, the "elder brother"

the judicial arrangements were of a more refined character." If now, as I have shown, the council of the Kin exercised power over life and death among them, it certainly had the same power among the ancient Mexicans. Besides, the same thing is inferable from the nature of many of the crimes punished by death. Conspicuous among these are the cases wherein tenure of lands became affected. If a member of the kin changed the limits of a "tlalmilli," it was a crime over which the calpulli alone had jurisdiction, and the same occurred if any one member neglected to attend to the lots of children placed in his care. We have seen that in both instances the penalty was death.

It is of course understood, that this power did not go beyond the limits of the kin and of such outcasts as were attached to its members. Over members of other kins it had no jurisdiction. The adjustment of matters between kin and kin became exclusively the duty of the tribe.

One of the most characteristic remarks, however, on the general functions of the kin is that of *Zurita* ("*Rapport*," etc., p. 53): "Finally, what is called in New Spain Calpulli, answers to what among the Israelites was called a tribe."

[153] *Zurita* ("*Rapport*," p. 50): "The chiefs of the third classes are still called Calpullec in the singular, and in the plural Chinancallec, that is to say: chiefs of very ancient race or family, from the word Calpulli or Chinancalli, which is the same, and signifies a quarter (*barrio*) inhabited by a family, known as of very ancient origin, which for a long time owns a territory with well defined boundaries and all the members of the same lineage." This statement is copied by *Herrera* (Dec. III, lib. IV, cap. XV, p. 135), with the exception that he omits the names, substituting that of "pariente mayor." In regard to this it is added by *Zurita* (pp. 60 and 61): "The calpullis have always a chief necessarily in the tribe. He must be one of the principal inhabitants, an able subject who can assist and defend them. The election is made among them. They are much attached to him, as the inhabitants of Biscay and of the mountains are to him who is called *pariente mayor*. The office of these chiefs is not hereditary: whenever one dies they elect in his place the most respected, the ablest and wisest old man. If the deceased has left a son who is qualified, he is chosen, and a relative of the former chief is always preferred." *Herrera* (Id. p. 135).

Although the above two authors speak but indefinitely of the "chief" of the calpulli, it is likely that they mean *two* chiefs, one of which is the calpullec, and the other the teachcauhtin. This is indicated by the name of "pariente mayor." Zurita does not say, according to Mr. Ternaux's translation, that this chief was thus called, but Herrera, who copies him, writes very distinctly: "que *llamaban* parientes maiores." Now, according to *Molina* (II, p. 91), "teachcauhtin" signifies elder brother. *Torquemada* (Lib. XIV, cap. VI, p. 544) gives to each "barrio ó parcialidad" two officers, namely, a calpixqui or gatherer of tribute or stores, and a "regidor, un Tecuhtli, que se ocupaba en executar lo que mustros Regidores executan, y hacen." But it is plainly evident, from the details given by the celebrated Franciscan, that he has lost sight of the peculiar position of officers of a *kin*, and looks to *tribal* functions and offices. Else, how could he assert of his "Regidor" that he was always in the "palace:" "y todos los Dias se hallaban en el Palacio, á ver lo que se les ordenaba, y mandaba; y ellos, en una grande Sala, que llaman Calpulli, se juntaban, y trataban de los negocios tocantes á su cargo."

"*De l'ordre de succession observé par les Indiens*" ("1st Recueil" of Ternaux, p. 225): "quant au mode adopté pour régler la juridiction et l'élection des alcades et des régidors des villages; ils nommaient des personnes notables qui portaient le titre de *achcacaulitin* qui est un nom de charge, comme l'est aujourd'hui celui d'alguazil. Les tribunaux de ces officiers étaient établis dans la capitale." . . . "Il n'y avait pas d'autres élections d'officiers." And further on the same document says (p. 227): "Ces achcacau-

"teachcauhtin" or "achcacauhtin."[154] Both were, in turn, ex-officio members of the council itself.[155] The "calpullec" or "chinancallec" was, in fact, what is still known among Indian communities of Mexico, Central America and New Mexico, as the "governor;" or rather his office was, for the *kin*, what the office of "gobernador" now is for the whole *tribe*.[156] Upon his

litis, c'est ainsi qu'on les nommait, remplissaient les fonctions d'alcade. Pour le moindre petit vol, c'est á dire pour avoir dèrobé seulement du mais, ils condamnaient à la potence." The singular feature is here asserted to exist, that the same officer should have been Judge ("alcalde") and executioner of his own decrees ("alguazil"). We meet also with the flagrant contradiction of "alguazils," elected for the villages, but whose courts resided "at the capital." Everywhere the same lack of distinctness is witnessed; the confusion between aboriginal institutions and Spanish organization is apparent.

Sebasti n Ramirez de Fuenleal ("Lettre," 3 Nov., 1532, p. 247) gives quite a clear picture of the "calpulli," adding: "Ces contribuables ont un chef et des commandants"; (p. 249): " Ils ont parmi eux des officiers que nous appelons principales (chefs); *il y en a deux dans chaque quartier qui portent aujourd'hui le nom de paroisses.*"

Finally, I refer to what has been said in the preceding note (152) about Tezcuco and the two officers of each so-called "pueblo." The fact that there were two of them is thus fully established, likewise that of their election; and as for their titles, they are found in the quotations just referred to and copied.

It is further confirmed through a statement of *Vetancurt* ("*Teatro Mexicano,*" Vol. I, p. 371): "en cada parcialidad, que llamaban calpulli y ahora tlaxilacalli; hábia uno como regidor que llamaban teuhtli: estos asistian á palacio todos los dias á saber lo que el mayordomo les ordenaba; éstos entre si elegian cada año dos en lugar de alcaldes, que llamaban tlayacanque y tequitlatoque, que ejecutaban lo que por los teuhtles se les mandaba; y para ejecutores tenian unos alguaciles que hoy llaman topile."

The term "tlayacanqui" is defined by *Sahagun* (Lib. II, cap. XXIX, p. 142) as "cuadrillero." *Molina* (II, p. 120) has "tlayacantli," "el que es regido, guiado, y gouernado de otro, o el ciego que es adiestrado de alguno" ("Tlayacati," "cosa primera, o delantera"). *Torquemada* (Lib. XIV, cap. VI, p. 545) calls the Tlayacanque "en lugar de merinos."

[154] *Molina* (I, p. 56).

[155] This results necessarily from the duties of the officers alone, as permanent representatives of the council of the kin or calpulli.

[156] The "Gobernador," as we shall hereafter see, was the successor to the "Cihuacohuatl," according to the Spaniard's notion of the nature of the latter's office. It is very interesting to notice that the "Cihuacohuatl" was, in the tribal government, the exact counterpart of the "Calpullec" in the kin. I am indebted to *Sr. Don Juan Gavarrete,* of the City of Guatemala (la Nueva), for the following description of the office of " Gobernador," as it is still found among the aboriginal settlements of Guatemala. This gentleman, (whose name is associated with that of my friend Dr. Valentini, in a noble effort to preserve the historical treasures of his country), writes to me under date of 14th of March, 1879: " Los pueblos formados por la antiguos misioneros ó por los conquistadores, y que son los que subsisten hasta el dia de hoy, han sido siempre gobernados por un *Gobernador* vitalicio elegido entre las familias nobles de la tribu (*cacique*). y un consejo á la usanza española compuesto de dos Alcaldes, cierto número de consejeros llamados Regidores entre quienes se distribuyen las comisiones de servici público y un secretario.

" La dignidad ó cargo de Gobernador, para la cual elegian en nombre del Rey los antiguos Capitanes Generales y despues los Presidentes de la República, es muy apetecida por los indios nobles y mientras el que la egerce no dá motivo por su mala conducta para ser removido puede contar con la perpetuidad y aun con dejarla á sus hijos

death " they elected, to fill his place, the most respected old man, the most able and most popular." It appears though that the choice often fell upon a son or near relative of the deceased, provided he evinced sufficient ability.[157]

It was the duty of this officer to preserve a plat of the territory dwelt upon by the kin, showing the location of each " tlalmilli," of the official tracts, of those of the " houses of the youth" and of worship; if the latter two were not, as we suspect, perhaps identical. These simple records he had to renew from time to time, according as mutations or additions occurred. The *stores* of the kin were under his supervision, though he could not dispose of them at his pleasure, but only for public purposes. Thus, aside from the presents, which always had to go with any public act of importance, it was his duty to provide, out of these stores, for everything requisite for the numerous religious and other festivities.[158] He had, under his immediate orders, the " stewards," " calpixqui," which attended to the details connected with the gathering, housing, and dispensing of all supplies.[159] It is prob-

si los tiene capaces de egercerla . . . . . . El cargo de Gobernador traia consigo los priviligos de usar *Don*, montar á caballo, ... usar baston y tener una numerosa servidumbre, no tenian jurisdiccion civil, pues esta competia á los Alcaldes, pero si la tenian en lo criminal en los délitos leves, siendo su poder principal sobre lo econórmigo y gubernativo."

[157] *Zurita* ("*Rapport*," etc., pp. 60 and 61).

[158] *Zurita* ("*Rapport*," etc., pp. 51 to 66). Copied in a condensed form by *Herrera* (Dec. III, Lib. IV, cap. XV, p. 134).

[159] The term " calpixqui," gatherer of crops, is so indiscriminately applied that it becomes necessary to investigate what class of officers were really meant by it. In general the " calpixca" were sent to subjected tribes, as representatives of their conquerors. For each such officer abroad there was one in the pueblo of Mexico, to receive and to house the tribute which the former collected and sent. The calpulli or kins, however, needed no officer of the same kind properly, because they owed no tribute to the tribe. The assertion of *Torquemada* (Lib. XIV, cap. VI, p. 545): " que el Maiordomo maior del Rei, se llamaba Hueycalpixqui, á diferencia de otros muchos, que havia, que se llamaban Menores; porque tenia cada parcialidad el suio," applies in this case to the tax-collectors and stewards themselves, and not to the stewards of the kins. The confused notions about the true nature of the office is also shown in the name of the official house. It is called by Torquemada alternately "tecpan," "calpul," finally also " calpixca, que era la casa del comun del Pueblo," (Lib. XIV, cap. I, p. 534). In confirmation of what has already been said in " *Tenure of Lands* " (pp. 413–428), I here refer to *Zurita* (pp. 236–242), " *De l'Ordre de succession* " (p. 229), *Motolinia et d'Olarte* ("*Lettre*," 27 Aug., 1554. pp. 403–406). We must never forget that tribute or tax was only due from a *conquered tribe* to its *conquerors*. No reference is made anywhere to tribute or tax gathered *inside* the pueblo of Mexico, but Tlatilulco, however, was obliged to pay a certain contribution (*Durán*, Cap. XXXIV, p. 270).

Nevertheless, the term " calpixqui" is found applied very distinctly to an office of the kin. *Durán* (Cap. XXI, p. 186) calls them " mandoncillos de los barrios." With equal propriety the calpixca are termed " governors " and " captains." It only proves that, while each kin had its stewards, they were under the direction of a " mandon,"

able that he himself, appointed the stewards subject to approval by the council.[160] Aside from these subalterns, the "calpullec" had his runners and attendants, mostly members of the household, perhaps " bonded " people. His judicial power was limited to minor cases, and it is more than doubtful if he held, alone, any authority to decide upon matters of life and death. But it is stated on high authority, that it was the duty of this officer, " to defend the members of a calpulli, and to speak for them."[161] We may be permitted to inquire, whether this, perhaps indicated, that the " calpullec" was also the " tlatoani" or speaker, who represented the kin in the tribe's supreme council. This must, however, be answered in the negative, for the obvious reason that he could not be in two places at the same time. The kin's official building was assigned to him as a residence, that he might be there on duty *always*, consequently he could not spend his time outside of it at the official house of the tribe.[162] Alongside of this officer (who corresponds almost to the " Sachem" of northeastern tribes), we find the " elder brother"—" teachcauhtin," " achcacauhtin," or through corruption, " tiacauh. ' He was, as already stated, the kin's military commander or war-captain, and the youth's instructor in warlike exercises ; but besides he was also the executor of justice—not the police magistrate, but the chief of police (to use a modern term of comparison) or rather " sheriff" of the calpulli.[163] As military commander he could

or superior officer. This could only be the " calpullec," since it is positively stated by *Zurita* (p. 62): "car lors des assemblées annuelles, qui sont trés nombreuses, il distribue gratuitement des vivres et des boissons." This had to be done out of the stores of the kin.

The term " tequitlato " is probably equivalent to " calpullec." It is derived from " ni-tequiti," to work or pay tribute (*Molina*, II, p. 105), and " ni-tlatoa," to speak (Id., II, p. 140); therefore "tributary speaker," or " speaker of tribute." But this is only used n the case of subjected tribes, where the "calpullec" was the one who cared for the tribute due by his kin, even collecting it. See *Fray Domingo de la Anunciacion* ("*Lettre*." Chalco 20 Sept., 1554, in 2*d Recueil*, p. 340), " les tequitlatos ou percepteurs." *Sahagun* (Lib. VIII, cap. XXXVIII, pp. 329–332) devotes a whole chapter to " De los grados por donde subian hasta hacerse Tequitlatos," without saying, however, what the latter means. I suspect it to be intended for " Tecuhtlatoques."

[160] This may be inferred from the nature of the office.

[161] *Zurita* (" *Rapport*." etc., p. 62): " Il a soin de défendre les membres du calpulli, de parler pour eux devant la justice et les gouverneurs."

[162] " *Tenure of Lands* " (p. 410 and note 52). *Zurita* (p. 266).

[163] It has already been shown that " achcauhtli," " achcacauhtli," and "teachcauhtin " or " tiacauh " are synonyms. I refer to "*Art of War*" (p. 119 and note 91) in regard to the various and contradictory notions about the nature of the office. Still, the prevailing idea is that, besides being the " teachers" and the " captains," they also were the " executioners" of the kin. " *De l'ordre de succession* " (p. 225): " ils nommaient des

appoint his subalterns in the field, and as executor of justice he had the same privilege while at the pueblo. The ",teachcauhtin," therefore selected his own assistants and runners. Accompanied by them and carrying his staff of office, whose tuft of white feathers intimated that his coming might threaten death,[164] the "elder brother" circulated through his calpulli, preserving order and quietness in every public place thereof. If he found or heard of any one committing a nuisance or crime, he could seize him forthwith and have him carried to the official house, there to be disposed of as the custom and law of the kin required. But it is doubtful whether, except in extraordinary instances, he was authorized to do justice himself without the council's knowledge and consent.[165]

Ere we pass over now from the functions of the kin to those of the ancient Mexican tribe, we must however dwell at some length on a peculiar institution, yet shared by the Mexicans in common with Indian tribes in general. We refer to the rank and dignity of CHIEF among them. Chieftaincy and office are far from being equivalent. The former is a purely personal, non-hereditary distinction, bestowed in reward of merit only, whereas the latter is a part of the governmental machinery.[166] Hence it follows that a chief might fill an office or not, and still remain a chief, whereas

personnes notables qui portaient le titre de achcacaulitin qui est un nom de charge, comme l'est aujourd'hui celui d'alguazils." *Sahagun* (Lib. VIII, cap. XVII, p. 305) calls the Achcacauhtli "(ó verdugos) que tenian cargo de matar á los que condenaba el señor." *Torquemada* (Lib. XI, cap. XXVI, p. 355), "llamabanse Achcauhtli, que quiere decir maiores." There is hardly any doubt as to their functions.

[164] White was the color of death. (Bleaching skulls and bones!) This is amply proven by their mode of declaring, or rather announcing, war. The custom of carrying "staffs of office" is well established.

[165] *Torquemada* (Lib. XI, cap. XXVI, p. 355). *Clavigero* (Lib. VII, cap. XVI, p. 482, calls those " who arrested " delinquents "topilli." But this word means simply "rod or baton of justice, staff, etc." (*Molina*, II, p. 150), and not office. There is no evidence that these officers might kill, without previous decision of the council, except perhaps in the great market place. *Cortés* ("*Carta Segunda*," Vedia I, p. 32): " Hay en la dicha plaza otras personas que andan continuo entre la gente mirando lo que se vende y las medidas con que miden lo que venden, y se ha visto quebrar alguna que estaba falsa." *Oviedo* (Lib. XXXIII, cap. X, p. 301) copies Cortés, adding, however, "é quiebran lo que está falso, é penan al que usaba dello." *Bernal Diez de Castillo* (Cap. XCII, p. 89) simply remarks: "y otros como alguaziles ejecutores que miraban las mercadérias," (Vedia, Vol. II). I hardly need any reference in regard to the manner of acting and mode of appearance of the "elder brothers." Their functions of "police" are repeatedly described in the older sources.

[166] *L. H. Morgan* ("*Ancient Society*," p. 71): " Nearly all the American Indian tribes had two grades of chiefs, who may be distinguished as sachems and common chiefs. Of these two primary grades all other grades were varieties. . . . The office of sachem was hereditary in the gens, in the sense that it was filled as often as a vacancy occurred; while the office of chief was non-hereditary, because it was bestowed in reward of per-

it was not necessary to become a chief in order to fill certain offices.   Still it is evident that, as chiefs were always men of peculiar ability, the higher charges were generally filled by chieftains.

The title and rank of "grandfather" ("Tecuhtli,")[167] which was the Mexican term for chieftain in general, was open to any one who strove to deserve it.   It was conferred:

1. In recompense for warlike prowess, and actions of personal intrepidity and superior shrewdness. Courage alone could not secure it; therefore the "distinguished braves" were not always chiefs.[168]

2. In reward for actions denoting particular wisdom and sagacity, and in acknowledgement of services in the councils, or as traders.[169]

sonal merit, and died with the individual." I have selected the term "*officer*" as a substitute for Mr. Morgan's "*sachem*," because the latter is a northern Indian word, whereas the former, while it expresses the nature of the charge and dignity, is more widely known, and therefore better understood. It is out of the union of the attributes, of both officer and chief, that nobility and monarchy have been claimed to exist. Among the Mexicans, in fact among the most highly advanced Indian tribes (the Inca of Peru not excluded), the dignity of chief was still a personal matter, and not necessarily connected with office. The chiefs are the "knights," mentioned by *Garcilasso de la Vega* ("*Histoire des Yncas*," Lib. VI, cap. XXIV, XXV, XXVI) and *Herrera* (Dec. V, Lib. IV, cap. VII, p. 63; Lib. IV, cap. I, p. 83). With the Muyscas of Bogotá, compare *H. Ternaux-Compans* ("*L'ancien Cundinamarca*," § XXVII, pp. 57 and 58). *Oviedo y Valdés* (Lib. XXVI, cap. XXXI, p. 410). *Herrera* (Dec. VI, Lib. V, cap. VI, pp. 116 and 117). Compare also, in regard to the dignity of "military chief" among the wild tribes of the Rio Orinoco and of its tributaries, *P. José Gumilla* "*Histoire naturelle, civile, et géographique de l'Orénoque*," translated by Mr. Eidous, 1758, (Vol. II, chapter XXXV, pp. 280-292). Very important.

[167] *Molina* (II, p. 93), "ahuelo," "tecul." It evidently should be "abuelo," and is therefore only a misprint. The older reports have the word "tecle," and only the later writers (those after the year 1530) begin to write it "tecutli," "tecuhtli," "teuctli." Whether the "teules" meant really "gods," or rather "tecuhtin," as plural of "tecutli," is yet doubtful. It is almost a truism to recall here the Roman "senex," and the German "grave" or "Graf." Among American tribes we have, in QQuiché, "ama" old, "ahau,"—chief; in Maya, "Hachyum,"—father, and "ahau,"—chief—also "achi,"—brave.

[168] *Sahagun* (Lib. VIII, cap. XXXVIII, pp. 329-332): "De Los grados por donde subian hasta hacerse Tequitlatos," especially (p. 331): "y á los que por si prendian cuatro cautivas, mandaba el rey que los cortasen los cabellos como á capitan, llamalbanle tal diciendo . . . . el capitán mexicatl, ò el capitan tolnaoacatl, ú otros nombres que cuadraban á los capitanes. De alli adelante se podian sentar en los estrados que ellos usaban de petates é icpales en la sala donde se sentaban los otros capitanes y Valientes hombres, los cuales son primeros y principales en los asuntos, y tienen barbotes largos, orejeras de cuero, y borlas en las cabezas conque están compuestas;" *Zurita* ("*Rapport*," p. 47): "Les chefs qui, comme nous l'avons dit, se nommaient Tec Tecutzcin, ou Teutley au pluriel, n'exerçaient le commandement qu'à vie, parce que les souverains suprémes ne les élevaient á ces dignités qu'en récompense des exploits qu'ils avaient faits à la guerre, et des services rendus à l'état ou au prince"). *Mendieta* (Lib. II, cap. XXXVIII, p. 156). *Torquemada* (Lib. XI, cap. XXIX, p. 361). *Clavigero* (Lib. VII, cap. XIII, pp. 471 and 472), and others.

[169] *Zurita* ("*Rapport*," p. 47). *Sahagun* (Lib. IX, cap. II, p, 342): "Estos mercaderes

In both the above instances (or kinds of instances) actions of particular merit facilitated, at least, the acquisition of the title; but it could, also, be obtained : —

3. By the observance of rigorous and even cruel rites of " medicine " for a stated time, which put the courage, fortitude, and self-control of the candidate to the severest tests.[170] Although a detailed account of these rites might perhaps be withheld for a subsequent sketch of ancient Mexican worship, yet they equally deserve a place here.

The candidate appears to have been presented at the great central place of worship by the representatives of his kin, perhaps, also, by the other chiefs of his tribe. There he underwent four days and four nights of the most cruel torments. While but little nourishment was allowed him (some went even so far as not to eat anything at all during this time), his blood was drawn freely, and no sleep was permitted to settle on his weary eyes. From time to time he was exposed to taunts, to injurious words, to blows and even to stripes. While he was thus hungry and thirsty, weakened from loss of blood through self-sacrifice, others ate and drank plentifully before his eyes. Finally, his clothes were torn from his body, and with nothing on but the breech-cloth or diaper, he was at last left alone at the " calmecac," there to do the rest of his penance. When these four initiatory days were past, the candidate went back to his calpulli, to spend the remainder of the 'time (about a full year), in retirement, and abstinence, frequently attended with more or less self-inflicted bodily suffering. When the kin had secured the necessary amount of articles to be offered up in worship, or given to the medicine-men, officers, chiefs, and guests attending the installation, this final solemnity was allowed to take place, provided always that the courage and personal strength of the novice had not forsaken him. Another period of fasting, sacrifice, and torture, similar to the one at the opening of the career of preparation, closed the probation. Some of the ordeals were again of the most trying nature. Finally the store of gifts was distributed ; eating and drinking alternated with

eran ya como caballeros, y tenian divisas particulares por sus hazañas." . . . *Fray Alonzo de Montufar* (' *Supplique*," etc., 30 Nov., 1554. " *Treizième relation d'Ixtlilxochitl*," Appendix. p. 257). " *Des Cérémonies observées autrefois par les Indiens lorsqu'ils faisaient un Tecle*," (1st " Recueil," p. 232). *Mendieta* (Lib. II, cap. XXXVIII, p. 156).

[170] *Gomara* (" *Conquista*," Vedia I, p. 435). " *Des Cérémonies observées*," etc. (pp. 232, etc.). *Mendieta* (p. 156). *Torquemada* (Lib. XI, cap. XXIX and XXX, etc.).

solemn dances to the monotonous rythmic noise called Indian music. The candidate was, at last, once more dressed in becoming apparel, and could recuperate, being himself now the " feasted one." [171]

Men, however young in years, who had successfully endured such great trials, certainly deserved to be looked upon thereafter as persons of uncommon fortitude. Hence indeed the chiefs or " tecuhtli" were particularly fitted for responsible offices of any kind. They were looked upon with deference, their voice was heard and listened to, and it is no wonder if higher charges, especially those of a military nature, were filled by such as had, in one way or another, achieved this distinction.[172] But no privilege was connected with their dignity, except that of wearing certain peculiar ornaments, and none was transmitted through them to their descendants.[173] That the " tecuhtli," besides, did

[171] For the above description of the formalities of creating a " Tecuhtli," I refer to the sources quoted in the preceding three notes. It is interesting to compare similar ceremonies used by the Indians of the Orinoco, *Gumilla* (" *Histoire*," etc., Vol. 11, cap. XXXV). Of the Yncas. *Garcilasso de la Vega* (Lib. VI, cap. XXIV to XXVI). *Cristoval de Molina* ("*An account of the Fables and Rites of the Yncas*," translated by C. R. Markham, in Hackluyt Society's Volume of 1873). " *Narratives of the Rites and Laws of the Yncas*." *Herrera* (Dec. V, lib. III, cap. VII, p. 63, etc.). We are forcibly reminded of the words of the quaint old poet and soldier, *Alonzo de Erxcilla*.

> "Los cargos de la Guerra, y preheminencia
> No son por flacos medios proveidos,
> Ni van por calidad, ni por herencia,
> Ni por hacienda, i ser mejor nacidos;
> Más la virtud del brazo, y la excelencia,
> Esta hace á los hombres preferidos,
> Esta ilustra, habilita, perficiona,
> Y quilata el valor de la persona."

(" *La Araucana*," Parte Ia, Canto 1°. Edition of 1733, p. 2).

[172] *Mendieta* (Lib. II, cap. XXXIX, p. 161: "Los que tenian el ditado de Tecutli, tenian muchas preeminencias, y entre ellas era que en los concilios y ayuntamientos sus votos eran principales." *Gomara* (" *Conquista*" Vedia I, p. 436). *Torquemada* (Lib. XI, cap. XXX, p. 366). It should always be remembered, that the dignity of Tecuhtli appears most prominent in Tlaxcallan. This people however, was but a league, very similar to that of the northern Iroquois, only consisting of four, instead of six tribes. Among them, the peculiar nature of the dignity of chief became more evident than it was among the Mexicans to the Spaniards. But there is no difference between the " Tecuhtli" of Tlaxcallan, and the " Tecuhtli" of Mexico or Tezcuco. That the head-chiefs of Mexico were always " Tecuhtli" themselves, previous to their election, needs hardly any proof. *Domingo Munoz Camargo* (" *Histoire de la République de Tlaxcallan*." Translation by Mr. Ternaux-Compans, in Vol. 98 and 99 of " *Nouvelles Annales des Voyages*," 1843. See Vol. 98, p. 176, etc.)

[173] About the privileges of the Tecuhtli, compare *Gomara* (" *Conquista*" Vedia I, p. 436), *Mendieta* (Lib. II, cap. XXXIX, p. 161), *Torquemada* (Lib. XI, cap. XXX, p. 366), *Zurita* (p. 48, etc.). It is evident however, that the latter confounds the rank of chief with the particular office which might have been entrusted to him, else the " cultivation of lands" could not be included in the list of advantages derived from the position. Compare "*Tenure of Lands*." *Bustamante* (" *Tezcoco*," etc., p. 235). Sr. Bustamante frequently copies Zurita. *Herrera* (Dec. III, Lib. IV, cap. XV, p. 135). In regard to the non-heredity of the dignity, I refer to the above authorities, and more especially

not form as it is often stated, an order of chivalry, is amply proven by the fact that the bond of kinship interposed a barrier between them and such an imaginary association and furthermore, because their number could not be very great. The formalities required were so numerous and dilatory, the material for distribution in the shape of gifts was so large, that a frequent repetition of the occurrence lay beyond the power of the kin.[174] After this necessary digression, we return once more to the Mexican calpulli.

Besides being as already established in "Tenure of Lands," the unit of territorial possession, we found the Mexican kin to be a *self-governing*, therefore *democratic* cluster. Every one of these clusters had, within itself, all the elements required for independent existence as an organized society. Except for assistance and protection against outsiders, it needed no associates. Hence it follows, that since we find twenty Mexican kins aggregated into a tribe, this tribe was a *voluntary* association, formed for mutual protection.

Three attributes of the tribe are next to self-evident:

1. A particular territory ;
2. A common dialect ;
3. Common tribal worship.[175]

to *A. de Zurita* ("*Rapport*," p. 49: "Lorsqu'un de ces chefs mourait, le prince accordait sa charge á celui qui s'en était rendu digne par ses services, car les fils du défunt n'en héritaient pas s'ils n'en étaient investis." The very fact of the election, and the manner in which it was performed is also evidence. See the various documents in *Ternaux-Compans, 2d Recueil.*

[174] That such a festival or ceremony necessitated the accumulation of much provision and many articles for presents and offerings, is proven by numerous authorities. *Gomara* ("*Conquista*" Vedia I, p. 436): "En fin, en semejantes fiestas no habia pariente pobre. Daban á los señores tecutles y principales convidados plumajes, mantas, tocas, zapatos, bezotes, y orejeras de oro ó plata ó piedras de precia. Esto era mas ó menos, segun la riqueza y animo del nuevo tecuitli, y conforme á las personas que se daba. Tambien hacia grandes ofrendas al templo y á los sacerdotes." *Zurita* ("*Rapport sur les différentes classes de chefs* etc.," p. 28): "Ces solemnités occasionnaient de grandes dépenses, car les assistants étaient fort nombreux; c'étaient les parents, les alliés et les domestiques du nouveau dignitaire. L'on faisait aussi des aumoṇes considérables aux pauvres." "*Des Cérémonies observées autrefois par les Indiens lorsqu'ils faisaient un Tecle.*" (1st *Recueil*, p. 233): "Celui que l'on nommait *Tecle*, devait d'abord posséder de grands biens, qn'il put donner aux prĕtres et aux autres nobles." (P. 237): "Un grand nombre ne poùvait pas se procurer en si peu de temps la quantité suffisante, etc., etc." *Mendieta* (Lib. II, cap. XXXVIII, p. 156): "Y asi les costaba excesivo trabajo y gasto, como aqui se dirá." (Id., cap. XXXIX, pp. 160 and 161.) *Veytia* ("*Historia Antigua*," Lib. II, cap. IX, pp. 65 and 68): "Y era exhorbitantisimo el gasto, por cuya causa algunos, cuyas facultades y caudal no era suficiènte á reportarlos, dejaban de tomar este dictado." *H. H. Bancroft* (Vol. II, p. 199): "As before remarked, the vast expenses entailed upon a Tecuhtli debarred from the honor many who were really worthy of it."

[175] For these three attributes of tribal organization I refer to *Morgan* ("*Ancient Society*," p. 113).

All three we find very plainly among the ancient Mexicans.[176] Since the tribe was formed of kins associating together voluntarily, it must be admitted that they stood on an equal footing, and had, all, an equal share in the tribal government. It was scarcely possible, however, from what we know of the population of aboriginal Mexico, that all the male members of the kins, at a general gathering, could form its directive power.[177] The latter consisted of delegates, elected by the kins to represent them; which body of delegates was the supreme authority, from whose decisions there should be no appeal.[178]

[176] "*Ancient Society*," (Part II, cap. VII).

[177] There is no evidence of a general gathering of the tribe of Mexico, subsequent to the election of "Humming-Bird" (Huitzilihuitl) to the office of "chief of men." This occurrence which, according to the *Codex Mendoza* (Plate III), took place in 1396, is mentioned by *Durán* (Cap. VII, p. 53): "Y asi haciendo su consulta y cauildo entre los grandes y mucha de la gente comun." *Tezozomoc* ("*Crónica Mexicana*" edited by *Sr. Jose M. Vigil* and annotated by *Sr. Orozco y Berra*, Mexico, 1878, cap. IV, p. 233), distinctly mentions delegates: "Casi con esto los mas principales, viejos, y sacerdotes de los Mexicanos, de los cuatro barrios." The "*Codice Ramirez*" ("*Relacion del Origen de los Indios que Habitan esta Nueva-España segun sus Historias*." "*Biblioteca Mexicana*," p. 39), uses the same words as Durán. *Sahagun* (Lib. VIII, cap. XXX, p. 318), gives probably the best and clearest picture of the most important meetings of the tribe,—those for election of the chiefs, and distinctly mentions only old men, officers and medicine-men.

[178] Evidence in regard to the existence and to the supreme authority of this body is found in many authors. In the first place we have the direct admission, that they elected the "chief of men" or so-called "King," and that the "matters of government" lay in their hands, in that (yet) anonymous Relation taken from the Archives of Simancas, translated and printed by Mr. H. Ternaux-Compans under the title: "*De l'ordre de Succession observé par les Indiens*" (1er *Recueil*, p. 228): "Des conseilleurs étaient chargés des affaires d'état; c'étaient pour la plupart des gens de distinction et des tecuclis ou chevaliers comme nous les appelons. On choisissait toujours des personnes âgées, pour lesquelles le souverain avait beauçoup de vénération et de respect, et qu'il honorait comme ses pères." The supremacy of the council is positively affirmed, besides, in the following authorities:—

(1). In a fragmentary MSS. of the sixteenth century, found along with the "*Codice Ramirez*," and incorporated with the latter in the "*Biblioteca Mexicana*" ("*Crónica*," *Fragmento* 2, Cap. . . p. 147): "Considerando el nuevo Rey de México la fuerza que el español traia, juntó á consejo y hizòles representacion de aquesto, y lo que estaba prometido que de Ixtlilxuchitl habia de salir la ruina de los Mexicanos, que se diesen con buenas condiciones, pues era menos mal que no morir á sus manos y á las de los españoles. No quisieron por tener concepto destos que eran insufribles y cudiciosos. Tornóles otra vez á tratar aquesto, y aún otras dos, diciéndoles ser entónces tiempo cómodo: dijéron que querian mas morir, que hazerse esclavos de gente tan mala como los españoles; y asi quedó combenido que era mejor morir; la qual determinacion sabida por Cortés andaba dando órden á Ixtlilxuchitl de como sitiar la ciudad." This shows how decisive the voice and vote of the council was, over and above the wishes and counsels of the so-called "King" (at that time Quauhtemotzin), even at the time of greatest danger, immediately before the last siege. Compare "*Art of War*" (p. 160) on the same subject.

(2). In same collection—*Fragmento* 1 (pp. 124 and 125), acknowledging the final decisions of the council at the time of the older "wrathy chief": "y assi en este tiempo

It is therefore a TRIBAL COUNCIL, called in the Mexican language " place of speech " (" Tlatocan "), which constituted the highest power among the ancient Mexicans.[179] In all probability it consisted of as many members as there were kins in the tribe,[180]

comenzó á edificar el templo á su dios Huitzilopochtli á imitacion de Salomon. por consejo de Tlacaellel y de todos sus grandes." Idem (p. 117): "y luego llamó á Tlacaellel y á sus consejeros, y diziendóles lo que pasaba, de comun acuerdo se determinó que se hiziesse guerra á los de Tepeaca."

(3). The proper words of the last "wrathy chief" (Montezuma II), as reported by *Tezozomoc* ("*Crónica Mexicana*," Vol. IX of Kingsborough, Cap. XCVII, p. 172) are: " hijos y hermanos, seais muy bien venidos, descansad, que aunque es verdad yo soy rey y señor, yo solo no puede valeros, sino con todos los principales Mexicanos del sacro senado Mexicano descansad." This reply was given by the reputed "despot" to the delegates from Huexotzinco, who came to negotiate for peace and alliance against the Tlaxcallans. In connection with this we meet with the remarkable passage already quoted, which, while proving the fact that the Mexican tribe could not, alone, even treat, for itself, with a hostile tribe, establishes incidentally, also, the supremacy of the Mexican council over its head-chief: " Habiendo venido ante Moctezuma todo el senado Mexicano, y consultado sobre ello, dijo Zihuacoatl resoluto: Señor, como será esto, si no lo saben vuestros consegeros de guerra los reyes de Aculhuacan Nezahualpilli, y el de Tecpanecas Tlaltecatzin? hagase entero cabildo y acuerdo: fue acordado asi."

(4). *Diego Durán* (Cap. XI, p. 103): "A estos quatro señores y ditados, despues de eletos principes los hacian del consejo real como presidentes y oydores del consejo supremo, sin parecer de los quales nenguna cosa se auia de hacer." (Cap. XII. p. 108): " El rey tomó parecer con los grandes de lo que auia de hacer. Tlacaelel, príncipe de los éxercitos, y los quatro del supremo consejo." (Cap. XIV, pp. 117 and 118) describes a called meeting of "los mas principales de toda la ciudad de México" with the two chiefs. (Cap. XVI, p. 132): " Tlacaellel respondió, que le parecia cosa muy acertada y justa, y todos los del consejo determinaron de que se hiciese." (P. 133): " Monteçuma aprobó el consejo y dixo: perdonad me, señores, que yo aunque soy rey no acertaré en todo: para eso tengo vuestro favor, para que me auiseis de lo que á la autoridad desta ciudad y nuestra conviniere." I further refer to Cap. XVIII (p. 156), and other places.

(5). *Acosta* (Lib. VII, cap. 11, p. 477): " De donde se puede entender, que entre estos el Rey no tenia absoluto mando é imperio, y que mas gouernaua a modo de Consul, o Dux, que de Rey, aunque despues con el poder crecio tambien el mando de los Reyes, hasta ser puro tyrannico, como se vera eu los ultimos Reyes." This latter assertion has already been refuted in a previous note. (Lib. VI, cap. XXV, p. 441): " Todos estos quatro eran del supremo Consejo, sin cuyo parecer el Rey no hazia, ni podia hazer cosa de importancia."

(6). *Herrera* (Dec. III. lib. II, cap. XIX. p. 76): " Estos quatro Ditados, eran del Consejo supremo, sin cuyio parcer no podia hacer el Rei cosa de importancia."

(7). Indirect evidence of the supreme power of the council is found in the descriptions of the mode of consultation about war or peace, as given by *Mendieta* (Lib. II, cap. XXVI. p. 129), *Torquemada* (Lib. XIV, cap. II, p. 537). The latter even mentions old women along with the men, as participating in the debate on peace or war, and describes this debate as truly " Indian."

[179] *Molina* (II, p. 140): " *tlatocan*," " corte ó palacio de grandes señores." (Id., I, p. 29): " consejo real," " tlatocanecentlaliliztli." *Torquemada* (Lib. XIV, cap. VI. p. 545): " si no era en la corte, á la qual llaman Tlatocan, que es lugar de Juzgado, ó Audiencia."

[180] We have already noticed that there were twenty " barrios " (kins) in the tribe. Now we are told by *Bernal Diez de Castillo* ("*Hist. verdadera.*" etc., Vedia II, cap. XCV, p. 95): "y siempre á la contina estaban en su compañia veinte grandes señores y consejeros y capitanes, y se hizo á estar preso sin mostrar pasion en ello." (Cap. XCVII, p. 99): "Ya he dicho otra vez en el capitulo que de ello habla, de la manera que entraban á

each calpulli sending a " speaker " (" Tlatoani ") to represent it. Such positions could only be filled by men of acknowledged ability and reputation, who had acquired the distinction of *chiefs*, and hence their other title — " speaking chiefs " (" Tecuthatoca,") which was everywhere recognized, in aboriginal Mexico, as the highest office and charge.[181]

negociar y el acato que le tenian, y como siempre estaban en su compañia en aquel tiempo para despachar negocios veinte hombres ancianos, que eran jueces; y porque está ya referido, no lo tornó á referir " Furthermore, it is positively asserted by *Torquemada* (Lib. XIV, cap. VI, p. 544): " En lugar de Regidores, ponian en cada Barrio, ó Parcialidad, un Tecuhtli, que se ocupaba en executar lo que nuestros Regidores executan, y hacen, y todos los Dias se hallaban en el Palacio, á ver lo que se les ordenaba, y mandaba." Consequently each calpulli or kin held one representative constantly at the official house of the tribe, and as there were twenty kins, we necessarily have here the twenty chiefs or "Judges," mentioned by Bernal Diez. The above statement of Torquemada is repeated (or copied?) by *Vetancurt* ("Teatro," Vol. I. p. 371).

Durán (Cap. XXVI, p. 215) mentions: " los grandes señores, que eran hasta doce." *Ixtlilxochitl* ("*Histoire des Chichimèques*," Cap. XXXIV, p. 236) says "there were fourteen great lords in the kingdom of Mexico." *Tezozomoc* (Cap. XXXVI. p. 57, Kingsb., Vol. IX) enumerates first twelve, then three more. This is the more singular after the detailed list giving *twenty* chiefs, which list I have already referred to in a previous note,

That the members of the tribal council were elected each one by his calpulli or kin. follows from the statements of *Zurita* ("*Rapport*," etc., p. 60): " Les calpullis ont toujours un chef pris nécessairement dans la tribu. . . . L'élection se fait entre eux. . . . La charge de ces chefs n'est pas héréditaire. . ." (P. 61): "Ce chef est chargé du soin des terres du calpulli et d'en défendre la possession. . . . . ." (P. 62): " Il a soin de défendre les membres du calpulli, de parler pour eux devant la justice et les gouverneurs." Consequently this officer *represented the kin* towards the other kins of the same tribe, and this could only be done in the tribal council, as one of its members. How this election took place, the same authority tells us (p. 61), also that the office was for life, and that as capacity was the first condition, incapacity or unfaithfulness necessarily brought about removal.

[181] *Molina* (II, p. 14): " Tlatoani," " hablador. ó gran señor." The plural is " Tlatoca." *Pimentel* ("*Cuadro*," p. 174). There is ample evidence of the high offices which bore this title. Compare *Torquemada* (Lib. IV, cap. XVI, p. 626): " los Tlatoques (que son los Señores, y Poderosos.)" . . . . *Tezozomoc* uses the term " Zemanahuac-tlatoani." *Zurita* (p. 43): " Les souverains se nommaient et se nomment encore Tlatoques, mot qui vient du verbe tlatoa, qui veut dire parler." *Bernal Diez de Castillo* (Cap. XXXVIII, p. 32, Vedia, II). "*Real Ejecutoria*" (Col. de Doc., Vol. II, p. 12 and note 36). In this document the word is used in the *plural*: "y diciendo que ya habian estado alli los Tlatoanis Teacames." It would be useless to quote further authorities. I shall only state that, according to *Sr. D. Juan Gavarrete*, the term, as applied to "principales" or "old men," is still used among the Indians of Guatemala: "Los ancianos que á su edad agregan servicios publicos se llaman en algunos pueblos Tatoques; pero esta denominacion casi ha desaparecido." (*Letter to the writer* 14 *March*, 1879.)

The term "tecutlatoca" decomposes into "tecutli" and "tlatoca." It is found in *Molina* (II, p. 93), as "in Tecutlatoa," "tener audiencia, o entender en su oficio el presidente, oydor, alcalde, etc., etc." "Tecutlatoliztli." "judicatura, o el acto de exercitar su oficio el Juez." *Torquemada* (Lib. XI, cap. XXVI, p. 355): " y á los Jueces, Tecuhtlatoque, Señores, que goviernan el bien publico, y lo hablan." I have already noticed that the "Tequitlato" mentioned by *Sahagun* (Lib. VIII, cap. XXXVIII, p. 329) might be a misprint or misspelling for "tecutlatoca." The same author says (Id., Cap. XXV. p. 314): "Estos tales eran los mayores jueces, que ellos llamaban *tecutlatoque*." *Molina* (I, p. 108): "senador," " tecutlatoca."

The place where this council assembled, was necessarily the official house of the tribe or " tecpan,"[182] and there they met at stated intervals, possibly twice every Mexican month of twenty days.[183] Such meetings were fully attended, and they could be called, besides, at any time.[184] There is evidence that, during

Bustamante (" *Tezcoco*," p. 191): "Habia tambien abogados y procuradores; á los primeros llamaban Tepantlátoani (el que habla por otro)."

[182] *Molina* (II, p. 93): "casa ò palacio real, ó de algun señor de salua." But of special importance is the following definition (I, p. 91): " Palacio real " — " tecpan, tlatocan, totecuacan." This shows that the tecpan was really the place where the council met." *Sahagun* (Lib. VIII. cap. XIV, pp. 302 and 303. Cap. XXV, p. 314). *Mendieta* (Lib. II, cap. XXVIII, p. 134). *Ixtlilxochitl* (" *Histoire des Chichimèques*," Cap. XXXVI, pp. 247–252). *Veytia* (III. cap. VII, p. 199). *Torquemada* (" *Monarquia*," Lib. XIV, cap. VI, p. 544), identifying "la Corte" with the "lugar de Juzgado, ó Audiencia." Further quotations are useless.

[183] This fact is implied by *Ixtlilxochitl* (" *Hist. des Chichimèques*," cap. XXXVIII, pp. 267, 268 and 269), when he affirms that, in notifying a hostile tribe of the intention to make war upon it, the notification was repeated thrice, at intervals of twenty days. *Veytia* (" *Historia antigua de* Méjico," Lib. III, cap. VII, p. 209), says that every twelve days "cada doce dias," the courts met to report to the "emperor." This is rather strange since (Id., p. 202, etc.), he says that these courts sat daily in what he calls the " palace." *Torquemada* (Lib. XI, cap. XXVI, p. 355): " De diez à diez Dias, y á mas tardar, de doce à doce, hacia junta el Rei de todos los jueces, asi de las Audiencias del Reino, como de los de sus Consejos." In this case he speaks of Tezcuco. *Mendieta* (Lib. II, cap. XXVIII, p. 135): " Y asi, á lo mas largo, los pleitos árduos, se concluian á la consulta de los ochenta dias, que llamaban nappoaltlatolli, demas que cada diez ó doce dias el señor con todos los jusces tenian acuerdo sobre los casos árduos y de mas calidad." *Zurita* (" *Rapport*, etc.," p. 101): " Tous les douze jours il y avait une assemblée générale des juges présidié par le prince. On y jugeait les affaires difficiles, celles de crimes qualifiés, et l'on examinait minutieusement tous les détails." *Clavigero* (Lib. VII, cap. XVI, p. 482), is very positive: " Each Mexican month, or within twenty days, a meeting of all the judges was held in presence of the King, to decide upon all cases not yet disposed of." He evidently bases the statement upon *Gomara* (" *Conquista*," etc., Vedia I, p. 442). " Consultan con los señores cada mes una vez todos los negocios," according to *Sr. Orozco y Berra* (" *Ojeada sobre Cronologia Mexicana*," Introduction to the " Crónica Mexicana," published under the supervision of Señor José M. Vigil, pp. 174 and 175). Gomara rests principally upon an unpublished series of documents, entitled " *Libro de Oro*," now in possession of my friend, Sr. Icazbalceta, which collection was formed by the Franciscans under the auspices of the unjustly abused Fray Juan de Zumárraga, between 1531 and 1547. The statement of Clavigero is, therefore, not to be rejected. The " *Codice Ramirez* " (p. 65) says: "los quales daban noticia al Rey cada cierto tiempo de todo lo que en su Reyno pasaba y se habia hecho." It is, therefore, to say the least, likely, that the full council met *once* a month, but, as we have stated in order to be just towards all, it is equally possible that it may have met twice. The reference to " Judges " needs no explanation. It is self-evident that for judiciary matters, alone, such meetings of executive officers were superfluous. Matters of government came up also,— and this is decisive of the kind of officers that were members of the tribal council, since they alone could fill such positions. These meetings were, therefore, full meetings of the council, and nothing else.

[184] This is abundantly proven by what has at last been recognized by *Sr. Orozco y Berra* as well as by my friend, *Sr. Chavero* (" *Ojeada*," etc.) as specifically Mexican sources of aboriginal history. See for inst.: " *Codice Ramirez* " (pp. 52, 62, 66, 67, 80). " *Fragmento No. 1* " (pp. 124, 127, 133, etc.). " *Fragmento No. 2* " (pp. 137, 147, etc.).

the critical period of Cortés' first stay at Tenuchtitlan, the twenty "speakers" held daily meetings at the official house.[185]

In a society based upon kin we cannot expect a clear division of the powers of government, particularly as there were no written laws,[186] and custom alone ruled. The functions of the ancient Mexican council were not properly legislative, but they were rather *directive* and *judicial* combined. One of its first duties was, however, to maintain harmony among the kins.

The twenty independent social units composing the Mexican tribe, while bound together by the necessity of mutual aid to secure territorial independence, could not be expected always to live in peace with one another. Difficulties would necessarily arise between kin and kin, and to prevent such disputes from leading to actual warfare,[187] the council as a body of *official arbitrators* was needed.

According to the rules of kinship, the calpulli was not only bound to avenge any wrongs suffered by one of its members, but it was also responsible for the offences committed by the kinfolk towards any outsider.[188] Hence theft committed outside of the

Durán (cap. X, p. 83, XI, pp. 107, 108, 109, XIV, pp. 117, 123, XVI, p. 132, XVIII, p. 156), etc., etc. We forbear further quotations, since they would be too numerous. All go to prove that the council was frequently called together between the times of regular meeting. Quotations from *Tezozomoc* ("*Crónica Mexicana*") are useless, since they are very numerous and agree with those of Durán in the main. The fact of irregular meetings of the council having been called during the conquest, is further proven by *Sahagun* (Lib. XII, cap. III, p. 7), and *Torquemada* (Lib. IV, cap. XIV, p. 385).

[185] *Bernal Diez de Castillo* ("*Historia verdadera*," Vedia, Vol. II, cap. XCV, p. 95): "y siempre á la contina estaban en su compania veinte grande señores y consejeros y capitanes." (Cap. XCVII, p. 99): "Ya he dicho otra vez en el capitulo que de ello habla, de la manera que entraban á negociar y el acato que el tenian, y como siempre estaban en su compañia en aquel tiempo para despachar negocios veinte hombres ancianos, que eran jueces."

[186] A number of paintings are mentioned as representing the customs and manners of the natives. Specimens of these are found in *Codex Mendoza*, Lam., 58 to 72 inclusive. But none of these contained, or could contain or express, anything like a *law*. Compare, on Mexican paintings in general and their value, "*On the Sources for aboriginal history of Spanish America*," in Vol. 27 of "*Proceedings of the American Association for the Advancement of Science*." Señor *Orozco y Berra* ("*Códice Mendozino,— Ensayo de descifracion geroglifica*," beginning in No. 3, of Vol. I, "*Anales del Museo Nacional de México*") has commenced a publication which can be expected to shed much light on such picture-leaves, and the true position which they held among the ancient Mexicans.

[187] Conflicts between the inhabitants of different "barrios" during festive turnouts and religious gatherings could not always be prevented.

[188] *Morgan* ("*Ancient Society*," pp. 76 and 77). *Davila-Padilla* ("*Historia de la Fundacion y Discurso de la Provincia de Santiago de México*," Lib. I, cap. XXVI, p. 83). The custom is general among other tribes and Mr. Morgan has adverted to it among the Maya of Yucatan and the Peruvians. It would be unnecessary display to produce further evidence: the remarkably clear statements of Mr. Morgan fully "cover the case."

calpulli, and especially the slaying, wilful or accidental, of members of one kin by those of another, became the cause of a claim by the offended calpulli upon that of the offender.[189] This claim was submitted to the tribal council by the "speaker" of the complainant kinship. He produced his evidence, sometimes even in the shape of paintings, not so much to prove the facts as to sustain his claim. From the opposite side, the "speaker" defended the interests of his clan, and he also supported his pleadings with whatever testimony he might command.[190] The remaining "tlatoca" listened attentively to both parties, and when the argument was concluded, they deliberated among

[189] *H. H. Bancroft* ("*Native Races*," Vol. II, pp. 458 and 459) was the first, to my knowledge, to call attention (in note 59) to the difference of opinion among authors, in regard to the punishment of murderers. He refers to the unpublished parts of the work of Fray *Diego Durán*. We find in the *Codice Ramirez* ("*Tratado de los Ritos y Ceremonias y Dioses que en su Gentilidad usaban los Índios desta Nueva España.*" Cap. I, p. 103): "El matar uno á otro era muy prohibido, y aunque no se pagaba con muerte, hazian al homicida esclavo perpétuo de la mujer ò parientes del muerto, para que les sirviesse y supliesse la falta del muerto, ganando el sustento de los hijos que dejaba." This is very interesting since it shows the autonomy of the kins. The murderer stood, towards the calpulli of the slain, in the same relation as, among northern Indians, a prisoner of war did towards the hostile tribe. Both could be adopted, and this condoned the deed. The offending kin lost one member; the offended kin obtained one in return for the one that had been killed. However, this was only in exceptional cases: the rule, as established by the majority of authors was that life alone could atone for life. In the same manner, and under the same head, the contradictory reports must be placed, about the punishment of theft, which have already been noticed. There are consequently, for each crime or kind of crime, two classes; one, of such as were committed within the kin, and the other, of such as were committed without.

[190] *Sahagun* (Lib. VIII, cap. XV, p. 304): "Otra sala del palacio se llamaba teccali, ó teccalco. En este lugar residian los senadores y los ancianos para oïr pleitos y peticiones, que les ofrecian la gente popular, y los jueces procuraban de hacer su oficio con mucha prudencia y sagacidad, y presto los despachaban; porque primeramente demandaban la pintura en que estaban escritas ó pintadas las causas, como hacienda, casas, ó maizales; y despues cuando ya se queria acabar el pleito, buscaban los senadores los testigos." I quote this passage, although it applies particularly to the judicial functions of the council, because the mode of proceedings is therein illustrated. *Veytia* (Lib. III, cap. VII, p. 207), speaking of Tezcuco, is very positive: "Habia tambien aboga os y procuradores; á los primeros llamaban tepantlatoani, que quiere decir *el que habla por otro*. . . . ." I need not recall here that "tlatoani" (plural "tlatoca") was the title of the members of the council, and that consequently these "attorneys" belonged thereto. The same statement (derived from Veytia also) is found in *Bustamante* ("*Tezcoco*," Parte II, cap: VII, p. 191). These two works contain (in the chapters indicated) the most detailed information as to the proceedings. Still, there is evident confusion in the minds of these authors in general: they fail to discriminate between arbitration and tribal jurisdiction. The bulk of the other authorities commit the same mistake. Compare *Zurita* ("Rapport," pp. 102-105), whom *Mendieta* (Lib. II, cap. XXVIII, p. 138) has almost verbally copied. *Torquemada* (Lib, XI, cap. XXVI, pp. 354 and 355).

The absolute lack of division of powers which characterizes so well ancient Mexican society is well established by *Veytia* (III, cap. VII, p. 206), speaking of what he.

themselves until they finally agreed upon an award.[191] The same thing occurred when two calpulli claimed possession or enjoyment of the same piece of land.[192] No appeal was possible to any higher authority; but every eighty days an extraordinary gathering took place at the "teepan," consisting of the council and the executive chieftains, the war-captains of the four great quarters, the "elder brothers" of the kins, and the leading medicine-men, and any cause pending before the "tlatocan" might be deferred until the next of these general meetings; and even in case a decision had been rendered, a reconsideration thereof, on that occasion, was sometimes agreed upon.[193]

calls " supremo consejo:" "Tratábanse en este consejo todo género de negocios de estado, justicia, guerra, hacienda etc., etc."

[191] This picture is mainly based upon *Veytia* (" *Historia antigua*," III, cap. VII), and *Bustamente* (" *Tezcoco*," pp. 191 and 192). The statement in the latter is only worthy of credit because copied from the former.

[192] *Veytia* (Lib. III, cap. VII, p. 207). *Clavigero* (Lib. VII, cap. XVI, y. 483). For a copy of the paintings reproduced, see *A. de Humboldt* (" *Vues des Cordillères*," etc., Vol. I, plate V. Ed. 8vo).

[193] I affirm this in the face of all the authorities on the subject, who, without exception, assert that there was an appeal to the " king." The *Codex Mendoza* (plate LXX, " Declaracion de la figurado ") is even very positive: " Y si era negocio de calidad del consejo, havia apelacion por via de agravio ante Monteçuma, en donde habia conclusion de la causa." My opinion is based on what precedes about the authority of the council, on what I expect to prove in relation to the true nature of the duties of the head-chiefs and which will hereafter follow, and on the contradictions among the authors themselves. Thus the " *Codice Ramirez*" (p. 58) places the supreme power into the hands of the councils "sin parescer de los quales ninguna cosa se habia de hacer," and (pp. 64 and 65) it does not mention any power of appeal whatever. *Zarita* (pp. 100 and 101): " Les appels étaient portés devant douze autres juges supérieurs qui prononçaient d'apres l'avis du souverain." It is queer to notice, how the writers of the tezcucan school, appear eager to place the power of final decree or the decision of final appeal in a "high tribunal," or rather simply a supreme council of their tribe. *Torquemada* (Lib II, cap. XXXXI, p. 146) mentions a supreme council, "á los quales avian de venir todas las cosas graves, y criminales, para que ellos, con el Rei, las determinasen." (Lib. XI, cap. XXVI, p. 354): " Para estos dos Jueces Supremos se apelaban las causas graves, los quales las admitian, pero no determinaban, ni sentenciaban, sin parecer, y acuerdo de el Rei." *Veytia* (Lib. III, cap. VII, p. 199) speaks of the establishment of " tribunals " by " Fasting wolf" (" Nezahualcoyotl "—properly " fasting coyote "), and adds: " pero concediendo á las partes el recurso de apelacion para el gran tribunal de justicia que erigió en su corte de Tezcuco." This so-called tribunal was, as we have shown at the close of note 190, the " Council of the tribe." *Mendieta* (Lib. II, cap. XXVIII, p. 135) almost copies Zurita. *Sahagun* (" *Historia general*," etc., Lib. VIII, cap. XXV, p. 314): " y los casos muy dificultuosos y graves, llevábanlos al señor para que los sentenciase, juntamente con trece principales muy calificados, que con el andaban, y residian." " Estos tales eran los mayores jueces, que ellos llamaban tecutlatoque. . . . " In this case the learned father speaks of tribal jurisdiction and not of arbitration. Still it is plain that he admits the *council's decrees as final*. The chief, " señor," appears only as member of this council, a position of which we shall hereafter speak. Without making any further quotations from similar authorities, I beg to revert to those which place, *by the side of the so-called " King*," an independent " supreme Judge "—the " Cihuacohuatl," whose tribunal

Aside from these arbitrative functions, other duties occupied the council's time at its full meetings. If any calpulli felt wronged in the distribution of the incoming tribute, it might through its delegate or "speaker,"[194] complain about the tribal officers answerable for it to the "tlatocan." The investiture of chiefs and officers of the kins belonged to the highest authority of the tribe

is positively mentioned as the final court of appeals. That this "Cihuacohuatl" occupied a high position, was already noticed by *Cortés* ("*Carta tercera*," Vedia I, p. 89), and subsequently, when he became still more prominent, by *Tezozomoc*. But *Torquemada* has been to my knowledge, the first one to establish his position as independent supreme Judge. It is not devoid of interest to notice what he writes about this office. ("*Monarchia Indiana*," Lib. XI, cap. XXV, p. 352): " Despues del Rei, havia un Presidente, y Juez maior, cuio nombre, por raçon de el oficio, era Cihuacohuatl . . . . De este Presidente no se apelaba para el Rei, ni para otro Juez alguno, ni podia tener Teniente, ni substituto, sino que por su misma persona havia de determinar, y decidir todos los negocios de su jusgado, y audiencia." He further adds; " lo qual no corria en este dicho Juez Cihuacohuatl; porque de su ultima determinacion no habia recurso á otro." *Fray Augustin de Vetancurt* ("*Teatro Mexicano*," Vol. 1, Parte 2a, Trat. 2°, cap. I, p. 369): " Despues del Rey . . . habia un virey que llamaban Cihuacohuatl, que el rey proveia y era su segunda persona en el gobierno, de cuya sentencia no habia apelacion á otro. Tan absoluta era la autoridad que le daba, que reservando el rey en si la autoridad real, era en la judicatura igual." These statements distinctly hint at the existence of an appellate judicial body, of which this Cihuacohuatl was foreman, and over which the so-called " King" had no control. *Clavigero* (Lib. VII, cap. XVI. p. 481) even states that while there was no appeal from the Cihuacohuatl whatever, there was one of these officers " at the court and the principal cities of the kingdom." These views in regard to the " Cihuacohuatl" have been plainly accepted by *W. H. Prescott* ("* Conquest of Mexico*," Vol. 1, p. 29): " There was no appeal from his sentence to any other tribunal, not even to the king," and *H. H. Bancroft* ("*Native Races*," Vol. II, cap. XIV, pp. 434 and 435).

The confusion is apparent, for we have here three different views of the same case. One is that the " head-chief" was the highest appellate authority, the other that the head-chief, *with the council*, formed the court of last resort, and the third that a " supreme Judge" was appointed by the so-called "King" to render final decisions. Now we have already seen that the supreme authority was the council or "tlatocan," consequently what is commonly called the "king" could not be the last resort in judiciary matters, still less could he appoint an officer for that purpose. Our proposition appears, therefore, sustained, that there was no appeal from the decisions of the council to any superior authority whatever.

But, finally, it was possible to reconsider, so to say, the cases decided by the council, and for such the so-called " *Nauhpohualtlatolli*" or " *eighty days-talk*" was instituted. Authorities are almost unanimous on this point, although it is commonly ascribed to Tezcuco alone, and I refrain from quoting them in detail, referring but to *Bancroft* ("*Native Races*." Vol. II, p. 439, etc.).

[194] This becomes evident from the relative positions of kin and tribe. As we shall hereafter see, the officers gathering and those receiving the tribute were tribal officers, consequently subject to the council. It was to the council, therefore, that any complaint had to be brought against them, and this could be done only through the " speaker" of a particular kin. That the tribute was distributed partly among the " calpulli" is indicated by *Durán* (Cap. IX, p. 79): " Tambien diéron á sus barrios para el culto de sus dioses, á cada barrio una suerte, etc.," and *Tezozomoc* ("* Crónica Mexicana*," Cap. X, p. 18): " y aunque venian á darlo á Ytzcoatl, era para todos los Mexicanos en comun."

also.[195] This "right to invest officers and chiefs of the kins" is commonly distorted into a right to appoint or at least to confirm an appointment or election,[196] whereas it was merely an act of courtesy ultimately converted into an established custom. But paramount in importance was the preservation of independence towards the outside world, and hence all relations with other tribes, and all final decisions concerning alliances, declarations of war and treaties of peace were, as we have elsewhere stated, in the hands of the council.[197] No raid or foray could be started unless by its direction; and delegates from foreign or hostile tribes, though not always admitted into the presence of the "tlatocan," always had to wait until that body agreed upon and formulated an answer.[198]

[195] *Torquemada* (Lib. XI, cap. XXIX, p. 361): . . "elegian Dia de buen signo: en el qual llamaban á todos los señores, y principales de la Republica, y á todos los Parientes, y Amigos: los quales acompañaban al mancebo, etc., etc." (Cap. XXX, pp. 364, 365). This author copies from *Mendieta* (Lib. II, cap. XXXVIII and XXXIX, pp. 156 to 161) who partly gathers from *Zurita* ("*Rapport*," pp. 25 to 29). *Gomara* ("*Conquista*," etc., Vedia I. p. 435): " Los señores, los amigos y parientes que convidados estaban, lo subian por las gradas al altar. . . . . El dia que habia de salir venian todos los que primero le honraron, y luego por la mañana le lavaban y limpiaban muy bien, y le tornaban al templo de Camaxtle con mucha música, danzas y regocijo. Subianle á cerca del altar, etc., etc. . . ." Although these quotations apply mostly to Tlaxcala, the dignity of "Tecuhtli" was common among all the sedentary tribes, and the customs of investiture were also about identical. Compare, " *Des Cérémonies observées autrefois par les Indiens lorsqu'ils faisaient un tecle*" (" *Pièces relatives à la conquête du Méxique*," Ternaux-Compans, pp. 233 and 234.

[196] *Zurita* ("*Rapport*," etc., p. 47): " parceque les souverains suprêmes ne les élevaient á ces dignités qu'en récompense des exploits qu'ils avaient faits á la guerre." etc. Besides, there are numerous evidences that the older authors all believed the officers to be nominated by the highest tribal authority. The distinction was never made as between officers of the kins and officers of the tribe. I have formerly discussed the point.

[197] "*Art of War*" (p. 129). In addition to the authorities there quoted, and those alluded to in note 178 of the present essay, I beg to refer with great pleasure to a paper written by a learned Peruvian, Sr. *José Fernandez Nodal* ("*Législation civile comparée des Méxicains sous les empereurs Aztecs et des Péruviens à l'époque des Incas*"). This memoir was presented at the "Congrés international des Américanistes," at Luxembourg in 1877, but only a short summary of it was published in the "*Compte Rendu*" (Vol. I, pp. 235–237). Sr. Nodal states that among the Mexicans' monarchy (?) was elective and controlled by a Council, " Controlée par un conseil supréme." It is to be sincerely regretted that this interesting paper was thus neglected.

[198] Evidences in regard to this latter detail are numerous. Compare *Tezozomoc* (" *Crónica*" Kingsborough, Vol. IX, cap. XCVII, p. 172). *Durán* (Cap. XV, p. 127): " El rey Monteçuma le respondió con rostro muy alegre y amoroso, que se lo agradecia el amor que les tenian y quel era muy contento de conservar la paz y de tener con ellos perpetua amistad; pero para questas treguas estuviesen con mas seguridad y vinculo, quel lo queria communicar con sus grandes señores y principales y quel le daria su respuesta. El rey de Tezcuco fué aposentado á descansar en un aposento de la casa real, con mucha onra, y luego el rey mandó venir á todos los de su consejo y á los demas señores y principales, y estando presentes, luego los propuso la plática

Such were, in a general way, the higher functions of the Mexican council, and they appear, if we are permitted to characterize them to be only arbitrative and directive. Yet the members of that council had other duties of a purely judicial nature.

No conflict occurred between its jurisdiction and that of the kins. It was neither superior nor inferior to it, but wholly independent, even without any connection with it. Hence it extended:

1. Over the unattached class, the hangers-on to the tribe, or outcasts from the bond of kinship.[199]

2. Over all the people composing the tribe, irrespective of kinship, at places specially placed under tribal care, or reserved for tribal business, and therefore *neutral ground* for the members of all the calpulli. These neutral localities were the official buildings, the central or tribal "house of god," and especially the great "tianquiz" or market places.

The outcasts were, happily for the preservation of tribal society, not very numerous. Still, from their very origin, they were the most disorderly part of the people and crimes were certainly more common among them than among those upon whose passions the tie of kinship and the obligations resulting therefrom acted like a wholesome check. It required a judiciary power constantly on hand to repress and punish the misdemeanors committed among this class.

The "tecpan," the great central "teocalli" and the square on which it stood, and the market, were regular meeting-places of

siguiente, etc. . . . . . ." (Cap. LX. p. 473): "Monteçuma. apiadándose dellos, los mandó aposentar, y llamando su consejo, propusoles la demanda que traian." *Codice Ramirez* (p. 61): "El Rey Itzcohuatl mostró gran contento con la embajada respondiendo con muy gratas palabras; mandó aposentar á los mensajeros, y honrarlos, y tratar como á su propia persona, diziéndoles que descansassen, que el dia siguiente les daria la respuesta." See also *Torquemada* (Lib. XIV, cap I, p. 535): "Acabada la Embaxada, si el Embaxador no era de mui gran Principe, no se le respondia cosa, hasta otro Dia; salian con él algunos, acompañandole á la Calpixca. adonde se proveia de lo necesario. y en el entretanto el Señor comunicaba con los de su Consejo lo que se havia de responder, lo qual hacia uno de ellos, y no él." But the most complete picture of such delegations and the manner in which they were received is found in *Vetancurt* ("*Teatro Mexicano*," Parte II°, Trat. IIa, cap. II. pp. 378 and 379). It is too long to be copied. I merely allude to the words: "Acabada la embajada, le volvian á la posada mientras se juntaban para la respuesta." It has been adopted by *Clavigero* (Lib. VII, cap. XI, pp. 470 and 471).

[199] The unattached class was under protection of no kin; therefore, if such a "bonded man" made his escape to the Tecpan, he became liberated from his bond. Already mentioned by *Gomara* ("*Conquista*," Vedia, I, p. 442), and subsequently confirmed by others.

people from *all* the calpulli, but over which no single kin could exercise any control.[200] This control had been delegated to the

[200] In regard to the "tecpan," the simple term "casa de comunidad," used particularly by *Torquemada* (Lib. VI, cap. XXIV, p. 48, and again Lib. XIII, cap. XXX, p. 477): la "Tecpan, que es el palacio," explains much. It is, besides, self-evident that the tribal places of business and of worship were under the control of no particular kin, being expressly reserved for the tribe. There is, however, no definite expression as yet, in fact it hardly amounts to a clear conception, of the number and position or location of the original "tianquiz" of Tenuchtitlan. There are four eye-witnesses of the conquest reporting upon the markets: Cortés, Andrés de Tapia, the anonymous conqueror, and Bernal-Diez de Castillo. I quote these in succession. *Cortés* ("*Carta Segunda*," Vedia, I, p. 32): "Tiene esta ciudad muchas plazas, donde hay continuos mercados y trato de comprar y vender. Tiene otra plaza tan grande como dos vezes la ciudad de Salamanca, toda cercada de portales al rededor, donde hay cotidianameute arriba de sesenta-mil animas comprando y vendiendo, . . ." "*Carta Tercera*," (p. 74): "hasta otra puente que está junto á la plaza de los principales aposentamientos de la ciudad." Note 2 of the Archbishop Lorenzana: "Antes de llegar á la plaza de la Universidad hay muchas puentes, y naturalmente habla aqui desta plaza ó mercado, que era muy grande." Id., (p. 78): "E porque este trabajo era incompartable, acordó de pasar el real al cabo de la calzada que va á dar al mercado de Temixtitan, que es una plaza harto mayor que la de Salamanca, y toda cercada de portales á la redonda;" (Id., p. 79): "seguimos nuestro camino, y entramos en la ciudad, á la cual llegados, yo reparti la gente desta manera: habia tres calles dende lo que teniamos ganado, que iban á dar al mercado, al cual los indios llaman Tianguizco, y á todo aquel sitio donde está llaman de Tlaltelulco; y la una destas calles era la principal, que iba á dicho mercado, . . Las otras dos calles van dende la calle de Tacuba á dar al mercado." Id. (p. 81), after the repulse of the Spaniards: "todos los españoles vivos y muertos que tomaron los llevaron al Tlatelulco, que es el mercado." Id. (p. 85): "E aquel dia acabamos de ganar toda la calle de Tacuba y de adobar los malos pasos della, en tal manera que los del real de Pedro de Albarado se podian communicar con nosotros por la ciudad, é por la calle principal, que iba al mercado, se ganaron otras dos puentes y se cegó bien el agua, . . . " Id., "y seguimos la calle grande, que iba á dar al mercado;" (p. 86): "Otro dia siguiente, estando aderezando para volver á entrar en la ciudad, á los nueve horas del dia vimos de nuestro real salir humo de dos torres muy altas que estaban en el Tatelulco ó mercado de la ciudad." *Andrés de Tapia* ("*Relacion*," etc., in *Col. de Doc.*, II, p. 582): mentions only the "patio de los idolos." "*El Conquistador anónimo*" (Col. de Doc., I. p. 392): "Sono nella cittá di Temestitan Messico grandissime et bellissime piazze, dove si vendono tutte le cose che usana fra loro, et specialmente la piazza maggiore che essi chiamano el Tatelula, che puo esser cosi grande como sarebbe tre volte la piazza di Salamanca, et seno all'intorno di essa tutti portici; . ." (p. 394): "Et oltra q'uesta gran piazza ve no sono dell'altre et mercati in che si vendono cose da mangiare in diverse parti della cittá." *Bernal Diez de Castillo* ("*Historia verdadera*," Vedia. II, cap. XCII, p. 89): "y cuando llegamos á la gran plaza, que se dice el Tatelulco, como no habiamos visto tal cosa, quedamos admirados de la multitud de gente y mercaderias que en ella habia, . ." He also states that the "gran plaza" was "cercado de portales." (Cap. CLII, p. 183): "que si nos parecia que fuesemos entrando de golpe en la ciudad hasta entrar y llegar al Tlatelulco, que es la plaza mayor Méjico, que es muy ancha, . . ." (Cap. CLV, p. 193): "que les entrásemos todo cuanto pudiésemos hasta llegalles al Tlatelulco, que es la plaza mayor, adonde estaban sus altos cues y adoratorios." We notice at once a contradiction. Cortés first mentions a market of Tenuchtitlan, and afterward he calls it of Tlatelulco. Archbishop Lorenzana identifies it with the "plaza de la Universidad," or in the neighborhood of the Cathedral. See *Cervántes-Salazar* ("*Tres Dialogos*," p. 9): "en la esquina de las calles del Arzobispado y Seminario."

There were two great market-places in ancient Mexico, one of which was in Tenuchtitlan, and the other in the conquered neighboring pueblo of Tlatelulco. This is very

" tlatocan " as a conseqnence of the formation of the tribe. Crimes committed at such localities were punished with unusual severity, because they were offences desecrating *neutral* ground which was

plainly stated by *Torquemada* (Lib. XIV, cap. XIII. p. 555), and it would even appear as if, notwithstanding the importance attached to Tlatelulco by many authors, that the principal market was the one mentioned by this author as " el que está en la Poblacion de San Juan . . . ," and consequently the proper " tianquiz " of the Mexican tribe. This could only be neutral ground, over which no single kin exercised any authority. It may have been different in regard to the " tianquiz " of Tlatelulco; at least the following indications of *Durán* (Cap. XXXIV, p. 270) deserve full attention : " Fecho esto mandó el rey que aquella plaça y mercado que ellos ganaron, pues los tlatelulcas no tenian mas tierra, que fuese repartido entre los señores y que la parte que á cada uno cupiese, que de todos los tlatelulcas que allí hiciesen asiento, de todo lo que vendiesen les diesen alcauala, de cinco uno, y así se repartió la plaça entre todos, de donde cada uno oabraua alcauala de lo que en el lugar que le auia cauido se vendia." The above is not quite definite enough, because the " plaza y mercado " of which the friar speaks, is evidently the one mentioned by him (p. 260): " y encerrándoles en la plaça de su mercado, haciéndose los tlatelulcas fuertes, no dexauan entrar á la plaça nenguno de los Mexicanos en ella," whereas he says (p. 270): " que allí hiciesen asiento," as if the place was built over. The fact that the " tianquiz " of Tlatelulco was " distributed among the Mexicans " is further asserted by *Tezozomoc* (" *Crónica Mexicana,*" Cap. XLVI, p. 75. Kingsborough, Vol. 9): "Axayaca mandó tambien se hiciese repartimiento del tianquiz de Tlatilolco á los Mexicanos, y comenzaron á medir primera suerte Axayaca, luego á Zihuacoatl Tlacaeleltzin, luego par su orden Tlacochcalcatl, y á todos los capitanes, que fué tenido el tianquiz en mas de sí ganaran cien pueblos." It would therefore appear, if we interpret this " distribution " as it should be done, namely : *as a division of spoils among the kins*, that the latter claimed a share of tribute from the traffic or barter going on in the " tianquiz " of Tlatelulco, a fact corroborated besides by that other statement of *Durán* (p. 269): " El rey le mandó, que pues auian sido traidores á su corona real, que de allí adelante queria y era su voluntad que aquella parcialidad Mexicana del tlatelulco le fuesen tributarios y pecheros como las demas ciudades y provincias, . . ." This, and the uncertainty as to which tianquiz is always meant, favors the assumption that *Gomara* (" *Conquista,*" p. 349. Vedia I) mentions Tlatelulco when he says: "Los que venden pagan algo del asiento al Rey, ó por alcabala ó porque los guarden de ladrones." *Cortés* (" *Carta Segunda,*" pp. 32, 33 and 34) does not mention it, for the words : " donde están personas por guardas y que reciben certum quid de cada cosa que entra " do not apply to the market which he describes as having visited and which, in spite of *Bernal-Diez* (" *Hist. Verdadera,*" Cap. XCII, p. 89) I still believe to have been that of Tenuchtitlan, and *not* that of Tlatelulco. Cortés is strictly followed by *Oviedo* (Lib. XXXIII, cap. X, pp. 300 and 301) whereas *Herrera* (Dec. II, lib. VII, cap. XVI, p. 195) copies Gomara.

I have dwelt thus long on this question because it disposes of the notion that the " government " of Mexico levied a tax on the traffic of the members of the tribe. This tax limits itself to a tribute paid by the subjected tribe of Tlatelulco alone, because, as *Durán* says (p. 270) " they had no more soil than that of their tianquiz." This tax was distributed among the kins, like any other tribute. But it does not follow that therefore the kins exercised judicial power over the Tlatelulcan market. This power either remained with the Tlatelulcan tribe, or devolved upon the officers of the tribe of Tenuchtitlan. The former is more likely, although the latter might also have been the case since the Tlatelulcans were treated with great severity, as traitors and outcasts (*Durán*, Cap. XXXIV, pp. 269–271), in which case the tribal authorities would have had to punish them.

That the central or tribal " teocalli " and the courts surrounding it were committed to the care of the tribe, as representing all the kins, on equal terms, in the share which each had in it, is self-evident, and needs no further proof.

then respected as open to use for all the kins in common.[201]
So many people met there daily, that the daily exercise, at least
the presence, of judicial authority was absolutely necessary.[202]

[201] *Las Casas* ("*Historia apologética.*" Cap. 214, in note XLV of Lord Kingsborough,
Vol. VIII. p. 124): "pero cuando reñian en los mercados, como á escandalosos y alboro-
tadores del pueblo eran muy gravemente castigados." *Sahagun* (Lib. VIII. cap.
XXXVI. p. 325) says even of those who disposed of stolen articles: "the Judges and
chiefs took them and sentenced them to death." *Torquemada* (Lib. XII, cap. V, p. 381):
" El que hurtaba en la Plaça ó Mercado, que llaman Tianquizco, luego allí era muerto á
palos, por tener por muy grave culpa, que en semejante lugar, y tan publico, huviese
tanto atrevimiento." *Clavigero* (Lib. VII. cap. XVII. p. 484): " He who changed the
measures established by the government, in open market, was executed on the spot,"
and (p. 487): " He who stole in the market, was at once beaten to death." *Mendieta*
(Lib. II, cap. XXIX, p. 138): " Porque tenian por grave el pecado cometido en la plaza
ó mercado."

[202] We have again here the eye-witnesses. *Cortés* ("*Carta Segunda.*" Vedia. I. p. 32):
" Hay en esta gran plaza una muy buena casa como de audiencia, donde están siempre
sentados diez ó doce personas, que son jueces y libran todos los casos y cosas que en
el dicho mercado acaecen, y mandan castigar los delinquentes. Hay en la dicha plaza
otras personas que andan continuo entre la gente mirando lo que se vende y las medidas con que miden lo que venden, y se ha visto quebrar alguna que estaba falsa."
Bernal Diez de Castillo (Cap. XCII. p. 89): Vedia, II, "y tenian alli sus casas, donde
juzgaban tres jueces y otros como alguaciles ejecutores que miraban las mercaderias."
These two statements, with more or less variation, are at the base of all that has
been subsequently said on this subject, except by *Sahagun* (Lib. VIII. cap. XXXVI.
p. 323): "El señor tambien cuidaba del tianguiz y de todas las cosas que en el se
vendian por amor de la gente popular, y de toda la gente forastera que alli venia,
para que nadie los hiciese fraude, ni sin razon en el comercio de la feria. Por esta
causa ponian por órden todas las cosas, que se vendian cada una en su lugar, y elegian
por la misma oficiales que se llamaban tianquizpantlayacaque, los cuales tenian cargo
del mercado, y todas las cosas que alli se vendian de cada género de mantenimientos
ó mercaderias; tenia uno de estos cargo para poner los precios de las cosas que se vendian y para que no huvrise fraude entre los compradores y vendedores." "Tianquizpantlayacaque" decomposes into "Tianquizpan," "feriar, o tratar en mercado." *Molina*
(II, p. 113), and "Tlayacatia," "cosa primera o delantera" (Id., p. 120); consequently,
" the foremost or first ones of those who trade in open market." We have to discriminate therefore between these and such officers as " *sat* " ("están siempre sentados,"
says Cortés) within that " very good house " in the market, or rather close by, and acted
as Judges. *Herrera* (Dec. II. Lib. VII. cap. XVI, p. 195) says this house was " cerca
del Mercado"— a statement which he afterwards changes to "en la plaza de Mexico"
(Dec. III, Lib. IV, cap. XVII, p. 137). We are now informed by *Torquemada* (Lib. XIV,
cap. XIII. p. 555) that the *tecpan* of Tlatelulco "que son las Casas de Cabildo, y Audiencia" was, at his time, on one of the sides (" acera") of the *market* of Tlatelulco,
and it appears to have been customary for the natives to have the official building
facing the " tianquiz." Such was the case at Tezcuco if we are to believe *Ixtlilxochitl*
(" *Hist. des Chichimèques,*" Cap. XXXVI, p. 247): " Le palais avait deux cours, dont la
première, qui était la plus grande, servait de place publique et de marché; elle est même
encore aujourd'hui destinée à cet usage;" and if the market of Tenuchtitlan really
was where Archbishop Lorenzana places it (see note 200), then it is evident that the
Mexican tecpan must have been very near it, if not actually facing the square. The
" great house " mentioned by the eye-witnesses quoted, was therefore, in all probability,
but the council or official-house of the tribe, and the old men who, in number from
three to twelve, are said to have officiated as " Judges," were members of the
" tlatocan " or supreme council on judicial duty, as we shall hereafter see. Those
officers who circulated among the people maintaining peace and order, were executive

It therefore demanded the daily attendance at the official house of the tribe of a body of men sitting as "judges." The decisions of these judges had to be final even in matters of life and death. Therefore the chiefs composing the highest authority of the tribe, the members of the council or "tlatoca," were also its supreme judges. It is stated that for this daily work the twenty "speakers" were subdivided into two bodies sitting simultaneously in two different halls of the "tecpan." One of these bodies is called "court of the nobles" because it attended, not merely to tribal cases, but especially to the preparatory business of government in general, whereas the other limited its decrees to judicial questions only.[203]

officers delegated for that special purpose, and, as we shall find, probably under orders of the military commanders of the tribe.

[203] This division of the council into two bodies for the purpose of greater dispatch of judicial work is particularly affirmed by *Sahagun* (Lib VIII, cap. XIV, p. 303, Cap. XV. p. 304, and Cap. XXV, pp. 313 and 314), who, however, contradicts himself in regard to the position and rank of his "Judges." Thus (p. 303) he calls his officers of the "sala de la judicatura," "el rey, los señores, cónsules, oidores, principales nobles" as distinguished from those of the "audiencia de la causas civiles," whom he designates as "los senadores y los ancianos," thus intimating, if not asserting, that the former were superior to the latter in rank and power. The hall wherein the former met, is called "tlacxitlan," the latter "teccalli." I shall return to these terms again. He further asserts (p. 314), speaking of the former: "Estos tales eran los mayores jueces, que ellos llamaban tecutlatoques," and establishes them as a court of appeal for the lower court. Now (Cap. XXX. p. 318) he says: "juntábanse los senadores que llamaban tecutlatoques . . ." Consequently, he tacitly admits that the "senadores" who, according to him, composed the "lower" court were also the *equals* of those of the higher, and all belonged to the same class of officers. Finally, his picture of the duties of both bodies is rather obscure. He even (p. 314) might be construed so as to establish *three* courts. If we now examine the names given by him, we find that of the "lower" to be "house of chiefs," from "tecuhtli" and "calli," house. Indeed, *Molina* (II, p. 92) has "teccalli," "casa, o audiencia real." "Tlacxitlan," however, signifies (II, p. 120) "en lo baxo, o al pie de los arboles, o de cosa semejante." The proper derivation, however, is from "ni tlacxitoca" "to correct writings, or count over what has been already counted" (p. 120), which would indeed correspond to a "court of appeals." "To appeal" is "nitlacuepa;" "appeal," "tlacuepaliztli; occecean neteihuiliztli," *Molina* (I. p. 12). It stands properly for the act of demurring, or of returning, folding, doubling up, and it is not likely to have been used by the natives to define an appeal in our sense of the word. Father Sahagun has probably introduced the word "tlacxitlan" himself. At all events, he is responsible for the notion of a superior body of judges, to whom a lower court, sitting in the same house, referred all cases of importance, contenting itself with taking testimony and despatching unimportant cases; while at the same time he tells us that the members of *both* groups *held the same office*, and were consequently equal and had the same title. This title we have found to be that of the members of the council, consequently the two groups formed but fractions of that body, co-ordinated and assisting each other, and not a higher and a lower branch of a tribal judiciary.

Father Sahagun and contemporary authors of the Franciscan school, whose writings have just now come to light in the "*Libro de Oro*," can easily be traced as the source of most of the later pictures of Mexican judicial customs as in the present instance. Thus his highest tribunal of *thirteen* "senadores" reappears in *Gomara* ("*Conquista*," p. 442,

We thus have found in the " tlatocan " or council, the high directive authority of the tribe, the arbitrator between its organic component parts, and the chief judicial power within the tribe. It is easy to recognize in it a counterpart to the council of the kin.

Like the kin also which, subordinate to its councils decrees had two superior officers for the execution thereof, the tribe had *two chief executive functionaries.*

Even at a comparatively remote period in the history of the ancient Mexicans we may discern two offices, not formally created, but naturally growing from what was left of tribal organization, which mark the beginning of a chief tribal executive. One of these is the " wise old man" conducting the " talk ;"[204] the other is the " big warrior" who led the braves to battle.[205] The former subsequently became "foreman" in the council, the latter " war-chief" to the tribe. There are indications to the effect that, for a while, both offices were held by one person. From the time the confederacy had been formed, however, we recognize two chief executive agents, [206] one of which is called the " Snake-woman "

Vedia I): " Los Jueces eran doce . . ." with a higher court of two; therefore, in all fourteen, equal to the thirteen of Sahagun with the " Señor" added. *Zurita* (" *Rapport,*" etc., pp. 100 and 105): " Les douze juges d'appel . . ." *Mendieta* (Lib. II. cap. XXVIII, p. 135) copies Zurita almost literally. By the side of this early Franciscan group of writers, there is the picture drawn by the two great Franciscans. Torquemada and Vetancurt, representing a supreme Judge, " Cihuacohuatl," and four tribunals beneath him in authority. This picture is evidently based on such paintings as the " *Codex Mendoza*" (plates LXIX and LXX). In my opinion the thirteen Judges of Sahagun should be connected with the judicial offices mentioned by Cortés as sitting at the " tecpan " (see note 202), rather than regarded as constituting a court of appeals.

Finally, I refer to *Ixtlilxochitl* (" *Hist. des Chichimques.*" Cap. XXXVI and XXXVII), *Veytia* (Lib. III, cap. VII, pp. 199 and 200) and others, in regard to Tezcuco. While they distinctly prove the subdivision, for judicial work, of the supreme council into two sections, they also show in a very marked manner, the confusion and contradiction arising from a misconception of the real case.

[204] Perhaps the earliest mention of such a " wise old man," foremost in the " talk." among the Mexicans proper, is that of the tale of the crafty old men. Huitziton and Tecpatzin, who are said to have persuaded the Mexicans to emigrate from Aztlan, as related by *Torquemada,* who is often copied (Lib. II, cap I, p. 78). In early times they are also called Captains and leaders, and must not be confounded with the " medicine-men " (Id., p. 78). Subsequently these latter sometimes appear as leading speakers. Much information can be gathered on this point by carefully and critically reading *Veytia* (Lib. II, cap. XII. XIII, XV and XVIII), *Codice Ramirez* (pp. 25 to 38), *Durán* (Cap. IV, V and VI), *Tezozomoc*(Cap.I, II and III).

[205] *Torquemada* (Lib. II, cap. II. pp. 80 and 81). *Vetancurt* (" *Teatro Mexicano,*" Parte IIa, Trat. I, cap. IX, pp. 260, 261 and 262). They merely show that the office of " big warrior," existed.

[206] This apportionment of the duties of chief-executive among two heads is found in many tribes of Mexico and Central America. Thus in Tlaxcallan, Maxiscatzin and Xicotencatl. the two head-chiefs, were alike and equal in power. (*Cortés,* " *Carta Segunda*" (pp. 18. 46). *Bernal Diez de Castillo* (Cap. LXVII, p. 60): " los dos mas prin-

("Cihua-cohuatl,") and the other (erroneously termed "King"), the "chief of men" ("Tlaca-tecuhtli").

The "CIHUA-COHUATL" was elected by the council for life, or

cipales caciques." "*Anonymous Conqueror*" (p. 388): "anchora che in certo modo si habbia rispetto á uno che e'el maggior Signore, che tiene teneva un Capitano generale per la guerra." *Motolinia*, "*Hist de los Indios*," etc. (Trat. III. cap. XVI, pp. 229 and 230). *Oriedo* (Lib. XXXIII. cap. III, p. 272) copies Cortés. *Gomara* (p. 332). *Torquemada* (Lib. XI. cap. XXII, p. 347) says four, of which Maxiscatzin was captain; though this is contradicted by the conquerors, Xicotencatl being war-chief. *Herrera* (Dec. II, lib. VI, cap. X, p. 152) reports the speech of Xicotencatl: "que bien debia de saber, que era Xicotencatl Capitan General de la Republica de Tlaxcala." and especially his interesting tale of the Tlaxcaltecan council in Cap. III, pp. 139 and 140. *Tezozomoc* (Cap. LXXXVI. p. 150): "el rey Xicotencatl," (Cap. LXXXVII, p. 152): "el rey Maxiscatzin." About Chalco, compare "*Tenure of Lands*" (p. 397. note 16), also about Xochimilco and the Tecpanecas. In regard to the Matlatzinca, *Zurita* ("Rapport,' etc., p. 389) says there were three chiefs, who occupied the highest power in succession. This statement is copied by *Herrera* (Dec. III, lib IV, cap XVIII, p. 139). The *Totonacas* had two chiefs. *Durán* (Cap. XXI, p. 181. Cap. XXIV, p. 206). The "Cazonzi" of Michuacan is represented by *Herrera* (Dec. III. lib. III. cap. V, p. 86, VI, p. 87) as being assisted by "his captain-general," and the anonymous document copied by *Don Florencio Janér* from the Codex C–IV–5 of the Escurial Library and published, without date, though evidently written between 1534 and 1551, entitled "*Relacion de las ceremonias y ritos, poblacion y gobierno de los indios de la provincia de Mechuacan, hecha al Ill'mo Sr. D. Antonio de Mendoza, Virey y Gobernador de Nueva España*" says ("Primera Parte," p. 13): "pues habia un rey y tenia su gobernador, y un capitan general en las guerras, y componiase como el mismo cazonci." This is very significant, especially because it is represented as being instituted by divine will. "Dicho sea en la primera parte, hablando de la historia del dios Curicaberis, como los dioses del cielo le dijeron como habia de ser rey, y que habia de conquistar toda la tierra, y que habia de haber uno que estuviese en su lugar, que entendiese en mandar traer leña para los ques." The evidence is positive about the QQuiché of Guatemala, and furthermore very interesting. *Zurita* ("Rapport," etc., pp. 405 and 406) mentions three chiefs, in a manner exactly similar to those of Matlatzinco, and *Herrera* (Dec. III. lib. IV, cap. XVIII, p. 140) follows him implicitly. *Torquemada* (Lib. XI. cap. XVIII, pp. 338 and 339) is of the same opinion, although it is easy to see that in fact there were *two* head-chiefs and not three, since he says: "Era el primero de todos el Rey actual; es á saber, el Abuelo: luego el Rey electo para despues de sus Dias; tras él, el que tenia nombre de Electo, etc." Consequently there were always two with the principal title. *Pedro de Alvarado* ("Relacion á Hernando Cortés," Utlatlan, 11 of April, 1524. Vedia I, p. 458) speaks of "cuatro señores de la ciudad de Vilatan." Another eye-witness of the conquest of Guatemala, *Bernal Diez de Castillo* (Cap. CLXIV, p. 220) speaks of "dos capitanes señores de Utatlan." We have fortunately, in regard to the tribes of QQuiché language, a very positive source of great value. This is the "Popol-Vuh" (p. 339). Enumerating the "Nim-Ha Chi Cavikib." it specifies from the fourth generation on ("U. cah. le"), always *two* chiefs, stating positively: "Oxib-Quieh, Beleheb-Tzi, u cablahu-le ahauab. Are-cut que ahauaric ta x-ul Donadiu, x-e hitzaxic rumal Caxtilan vinak"(p. 338). Consequently Alvarado executed *two* chiefs. Besides (p. 340), it even mentions their last successors, with Spanish names. At the close three "great-elected ones" ("Nim-Chocoh") are mentioned, but only two are named, the one from "Nihaib" and the other from "Ahau-QQuiche." We find here the exact counterpart of the Mexicans, before their fight with Tlatelulco.—two chiefs of Mexico, and two chiefs of Tlatelulco, Moquihuix and Teconal. See the authors on that subject. In regard to the Maya of Yucatan, see *Lizana* ("*Devocionario de Nuestra Señora de Itzmal*," § IV), also *Villagutierre y Sotomayor* ("*Historia de la Conquista y Reducciones de los Itzaex y Lacandones*," Lib. VIII, cap. XVI, p. 514)

during good behavior.[207]   We find in the Codex Mendoza — the earliest date connected with the office — the symbol of "snake-woman" affixed to the head of "Handful of Reeds," who was inaugurated "chief of men" in 1375.[208]   The inference may be permitted, therefore, that at one time both offices were held by one and the same incumbent.   At all events, the "Cihuacohuatl" becomes prominent only after the formation of the tri-partite confederacy embracing the Nahuatl tribes of Mexico, Tezcuco, and Tlacopan.[209]   But the position which he occupies thereafter is a

---

[207] Most of the older authors assert that the "Cihuacohuatl" was appointed by the "King." How was it possible for an officer to appoint his own equal, or associate officer? *Torquemada* (Lib. XI, cap. XXV, p. 352), says: "Despues del Rei, havia un Presidente, y juez mayor, cuio nombre, por raçon de el oficio, era Cihuacohuatl: esto oficio se proveia por el mismo Rei;" and again he concedes to the Cihuacohuatl "porque de su ultima determinacion no havia recurso à otro . . . . aqui parece lo mismo que reservando el Rei Mexicano para si, la autoridad Real, le hace su igual en la judicatura; y añade, que parte de sus Determinaciones, y Sentencias, no tengan recurso al Rei, que es condicion, y calidad, que engrandece mas la Persona de el Cihuacohuatl." Now, either the Mexicans were under a constitutional monarchy of the most improved kind,— of which there is no evidence since there was not even a division of powers,— or else the Cihuacohuatl was not appointed, but *elected* in true democratic fashion   *Vetan-curt* (Parte II, Trat. II, cap. I, p. 369) is still plainer; "Tan absoluta era la autoridad que le daba, que reservando el rey en si la autoridad real, era en la judicatura igual." Such an officer could only be appointed (if he was appointed and not elected), by the highest authority of the tribe, which was the council. Such is the version of *Tezozomoc* (" *Crónica*" Cap. LXXIX, p. 137): "y acabado de celebrar su entierro y quemazon de su cuerpo, que lo sintió mucho el rey Ahuitzotl, *pusieron* en su lugar su hijo Tlilpotonqui, Zihuacohuatl por sobrenombre." *Codice Ramirez* (p. 67): "Antes que fuesse coronado recien electo adolesció el famoso y sabio capitan Tlacaellel, de la qual enfermedad murió; en el articulo de su muerte llamó al Rey electo y le encargó mucho á sus hijos, especialmente al mayor, que daba muestras de ser muy valeroso, y habia hecho grandes hazañas en las guerras. El nuevo Rey por consolarle despues de haberle hablado muy tiernamente con muchas lágrimas, hizo llamar á los de su consejo real y rodeados todos del lecho de Tlacaellel mandó llamar el Rey al hijo mayor de Tlacaellel. y alli en presencia de su padre y de su consejo, le dió el mismo oficio de su padre, de capitan general y segundo de su corte con todas las preeminencias que su padre tenia." Even if there had been such an officer as a "King of Mexico" he could not have "appointed" anybody before his coronation. The ceremony indicated was therefore an *election by the council*. This is fully confirmed by *Durán* (Cap. XLVIII, p. 381): "llamando al hijo mayor, con parecer de todos los grandes, lo puso en la misma dinidad que el padre auia tenido, que era ser segundo despues del Rey en la corte, y mandó fuese honrado con la mesma veneracion que su padre auia sido jurándoles todos por principe de México, al qual le fué puesto el nombre de Ciuacoatl."

[208] " *Codex Mendoza*" (Tab. II), and the explanation says: "Las dos figuras con sus titulos é nombres de Acamapichtli son una misma cosa reservida en substancia. por que la primera figura demuestra el principio subcesion del dicho señorio . ." In note (p. 8, Vol. VI) of " *Antiquities of Mexico*," Lord Kingsborough adds the very sensible remark: "The first figure probably denotes that Acamapichtli. before he was elected King, possessed the title of Cihuacohuatl. or supreme governor of the Mexicans; when Mexico afterwards became a monarchy, this title was retained." The token for "Cihuacohuatl" a female head surmounted by a snake, is also found in the pictures of *Durán* (Lam. 8a).

[209] *Durán* (Cap. XXIV, p. 205): "Monteçuma se voluió a ciauacoatl Tlacaellel, que

very important one. The most specific Mexican chronicles call
him "coadjutor to the King," "second King," "governor."[210]
By other authorities he is mentioned as "vice-roy,"[211] and more
frequently yet as "supreme judge."[212] Finally, eye-witnesses of
the conquest apply to the "snake-woman" the titles of "keeper
of the tribute"[213] and "captain-general" of the Mexicans.[214]

le auia puesto por renombre y grandeça aquel nuevo ditado que." *Tezozomoc* ("Crònica,"
cap. XXXIX, p. 35) mentions the title together with the first actions of "wrathy chief,"
the Elder. But it also appears to have been very much older. *Ixtlilxochitl* ("Relaciones históricas" Segunda Relacion, p. 323, Vol. IX of Kingsborough), speaking of the
migrations of the Toltecs says: "llegaron à Xalisco, tierra que estaba cerca de la mar,
y aqui estuvieron ocho años, siendo descubridor Zuihcohuatl, tambien uno de los cinco
capitanes inferiores." *Veytia* (Lib. I, cap. XXII, p. 220) attributes to the same the dis-
covery of another region. It appears as if this title,— whose origin we may speculate
upon but, as yet, without any hope of positive results,— was always in existence, but
appeared as a distinct office only after the confederacy had been formed. A historical
question of some interest looms up here: whether or not the first reported incumbent
of the office after the formation of the confederacy, Atempanecatl Tlacaeleltzin, really
existed. *Torquemada* (Lib. II, cap. LIV, p. 171) denies his existence, and perhaps hints
at the "Codice Ramirez" when he speaks of "la mala, y falsa Relacion, que de esto
tuvo, que yo tengo enuni poder escrita de mano, con el mismo lenguage, y estilo." *Sr.
José F. Ramirez* already noticed this sally of the provincial, in note 1 (p. 382) of *Durán,
"Hist. de las Yndias,"* etc., and recognized it at once as applying to the Codice R.
Veytia (Lib. II, cap I, p. 82, etc.) acknowledges the existence of Tlacaellel, so does of
course *Acosta* (Lib. VII, cap. 14, 15, 16, 17 and 18), and all those who followed the same
sources as the "Codex Ramirez." The present city of Mexico, however, has two
monuments which, to my judgment, establish beyond a doubt the existence of this
Tlacaellel. One of these is the "Stone of Sacrifice," and the other a commemorative
slab, figured and described in No. 2 of Vol. I. *"Anales del Museo Nacional de México,"*
by the great Mexican scholar, Sr. Orozco y Berra. See my article in No. I, Vol. II of
the *"American Antiquarian," "The National Museum of Mexico and the Sacrificial
Stone"* (pp. 23 and 27).

[210] For these titles I refer in general to the *Codice Ramirez, Durán,* and *Tezozomoc.*
Quotations are useless and would only serve to increase the size of the volume.

[211] Already *Tezozomoc* mentions him a "teniente" *Torquemada* (Lib. XI, cap. XXV,
p. 352). *Vetancurt* ("Teatro Mexicano," Parte IIa, Trat. II°, cap. I, p. 369): "Despues
del Rey que heredaba, como se ha visto guardando el órden de la sangre real, habia un
virey que llamaban Cihuacohuatl, que el rey proveía y era su segunda persona en el
gobierno, de cuya sentencia no habia apelacion al rey."

[212] *Torquemada* (Lib. XI, cap. XXV, p. 352). *Vetancurt* ("Teatro," p. 369). *Clavigero*
(Lib. VII, cap XVI, p. 481). *Prescott* ("Conquest," B'k I, cap. II, p. 29). *H. H. Ban-
croft* ("Native Races," Vol. II, cap. XIV, pp. 434 and 435). *Codex Mendoza* (Tab. LXIX,
"Myxcoatlailotlac, Justicia mayor").

[213] *Bernal-Diez de Castillo* ("Hist. verdadera, etc," Cap. XCI, p. 87, Vedia II): "Acuérdome que era en aquel tiempo su mayordomo un gran cacique que le pusimos por
nombre Tapia, y tenia cuenta de todas las rentas que le traian al Montezuma, con sus
libros hechos de papel, que se dice amatl, y tenia destos libros una gran casa dellos."
Now this "Tapia" reappears again as "governor" of Mexico in different places.
*"Relacion de la Jornada que hizo Don Francisco de Sandoval Acazitli, Cacique y Señor
Natural que fué del pueblo de Thalmanalco"* ("Col. de Documentos," Icazbalceta, p.
315, Vol. II): "y á solos los Mexicanos llevó, y fueron por sus caudillos Tapia y D.
Martin el de Tlatelulco." *"Cuarta Relacion Anónima de la Jornada de Nuño de
Guzman"* (Col. de Doc. II, p. 471): "Viendo el señor desta cibdad de México, que se
llama Tapia." *Letter of the "Oydores" Salmeron, Maldonado, Ceynos, and Quiroga*

Every one of these designations conveys a certain amount of truth, though none of them adequately defines the office, the true nature and position of which become clear only through a glance at its early history. Tribal executive as a permanent office, (which must always be distinguished from a hereditary dignity), was created under the pressure of extreme need. The warrior who enjoyed the confidence of the tribe, who was not only daring and brave, but had also given proof of wisdom in the councils, became the people's choice as leader. The Mexicans were then in an attitude of defence; their own existence was at stake, and it was but natural, therefore, that the leading " talk " should be on military subjects, and that consequently the prominent war-captain should become the prominent "speaker," or foreman of the council.[215] In this manner we come to notice but *one* executive chief until the confederacy was formed. His duties were plain, even simple, at that time. He resided at the official house and superintended the exercise of tribal hospitality there; he was foreman to the council, and the leading executor of its decrees as far as tribal jurisdiction extended; he controlled the receiving and housing of the modest crops gathered from the "lands of the official-house" (tecpan-talli),[216] which, together with the customary pres-

(2d " *Recueil* " of " *Ternaux Compans*," dated Mexico, 14 August, 1531): "Ainsi l'on dit qu'un certain Tapico, qui gouvernait la partie du Mexique que l'on appelle Temixtitan." I find also the following in the municipal records of Mexico: "*Actas de Cabildo*" (Vol. I. p. 75; "Viernes 17 de Agosto 1527, años"): " Este dia de pedimento de Diego de Ordáz vecino de esta Cibdad le hizieron merced de le confirmar cierta compra que hize de Guanachel cacique que se llama Tapia de un sitio de casa que esta cabe San Francisco."

The "gobernador" of Mexico, after the conquest, and restoration under Spanish rule, was the former " *Cihuacohuatl* " This is plainly stated by *Cortés* (" *Carta Cuarta*," Vedia I, p. 110): " hice á un capitan general que en la guerra tenia, y yo conocia del tiempo de Muteczuma, que tomase cargo de la tornar á poblar. Y para que mas autoridad su persona tuviese, tornéle á dar el mismo cargo que en tiempo del señor tenia, que es ciguacoat, que quiere tanto decir como lugar-temente del señor." Therefore the appellation of Bernal-Diez, applies evidently to this officer.

[214] *Cortés* (" *Carta Tercera*," p. 89). " *Carta Cuarta*," p. 110, both in Vedia I). *Gomara* (" *Conquista*," etc., Vedia I. p. 392): " Vino Xihuacoa, gobernador y capitan general." *Herrera* (Dec. III. lib. II, cap. VII, p. 53) calls him " Guacoazin, Principal consejero del Rei, i su Lúgar teniente," *Torquemada* (Lib. IV, cap. C, p. 567): " Salió un capitan, llamado Cihuacohuatl Tlacotzin."

[215] *Codice Ramirez* (pp. 34 and 35): " Mira, Señor, que vienes á ser amparo y sombra y abrigo desta nacion Mexicana . . . ." *Joseph de Acosta* (Lib. VII, cap. VIII, p. 468). *Torquemada* (Lib. II, cap. XIII, p. 95): " La causa de su Eleccion, fue, aver crecido en numero, y estár mui rodeados de Enemigos, que les hacian Guerra, y afligian."

[216] " *Tenure of Lands*" (pp. 405, 406 and 419). I beg leave to correct here a mistake of mine in note 75, p. 420. At the close of said note it reads: "The above quotations show conclusively that the soil of the " tecpantlalli" was held and vested in the *King*

ents, constituted the tribal stores; finally he commanded the people when in arms. The overthrow of the tribes of Azcaputzalco and Cuynacan, by rendering these pueblos tributary, and compulsory allies of the Mexicans in warfare, suddenly increased these duties to such an extent that an assistant or colleague, a second head-chief, became necessary. Finally, when the confederacy came into existence, the first of these two chiefs was made its military commander, thus burthening him with duties of an extra-tribal nature.[217] He, therefore, had to relinquish a corresponding share of tribal business, which naturally fell to his associate. This associate, as we have already stated, was the "snake-woman" or "Cihuacohuatl," the proper head-chief of the Mexicans.

As daily leader of the council's "talk," the foreman of its deliberations, the "snake-woman" appears in the light of a judge, even of a supreme judge. But while, on all important occasions, he was the spokesman[218] of the council, and the awards he declared and the sentences he pronounced, were final and admitted of no appeal, yet it was only so because they emanated from the council, and not because they were his own individual decrees He remained always subject to the authority of that body, and, in a general way, he can be said to have superintended the execution

. . ." In place of it, "ve-ted in the *Kin*" is the proper reading. The mistake is wholly and exclusively mine — a "slip of the pen," which I neglected to correct in time.

[217] The Tezcucan writers, represented by *Ixtlilxochitl* ("*Hist. des Chichimèques*," Cap. XXXII and XXXIV) claim the leadership for Tezcuco, but the facts disprove it. Compare also "*Tenure of Lands*" (pp. 416, 417 and 418).

[218] *Fragmento No. 1* ("*Biblioteca Mexicana*"—"*Noticias relativas al Reinado de Motecuzuma Ilhuicamina*," p. 124): "Juntos los principales Mexicanos, el Rey les dixo lo que el Rey de Tetzcuco pedia, y todos dieron la mano á Tlacaellel, el cual respondió en nombre de todos á su Rey." *Durán* (Cap. XIV, p. 118): "Tlacaellel, que en todo era el primer voto y á quien se dava la mano en responder." (Cap. XV, p. 128): "Todos dieron la mano á Tlacaellel para que respondiese al rey." (Cap. XXIX, p. 240): "Tlacaellel, poniendose en pié, dixo desta manera, etc., etc." (Cap. XXXII. pp. 254 and 255, Cap. LIII, p. 417.) *Tezozomoc* (Cap. XVIII. p. 28. Cap. XIX. p. 30): "Y asi oydo esto por los principales Mexicanos tomó la mano de hablar Cihualcoatl Tlacaeleltzin y dijo: hijo y nuestro muy querido rey, os encargaos que veais muy bien lo que quereis hacer . . ." (Cap. XXI. p. 32): "Pasados algunos dias dijo el rey Moctezuma á Zihuacoatl Tlacatleltzin general y oydor . . ." "Llegados todos los señores de los dichos pueblos al palacio del rey Moctezuma, y sentados cada señor segun su merecimiento y valor de sus personas, digéron el rey Moctezuma, y su presidente y capitan general Zihuacoatl Tlacatleltzin." (Cap. XXXI. p. 48). (Cap. XXXVI. p. 57): "que el primero era su real consegero Zihuacoatl Tlacaeleltzin, . . ." (Cap. XXXIX, p. 62. Cap. XLIII. p. 69): "Luego en el palacio del rey Axayaca sin salir los grandes, ni nadie, prosiguió Zihuacoatl Tlacaeleltzin . . ." Further quotations are superfluous, particularly from this author.

of its judicial decisions, although, as will be seen hereafter, this part of the duty was properly assigned to other officers.

The " Cihuacohuatl " was responsible to the council for the careful housing of the tribute received, as far as it was applied to tribal requirements, and for the faithful distribution of the remainder [219] among the kins. This, and the fact that he kept the paintings recording the tribute, has caused Bernal Diez de Castillo to call him " mayordomo mayor," or general Intendant, and " keeper of the tribute " as we have already mentioned.[220]

How the " snake-woman " was the actual associate and colleague of that other chieftain who, after having been originally principal war-chief of the Mexicans, became at last commander of the confederate forces, we have already noticed.[221] We shall yet recur

[219] This results from the authority exercised by the Zihuacoatl over the captives in war. I have already alluded to this feature, and now but recapitulate the following quotations: *Durán* (Cap. XIX, pp. 172 and 173). Also *Tezozomoc* (Cap. XXIX, p. 45, Cap. XL, pp. 64 and 65, Cap. LXII, p. 104, Cap. LXVI, pp. 110, 111, Cap. LXX, p. 119), etc., etc.

[220] *Bernal Diez de Castillo* (Cap. XCI, p. 87, Vedia II): "Acuérdome que era en aquel tiempo su mayordomo mayor un gran cacique que le pusimos por nombre Tapia, y tenia cuenta de todas las rentas que le traian al Montezuma, con sus libros hechos de su papel, que se dice amatl, y tenia destos libros una gran casa dellos."

[221] There is no doubt in regard to the *equality of rank*, though the duties were somewhat different. "*Codice Ramirez*," (p. 66): "Concluidas las obsequias, el capitan general Tlacaellel que todavia era vivo, juntó los del consejo supremo . . . . . Estos juntos . . . . trataron de elegir nuevo Rey, y todos se encaminaban al valeroso Tlacaellel, el qual como otras veces, nunca quizo admitir el Reyno, dando por razon que más útil era á la República que hubiese Rey y coadjutor que le ayudasse como era él, y no solo el Rey . . . . . Pero no por esto dejaba de tener tanta y mas autoridad que el mismo Rey, porque le respetaban y honraban, servian y tributaban como ã Rey, y con mas temor, porque no se hazia en todo el Reyno mas que lo que él mandaba. Y assi usaba tiara y insignias de Rey, saliendo con ellas todas las vezes que el mismo Rey las sacaba." (P. 67), when the old Zihuacoatl died, his successor was elected: "con todas las preeminencias que su padre tenia." The "*Fragmento No. 1*" ("*Noticias relativas al Reinado de Motecuzuma Ilhuicamina*") is very positive also, almost always mentioning both officers together. *Durán* (Cap. XXVI, p. 215): "Ordenóse que solo el rey y su coadjutor Tlacaellel pudiese traer çapatos en la casa Real y que ningun grande entrase calçado en palacio, so pena de la vida, y solo ellos pudiesen traer çapatos por la ciudad, y ningun otro . . . ."; (Cap. XXXII, p. 255): "Tlacaellel respondió: qué mas honra puedo yo tener que la que hasta aqui é tenido? qué mas señorio puedo tener del que tengo y e tenido? pues ninguna cosa los reyes pasados an hecho sin mi parecer y consejo en todos los negocios civiles y criminales . . ."; (Cap. LXI, p. 326), the speech of Tlacaellel there reported is rather too lengthy to copy. Its substance is contained in the closing words: "luego rey soy y por tal me aueis tenido; pues qué mas rey quereis que sea? y asi como asi tengo de tener el mismo oficio y exercicio, hasta que me muera . . . . Sosegaos, hijos mios, y hace mi voluntad, que ya yo soy rey, y rey me seré hasta que muera; . . ." (Cap. XLIV, p. 357): "el viejo Tlacaellel, ã la mesma manera, al qual, dice esta ystoria, respetauan como ã rey;" (Cap. XLVIII, p. 381): "el nombre de Ciuacoatl, que el padre tenia, el qual era ditado de mucha grandeça eredado de los dioses; y asi desde aquel dia le llamauavan Tlilpotonqui Ciualcoatl, que era sobre nombre diuino." *Tezozomoc* ("*Crónica*," Cap.

ŋo the relative positions occupied by both officers, and merely advert, here, to the fact, that, since the latter has commonly been called a monarch, the designations of "coadjutor to the King," "second-King," previously quoted, are explained, though not justified. The same explanation applies to the title of "vice-roy," or "royal lieutenant."

Finally, the "Cihuacohuatl" was ex-officio commander-in-chief of the Mexicans proper, whenever his colleague directed the entire confederate force.[222] If, however, this was not the case, then the

XXXIII. p. 53): "De la manera que fué vestido y adornado Moctezuma. lo fueron también Zihuacoatl y Tlacaelelzin;" (Cap. XXXVI. p. 58): "pues solos dos eran los que havian de tener catles, que eran Moctezuma, Zihuacoatl y Tlacaeleltzin, como segunda persona del rey. porque se entendiése havian de ser temidos de todos los grandes del imperio;" (Cap. XL, p. 66). Speech of Tlacaellel: "tocante ä lo que tratais del señorio, yo siempre lo he tenido y tengo, ... porque yo como segunda persona que siempre fui del rey y de los reyes pasados, etc." Further quotations from this author would become too numerous. consequently too bulky. Besides these sources. to which should be added *Joseph de Acosta* ("*Hist: nat: y moral.*" Lib. VII, cap. XVII. p. 494, Cap. XVIII, p. 495), we find significant testimony in two authors who certainly did not gather their information at the source, from which the above series of authors obtained theirs. I refer to *Juan de Torquemada* ("*Monarchia Indiana.*" Lib. XI, cap. XXV. p. 352): "Aqui parece lo mismo, que reservando el Rei Mexicano para si, la autoridad Real. le hace su igual en la Judicatura." *Vetancurt* ("*Teatro Mexicano,*" Parte IIa. Tratado II°, cap. I, p. 339): "Tan absoluta era la autoridad que le daba, que reservando el rey en si la autoridad real, era en la judicatura igual." In regard to the fact that both chiefs wore the same characteristic ornaments and dress, see *Durán* (Lámina 8a to Cap XXIII of Trat. I°), also "*Codex Telleriano-Remensis,*" comparing it with the head-dress of the leading figure of the sculptures on the rim of the cylinder known as the "stone of sacrifice," in the Museo Nacional of Mexico.

[222] "*Codice Ramirez*" (pp. 59, 60, 61, 62 and 63), treating of the "capitan-general Tlacaellel:" haziendo hazañas dignas de gran memoria por medio de su general Tlacaellel." The war against Chalco was waged by the Mexicans *and* their confederates, therefore we read (p. 4): "Y asi fué que acudiendo esto Rey en personas ä la guerra." (P. 67) his office was: "de capitan-general y segundo de su corte. . . *Durán* (Cap. XVII, pp. 147 and 148). war against Chalco. when both chiefs went along. (Cap. XVIII. p. 158), foray against Tepeaca. both chieftains in the field, as both Mexicans and confederates participated. (Cap. XIX), against the Huaxteca. (Cap. XXII, p. 189): "Tlacaellel, principe de la milicia." in the raid against Coayxtlahuacan. In place of Tlacaellel. "era ya viejo y que no podria ya ir á guerra tan apartada." Cuauhnochtli commanded the Mexicans. The most explicit and positive author of all is *Tezozomoc* ("*Crónica Mexicana.*" Cap. XIX. p. 32, Cap. XXI. p. 32): "Zihuacoatl Tlacaeleltzin general y oydor."—"y su presidente y capitan-general Zihuacoatl Tlacatleltzin." In regard to the protracted hostilities against the tribe of Chalco. it is stated that the "Cihuacohuatl" alone commanded (Cap. XXII. p. 34); but it follows from p. 35, that after the first bloody though indecisive fight. the allies were called upon for assistance, although Tezozomoc says it was only a delegation to insure their quiet. This explains the contradiction between him and the two preceding authors. In (Cap. XXIV. p. 37), he acknowledges that Montezuma Ilhuicamina went along, together with Cihuacohuatl. The fact, that the conquest of Chalco was made by the Mexicans. with the assistance of allies. is conceded by other authors. See *Torquemada* (Lib. II, cap. XLIV and L). *Ortega* ("Apendice" to Veytia, Cap. III, pp. 240–243). Therefore the Cihuacohuatl commanded the Mexicans. In the foray against Tepeaca and Tecamachalco. the confederate forces sallied out, (Cap. XVII): "cada uno con su capitan y

latter led the Mexicans in person, or a substitute for either of them might take the command.[223] During the last days of aboriginal Mexico, when warriors from different tribes, together with the head-chiefs of Tezcuco and of Tlacopan, crowded into the invested pueblo, the so-called " King of Mexico " appeared as the *confederate* commander, while the " snake-woman " only wielded the authority and performed the duties of " captain-general " of the *Mexican* contingent.[224]

All these different attributes may be united in the functions of one office, namely : that of head-chief of the tribe. As such, we must consider the " Cihuacohuatl," and as such was he recognized by Cortés when in 1521, he created the last " snake-woman " " governor " of the remnants of the Mexican tribe and of the so-called Indian wards within which they " were " subsequently settled.[225]

We have seen that the " snake-woman " was the colleague, or associate in matters of tribal importance, of another officer, who had originally filled his place, but whose sphere of action had been so much extended through the formation of the confederacy, that a colleague became needed in tribal affairs. This officer, commonly entitled " King of Mexico," sometimes even " Emperor of Anahuac," was the " chief of men," " Tlaca-tecuhtli ".[226]

capitanes señalados," and both war-chiefs of Mexico were present and in the field (p. 41). Not to increase the volume of quotations beyond measure, I shall simply add that, as the Cihuacohuatl grew older and could not well go to war, other captains took his place. These captains I will refer to hereafter. *Acosta* (Lib. VII, cap. XVIII).

[223] Evidence to that effect is found in *Durán* (Cap. XXII, p. 189), and especially in *Tezozomoc* (Cap. XLVIII. p. 78) : " Cuauhnochtli, capitan general " (Cap. LXXI. LXXII and XCI, pp. 160 and 161, etc., etc.). This explains why the title of chief-commander of the Mexicans is so variously stated. See the very sensible remarks of *Clavigero* (Lib. VII, cap. XXI. p. 494, etc.). These chiefs were, in this instance, temporarily appointed, since it was not the creation of an office, but simply a delegation of power for a certain special purpose. When the foray was over, the charge ceased to exist, the war-chief returning to his original rank.

[224] *Cortés* (" *Carta Tercera*," Vedia I. p. 89) : E dende a poco volvió con ellos uno de los mas principales de todos aquellos que se llamaba Ciguacoacin, y era el capitan y gobernador de todos ellos, é por su consejo se seguian todas las cosas de guerra." This fact is generally accepted, and needs no further proof.

[225] *Cortés* (" *Carta Quarta*," Vedia I, p. 110). *Petition to Charles V, by four Indian chiefs of Mexico*, June 18, 1532, in " *Cruautés horribles des Conquérants espagnols*," of Mr. Ternaux-Compans, 1st Series (Appendix, pp. 265, 266 and 269) : " Moi, don Hernando de Tapia, je suis feu de Tapia, et ancien Tucotecle, gouverneur de Mexico, sous le marquis del Valle." *Herrera* (Dec. III. lib. IV, cap. VIII, pp. 122 and 123). *Bernal Diez de Castillo* (Cap. CLVII, Vedia II, pp. 198 and 199). *Icazbalceta in Cervántes-Salazar* (" *Tres Diálogos*," Introd. to 2d Dialogue, pp. 75 and 76).

[226] I have used this title, perhaps for the first time among recent writers, in " *Art of War*," (p. 123). *Tezozomoc* (Cap. LXXXIII, p. 145). *Ramirez de Fuenleal* (" *Letter*,

In the year 1375, according to the Mendoza Codex, the first incumbent of this office was elected by popular vote.[227] From that time on, the office remained strictly elective and non-hereditary, in so far as, like the chief officers of the calpulli, the descendants of the former incumbent were preferred to succeed him; provided they were undoubtedly competent.[228] But no rule of succession

etc." in 1*st* *Recueil* of Ternaux-Compans, p. 247). *Codex Mendoza* (Plate XVIII): " Tlacatectli gobernador " also the " Declaracion de la figurado." *Sahagun* (Lib. VI, cap. XX, pp. 136 and 138). This very remarkable chapter deserves to be closely studied, since it embodies the principles upon which the aborigines of Mexico filled their offices, and the bases of their mode of government. It would be too long to attempt a full analysis of it, and anything short of a careful study would fail to give an adequate conception of its importance. I merely refer to the statements of the celebrated Franciscan in regard to the title under consideration: "porque ya está en la dignidad y estrado, y tiene ya el principal lugar donde le puso nuestro señor? ya le llaman por estos nombres tecatlato, tlacatecutli, por estos nombres le nombran todos los populares . . . ." This passage and the succeeding one: " y alguno de estos tomado de la república por rey y señor," clearly indicate that the title is that of the so-called " King " or " chief of men; " (p. 138); however, he mentions the " tlacatecutli " as one of " dos senadores para lo que toca al regimiento del pueblo." There is an evident contradiction here. which is very similar to the one already noticed in regard to the two sections of the council, in a former note.

[227] *Codex Mendoza* (Plate II). *Mendieta* (Lib. II, cap. XXXIV, p. 148). In regard to this Chronology, compare the late and highly valuable work of *Don M. Orozco y Berra*, (" *Ojeada sobre la Cronologia Mexicana* " in *the* " *Biblioteca Mexicana*," — an Introduction to a reprint of Tezozomoc). The learned author has brought to light many highly valuable facts. That " Acamapichtli " or " Handful of Reeds " was *elected*, is abundantly proven by many authorities, so that detailed quotations are useless.

[228] The fullest report is contained in *Sahagun* (Lib. VIII, cap. XXX, p. 318): " Cuando moria el señor ó rey para elegir otro, juntábanse los senadores que llamaban tecutlatoque, y tambien los viejos del pueblo que llamaban achcacauhti. y tambien los capitanes soldados viejos de la guerra que llamaban Iauequioaques (should be Iau-Tequioaques), y otros capitanes que eran principales en las cosas de la guerra, y tambien los Sátrapas que llamaban Tlenamacazques ó papaoaque: todos estos se juntaban en las casas reales, y alli deliberaban y determinaban quien habia de ser señor, y escogian uno de los mas nobles de la liné de los señores antepasados, que fuese hombre valiente y ejercitado en las cosas de guerra, osado, animoso, y que no supiese beber vino: que fuese prudente y sábio, y que fuese criado en el Calmecac: que supiese bien hablar, y fuese entendido, recatado y animoso, y cuando todos ó los mas concurrian en u io, luego le nombraban por señor. No se hacia esta eleccion por escrutinio ó per vo os, sino todos juntos confiriendo los unos con los otros, venian à concertarse en uno." To this should be added the testimony of the same author (Lib. VI, cap. XX, pp. 136–139). *Duran* (Cap. XI. p. 103): " y es de saner que no ponian hijo del que elexian por rey, ó del que moria. porque como ya tengo dicho, nunca heredaron los hijos, por via de herencia, los ditados ni los señorios, sino por election; y asi, agora fuese hijo, agora fuese hermano, agora primo, como fuese eleto por el rey y por los de su consejo para aquel ditado, le era dado, bastaua ser de aquella lingnia y pariente cercano; y asi iban siempre los hijos y los hermanos heredándolo, poco á poco, si no esta vez, la otra, ó si no la otra. y asi nunca salia de aquella generacion aquel ditado y señorio, eligiéndolos poco á poco." (Cap. LXIV, p. 498): " porque en aquel tiempo heredábanse los hermanos hijos del rey unos á otros, aunque de lo que desta hystoria e notado, ni auia herencia ni sucesion. sino solos aquellos que los electores escogian, como fuese hijo ó hermano del que moria. ó sobrino ó primo, en segundo grado, y este órden me parece que llevan en todas sus electionos, y asi cree que muchos de los que claman y piden venilles por herencia los señores, porque en su infidelidad sus padres fueron reyes y señores,

limited the choice to a family, perhaps not even to a kin.[229]   Like every other office it had to be *deserved*,[230] and could not be obtained by birth or through craft ;[231] neither could it be transmitted through inheritance.[232].

The history of this office may be divided into two periods : the first, closing with the formation of the confederacy in the first quarter of the fifteenth century ; the second, beginning at that time, and lasting until the final abrogation of the office by the Spaniards, in 1521.[233]   During the former period the "chief of men" was, as we have already said, but the executive chieftain

entiendo no piden justicia, porque en su ley antigua mas eran electiones, en todo género de señores, que no herencias ni sucesiones." The author of the above was a native Mexican. and knew the customs of his people. " *Codice Ramirez*" (p. 58): " porque como queda referido, nunca heredaron los hijos de los Reyes en los señorios, sino por eleccion daban el Reyno á uno destos quatro principes, á los quales tampoco heredaban sus hijos en estos ditados y cargos; sino que muerto uno escogian otro en su lugar al que les parescia, y con este modo siempre tuvo este Reyno muy suficientes hombres en sus Repúblicas, porque elegian los mas valerosos." *Tezozomoc* (Cap. LXXXII, pp. 142 and 143), confirming the mode of election as reported by Sahagun. *Zurita (" Rapport, etc.,*" p. 14): " Ainsi, ils préféraient laisser apres eux un successeur qui fut capable de bien gouverner, plutôt que d'abandonner cette charge ă leurs fils, ă leurs petits-fils ou ă leurs lieutenants, comme le fit Alexandre le Grand." *Mendieta* (Lib. II, cap. XXXVII, pp. 153 and 154). *Torquemada* (Lib. XI, cap. XXVII, p. 358): " Confieso de la Republica Mexicana esta manera de sucesion, y que se elegian algunas veces, sin diferencias, notando solamente las qualidades de las personas. y de estos fue Itzcohuatl, valeroso Rei Mexicano, que por el valor de su persona, y la grandeça de su animo, no se advirstió. ni reparó para eligirle, en que era Hijo de una Esclava; pero no es maravilla, que el bien publico, prefiera al particular." I forbear quoting the tales about the election of sundry Mexican chiefs, as related by the above and other authors.

[229] *Clavigero* (Lib. VII, cap. VI, p. 463). has distinctly formulated the idea : "that the crown should always remain in the house of Acamapitzin." Enough has been said about the Mexican family to dispel the notions of an "Indian dynasty" in Mexico. At best, a succession or perpetuation of the *office* in a certain *Kin* or *calpulli*, might be conceded. *Durán* (Cap. XI, p. 103), *Codice Ramirez*, (p. 58). and *Zurita* (p. 14), make even this somewhat doubtful; so does the election of Itzcohuatl, *as conceived* by *Torquemada* (Lib. XI. cap. XXVII. p. 358). The origin of " Flinty Snake " is, however, reported in too many different ways to justify any conclusion based on it. The fact, that one of the four leading war-captains should become " chief of men," militates against descent of office in a certain kin. See also *Joseph de Acosta* (" *Hist. nat. y moral de los Indias*," Lib. VI, cap. 24, pp. 439 and 440).

[230] *Sahagun* (Lib. VI. cap. XX; Lib. VIII, cap. XXX). *Acosta* (Lib. VI. cap. 24).

[231] *Las Casas* (" *Hist. apologética*" quoted on p. 124 of Vol. VIII of Lord Kingsborough's collection) : " Quando algun señor moria y dexava muchos hijos, si alguno se alzava en palacio y se queria preferir á los otros, aunque fuese el mayor, no lo consentia el Señor ă quien pertenecia la confirmacion, y menos el pueblo. Antes dexavan pasar un año. ó mas de otro, en el qual consideravan bien qual era mejor para regir ó gobernar el estado, y aquel permaneció por señor." *Zurita* (" Rapport, etc.," pp. 18 and 19). *Torquemada* (Lib. XI, cap. XXVII, pp. 358 and 359). Further quotations would be useless.

[232] In addition to the authorities named in note 228, I refer to *Clavigero* (Lib. VII, cap. VI, p. 463), with the restriction mentioned in note 229. " *De l'ordre de Succession, etc.*" (1st *Recueil of Ternaux-Compans*, p. 228).

[233] *Zurita* (" *Rapport*, etc.," p. 69). *Sahagun* (Lib. VIII, cap. I, p. 272). The death of Cuauhtemotzin put an end to the office in the eyes of the Spaniards, although it had

of the tribe, and the duties of his office, at that time embracing those of the " Cihuacohuatl," have been stated by us already. The confederation had so far wrought a change that he became " general " of its allied warriors,[234] and consequently to a certain extent, an extra-tribal officer residing at Tenuchtitlan, Mexico, because the military supremacy was vested in that tribe. We have previously alluded to the fact that it was the " chief of men " upon whom we have been heretofore accustomed to look as a monarch, even a despot. His office and its attributes have been the mainstays of the notion that a high degree of civilization prevailed in aboriginal Mexico, in so far as its people were ruled after the manner of eastern despotisms.

Not only was this pretended monarch strictly elective, but he could also be deposed for misdemeanor.[235] " Wrathy chief" the younger, better known as the last Montezuma, was removed from office and his successor elected before that ill-starred chieftain's violent death.[236]

been formally abrogated by the capture of that chieftain, to whom no successor was appointed by the whites.

[234] *" Tenure of Lands"* (p. 417). *Ixtlilxochitl* (*" Histoire des Chichimèques,"* Cap. XXXII, p. 219), claims for his Tezcucan chief the military command, in the shape of an " imperial " title: " He of Tezcuco was greeted by the title of Aculhua Tecuhtli, as also by that of Chichimecatl-Tecuhtli which his ancestors carried, and which was the distinctive mark of the empire." I believe this claim was disposed of in " *Tenure of Lands"* (p. 394, notes 9 and 10). See also *Vetancurt* (Part IIa, Trat. I, cap. XIV, p. 291): " y remataron la fiesta quedando Izcohuatl por rey supremo del imperio tepaneca, por ser primero que Netzahualcoyotl." See also the tacit acknowledgments by *Ixtlilxochitl* (" *Hist: des Chichimèques,"* Cap. XXXVIII, LXXIV, LXXV).

[235] *Vetancurt* (" *Teatro Mexicano,"* Parte II, Trat. II, cap. XV, p. 485): " Otras muchas leyes extravagantes que con el instinto natural, con maduro consejo confirmaron y que inviolablemente guardaban. tenian los Mexicanos y los de Guatimala, como el de deponer al rey con junta y consejo de la nobleza."

[236] That " wrathy chief" had lost all his authority during the time Cortés went against Narvaez, is clearly stated in " *Carta Segunda"* (Vedia I, pp. 41 and 42) already, though the fact of his removal from office is not noticed by the Spanish commander himself. It is, however, mentioned by *Bernal Diez de Castillo* (Cap. CXXVI, p. 132). Montezuma said to Olid and to the " Padre de la Merced:" " Yo tengo creido que no aprovecharé cosa ninguna para que cese la guerra, porque ya tienen alzado otro señor . . . ;" and again the Mexicans themselves are reported as answering to Montezuma: " Hacémosos saber que ya hemos levantado á un vuestro primo por señor." *Las Casas* (" *Breuissima Relacion,"* p. 49), Alvarado: " Ponen un puñal a los pechos al preso Motençuma que se pusiesse à los corredores, y mandasse, que los Yndios no combatiessen la casa, si no que se pusiessen en paz. Ellos no curaron entonces de obedecelle en nada; antes platicauan de elegir otro Señor, y capitan, que guiasse sus batallas." *Sahagun* (Lib. XII, cap. XXI, pp. 28 and 29): " Oidas estas voces por los Mexicanos y Tlatilulcas, commençaron entre si á bravear, y maldecir á Mocthezuma diciendo que dice el puto de Mocthezúma y tú bellaco con él? no cesaremos de la guerra; luego comenzaron á dar alaridos y á tirar saetas y dardos ácia donde estaba el que hablaba junto con Mochthecuzuma." This was before Cortés had even captured Narvaez, and shows that at that time the " chief of men " had already lost all authority. *Codice Ramirez* (p. 89). When the other chief who was with Montezuma had spoken:

Among the duties of the "chief of men," we notice first that of residence at the "tecpan" or official house.[237] This is commonly stated to be a royal privilege, whereas it was, in fact, a burthen, as it simply meant that he occupied the position of head of the official household of the tribe.[238] The formation of this household we have elsewhere described.[239] It was a communal group, consisting of the head-war-chief and his family, together with such assistants (and their families, if any), as were required for the transaction of daily business.[240] The "tecpan" is appropriately called : "house of the community," "casa de comunidad," by Fray Juan de Torquemada,[241] and its residents were placed and kept there for the purpose of extending tribal hospitality, and for the furtherance of tribal business and extra-tribal relations. This "official family" had to wait upon the officers and chiefs who

"un animoso capitan llamado Quauhtemoc de edad de diez y ocho años que ya le querian elegir por Rey dijo en alta voz :" "Qué es lo que dize este bellaco de Motecuczuma, muger de los españolos, que tal se puede llamar, pues con ánimo mugeril se entregó à ellos de puro miedo y asegurándonos nos ha puesto todos en este trabajo? No le queremos obedecer porque ya no es nuestro Rey, y como à vil hombre le hemos de dar el castigo y pago." *Fragmento No.* 2 (*Noticias Relativas á la Conquista,*" etc., p. 143): "y ellos le deshonraron y llamaron el Cobarde." *Torquemada* (Lib. IV, cap. LXVIII, p. 494): "soltó á un Hermano de Motecuhçuma, Señor de Iztapalapan, y los Mexicanos, ni hicieron el Mercado, ni le dexaron bolver ă la Prision, y le eligieron por su Caudillo" (Id. Cap. LXX, p. 497). *Vetancurt* ("*Teatro,*" Parte IIIa, Trat. I, cap. XIV, p. 125, cap. XV, pp. 130, 131). *Herrera* (Dec. II, lib. X, cap. VIII, p. 264). It is very interesting to notice that Torquemada and Herrera use identically the same words. Their versions are the fullest.

[237] *Tenure of Lands* (pp. 409 and 410). *Durán* (Cap. XXVI, p. 214): "Y asi. lo primero que se ordenó, fué que los reyes nunca saliesen en público, etc., etc." It is scarcely necessary to prove this at any length, by quotations.

[238] *Tenure of Lands* (p. 409). *Herrera* (Dec. III, lib. IV, cap. XVII, p. 138): "Estos Tributos eran para el bien publico, para las Guerras, para pagar ă los Governadores, i Ministros de Justicia, i Capitanes, porque toda esta Gente comia, de ordinario, en el Palacio del Rey, adonde cada uno tenia su asiento, i lugar conocido, segun su oficio, i Calidad, . . ." *Sahagun* (Lib. VIII. cap. XIII, p. 301): " Y despues que habia comido el señor, mandaba á sus pages, ó servidores, que diesen de comer á todos los señores y embajadores que habian venido de algunos pueblos, y tambien daban de comer á los que guardaban el palacio. Tambien daban de comer ă los que criaban los mancebos que se llaman telpuchtlatos y á los Sátrapas de los idolos. Asimismo daban de comer á los cantores, á los pages, á todos los del palacio, etc., etc. . . ." *Tezozomoc* (Cap. LXXXII, p. 144). The latter is very positive, mentioning it as a duty.

[239] *Tenure of Lands* (pp. 409 and 410).

[240] The information on this point goes back to *Cortés* (" *Carta Segunda,*" Vedia I, p. 35): "La manera de su servicio era que todos los dias luego en amaneciendo eran en su casa de seiscientos señores y personas personales, los cuales se sentaban, y otros andaban por unas salas y corredores que habian en la dicha casa, etc., etc." The other eye-witnesses are hardly as positive. The exaggerated reports of *Oviedo* (Lib. XXXIII, cap. XLVI, p. 505), *Torquemada* (Lib. III, cap. XXV, p. 296), *Vetancurt* ("*Teatro,*" Parte IIa, Trat. I°. cap. XXIII, pp. 356, 357, etc.), *Herrera* (Dec. II, lib. VII, cap. IX, pp. 183, 184) and others, simply prove that the "tecpan" was permanently occupied by a numerous household, of which the "chief of men" was the head.

[241] " *Monarquia Indiana*" (Lib. VI, cap. XXIV, p. 48).

daily transacted affairs at the " tecpan," to carry their victuals to the halls in which their sessions were held and also to wait upon the foreign official guests (often enemies) who were received in separate, even secluded, quarters.[242] But their main duty con-

[242] *Sahagun* (Lib. VIII, cap. XIII, p, 301, as copied in note 238). *Zurita* (" *Rapport*," etc., p. 96): " Il y avait dans les palais des souverains des appartements vastes, élevés de sept ă huit marches comme nos entre-sol, et destinés ă la résidence des juges." (P. 100): " De bonne heure on apportait au palais même les repas des magistrats." This would imply that the food was brought to the " tecpan " from the places where the members of the council (" tecutlatoca ") actually resided. This is positively contradicted by *Tezozomoc* (" *Crónica,,*' Cap. LXXXII, p. 144), who makes it one of the duties of the " chief of men." " con los viejos y viejas mucho amor, dándoles para el sustento humano: regalados los principales, teniéndolos en mucho, y dándoles la honra que merecen: llamarles cada dia al palacio que comán con vos, ganándoles las voluntades, que con ellos está el sostener el imperio, buenos consegeros, buenos amigos, que por ellos os es dado el asiento, silla, estrados, honra, señorio, mando y ser." Such an extensive meal of the tribal officers is also intimated by the same author as having been customary with the Xochimilcas,— a tribe well known as being closely allied to the Mexicans,— where he says (Cap. XVI, pp. 25 and 26): " Las Indias mugeres de las Xochimilcas, lavando muy bien el itzcahuitl, tecuitlatl, y otras cosas salidas de la laguna, y lavado, y limpiamente lleuándolo al palacio de Tecpan para que le comiesen los principales, y comenzandolo á comer estava muy sabrosa, y prosiguiendo en su comida, etc., etc. . . ." *Zurita* (" *Rapport*," etc., p. 49), speaking of certain chiefs, says: " Outre ces avantages, le souverain suprême payait une solde ă ces chefs, et leur faisait délivrer des rations. Ceux ci se tenaient continuellement dans son palais pour former sa cour." It is to these " chiefs," which were none other than the members of the council, that *Gomara* (Vedia I, p. 342) refers, copying *Cortés* (" *Carta Segunda*," Vedia I, p. 35), who adds, however: " E al tiempo que traian de comer al dicho Muteczuma, asimismo lo traian ă todos aquellos señores tan cumplidamente cuanto ă su persona, y tambien á los servidores y gentes destos les daban sus raciones. Habia cotidianamente la dispensa y botilleria abierta para todos aquellos que quisiésen comer y beber." The chaplain has added to Cortés' relation some items tending to increase or enhance the importance of the meals, whereas he has suppressed the above, very important, passage. Compare Vedia: (Tom. I, p. 345). His statements agree far better with those of *Bernal Diez* (" *Hist. verd.*" Vedia II, cap. XCI, pp. 86 and 87). The fact of the " official household " being entrusted with the dispensation of tribal hospitality is therefore certain. The members of the council ate there also, as proven by *Zurita* (p. 96), *Sahagun* (Lib. VIII, cap. XIII, p. 301), *Mendieta* (Lib. II, cap. XXVIII, p. 134): " traiänles algo temprano la comida de palacio," and it is implied by *Torquemada* (Lib. XI, cap. XXV, p. 352): " Estos Jueces oian de ordinario, en especial de causas criminales, todos los Dias ă mañana, y tarde, ... asistian en sus Salas, que las havia en la casa del Rei, particulares, ..." He is even very positive (Lib. III, cap. XXV, p. 296): " No solo tenia este Grande, y Magnifico Emperador casas muy cumplidas, y Salas, y Aposentos grandiosas, para su Morada, para sus Consejos, y Señores, y toda la demas Gente, que llegaba á ser digna de su hospedage, y recibimiento, donde como su misma Persona Real eran servidos, y acariciados . . ," also (Lib. IV, cap. L. p. 459). He also says of " Fasting Wolf," headchief of Tezcuco (Lib. II, cap. LIII, p. 167): " no fué menos en el gasto de su Casa, asi para su Persona, como para hacer Hospicio ordinario ă todos los que servian en su Palacio, y otros muchos Señores, que comian en su Casa, cada Dia, . . ." *Petrus Martyr of Anghiera* (" *De nouo Orbe*," etc., Dec. III, cap. X, pp. 231 and 232). *Clavigero* (Lib. VII, cap. XVI, p. 482), about Tezcuco. In regard to Mexico he is very positive (Lib. V, cap. III, p. 304). Further quotations are useless. I shall merely refer to the " *Codex Mendoza*" (plate LXX) and, for the sake of analogy with the tribes of QQuiché-stock in Guatemala, to the " *Popol Vuh*" (p. 305): " Are qui cuchbal quib ri-oxib chi nim-ha u bi cacmal, chiri cut chi c'uqah-vi c'uquiya, ..."

sisted in preparing and serving every day an extensive meal, of which not only all the members of the household, several hundreds in number, partook, but every one who, either on business or as an idler, happened to be on or about the premises.[243]   It was the duty of the " chief of men " himself to open this rude clannish feast,[244] and it pertained to his office to represent the hospitality and dignity of the tribe on such occasions.   Hence the peculiar

That the delegates from foreign tribes were quartered at the " tecpan " is plainly stated by *Sahagun* (Lib. VIII, cap. XIX, p. 308): " Habia otra sola que se llamaba Coacalli: en este lugar se aposentaban todos los señores forasteros, que eran amigos ó enemigos del señor. . . . . ." ; " *Codice Ramirez* " (p. 75): " Vinieron á estas fiestas hasta los propios enemigos de los Mexicanos. como eran los de Michhuacan y los de la provincia de Tlaxcala, ä los quales hizo aposentar el Rey y tratar como á su misma persona. y hazerles tan ricos miradores desde donde viessen las fiestas, como los suyos;" *Durán* (Cap. XL, p. 317, cap. XLIII. p. 347): " Fasting child" of Tezcuco " aposentándole en un lugar que ellos llaman Teccalli, que quiere decir, palacio Real." " Luego llegó el rey de Tacuba con todos sus principales y señores. . . . . ä quien no menos honra y cortesía se hizo que al de Tezcuco. poniéndole en el mismo palacio, junto à Neçaualpilli." The delegates from Tlaxcallan, Huexotzinco, and Cholula were: " Llevados al palacio real, donde les tenian aparejado un retraimiento oculto y escondido," and " fueron aposentados en el mismo lugar" those of Michhuacan and others (pp. 350 and 351), also (Cap. LIV, pp. 428 and 429, and LVIII, p. 459, etc.).   These authors are also fully confirmed by *Tezozomoc* (" *Crónica,*" Cap. LXIV. pp. 106 and 107; cap. LXVIII, p. 111; cap. LXXXVI. p. 151), *Ixtlilxochitl* (" *Histoire des Chichimĕ-ques,*" Cap. XXXVI, p. 254, speaking of Tezcuco). *Torquemada* (Lib. XIV, cap. I, pp. 534 and 535).   The latter distinguishes between the " calpixca" and " el palacio," stating that delegates were quartered at the former.   But since he himself (Lib. VI, cap. XXIV. p. 48) calls the " tecpan " casa del comun "—a name given by him to the " calpixca"—and we know from *Sahagun* (Lib. VIII. cap. XIX, p. 307) that the " calpixcacalli" was a hall of the " tecpan," there can be no doubt as to the fact, that the " tecpan " was also the place where delegates were received, lodged and fed, at the expense of the tribe.

When, in 1537, the Bishop Las Casas sent certain traders with full instructions and " implements for conversion." to the Indians of " Tuzulutlan " or of the " Tierra de Guerra " *Fray Antonio de Remesal* (" *Historia de la Provincia de S. Vicente de Chyapa,*" etc., etc., Lib. III. cap. XV. p. 135): Y como en aquel tiempo no auia mesones ni casas de comunidad, todos los forasteros que llegauan al lugar acudian á pasar en casa del señor, que los recebia humanamente, hospedaua y daua de comer conforme la calidad de la persona, y el forastero reconocia el bien recibido, ó que auia de recibir, poniendo á los pies del señor algun presente conforme á su posibilidad." The traders, therefore, " took lodgings " at the official house,— the tecpan,—and staid there (as we may read p. 136 of the Friar's history) until they had performed their work of opening the country to the preaching of the gospel. The comparison with Cortés, being also quartered at the " tecpan " of Mexico, is indeed striking.

[243] Descriptions of this meal are so abundant, that it is hardly worth while to refer to them in detail.   I would only call particular attention to the statements of *Cortés* (" *Carta Segunda,*" Vedia I. p. 35). *Bernal diez de Castillo* (" *Hist. verdadera,*" etc., etc., Cap. XCI. pp. 86 and 87, of Vedia II). *Andrés de Tápia* (" *Relacion sobre la Conquista de México,*" Col. de Doc's II. p. 581).   These statements. made by eye-witnesses, if viewed in their proper light and compared with those of subsequent writers, fully corroborate the views of *L. H. Morgan* (" *Montezuma's Dinner*" in *N. American Review.* 1876), that this meal was but an official communal one, given by the official household of the tribe, as part of its daily duties and obligations.

[244] I cannot refrain here from recalling the description of the meal given to the Clan McIvor by its chief " Fergus McIvor, Vich Ian Vohr," — so graphically pictured by Sir

earnestness of his manner which eye-witnesses have mistaken for the haughtiness of a tyrant.[245]

These duties not only necessitated official residence at the "official house," but even permanent stay there, unless important business required the chief's absence.[246] Such absence, however, could only be justified by official duties, and then the "chief of men" had to appear with all the tokens and emblems of his rank.[247] If otherwise, he might indeed, go about, but he lost all claim to official recognition.[248] Hence the statements are true in the main, however exaggerated in detail, that great decorum was observed towards the "chief of men" whenever he appeared in public, that he was addressed with marked deference, and that a certain pomp surrounded him on such occasions.[249] These occasions were, of course, opportunities for the display of Indian

Walter Scott in "Waverley." As to the part played by the "chief of men" see particularly *Bernal Diez* (Cap. XCI, p. 86, Vedia II).

[245] This particularly earnest mien is noticed by all authors. It is strictly Indian, and found among the rudest tribes.

[246] *Durán* (Cap. XXVI, p. 214): "Y asi, lo primero que se ordenó, fué que los reyes nunca saliesen en público, sino á cosas muy necesarias y forçosas." *Codice Ramirez* (p. 76): "De ordinario estaba retirado saliendo muy pocas vezes á vista del pueblo."

[247] *Durán* (Cap. XXVI, p. 214), *Sahagun* (Lib. VIII, cap. X, p. 291). It is distinctly asserted by the former that, what he has called "corona real" could only be worn by the "chief of men" and the "snake-woman." This head-dress, very appropriately termed by the Spaniards, "half mitre" ("media mitra") is figured by many authors of native origin. See *Codex Mendoza* (plates II to XIV, also LXX), *Durán* (Láminas 2 to 14, also 16, 18, to 24 etc.), *Codice Ramirez* (plates 4 and 5). It is called "Xiuhuitzolli" by the Mexicans. See also *Molina* (Parte Ia, p. 30 and IIa, p. 160) from "Xiuitl" turquoise or green stone, and is totally different from the head-dress worn by the "chief of men" in the field. Compare "*Art of War*" (p. 126).

[248] This explains the stories about the "incognito" ramblings of "Fasting Wolf" of Tezcuco, so frequently repeated after the Ixtlilxochitls, as well as that of the arrest of "Wrathy Chief" (the last Montezuma) for appropriating corn out of a field. The latter tale is beautifully told by *H. H. Bancroft* (Vol. II, pp. 451, 452) after the best authorities.

[249] No author has been more prolific in pictures of pomp, regal wealth and magnificence, than *Bernal Diez de Castillo* ("*Historia verdadera*," etc., etc., Cap. LXXXVIII, XCI and XCII, etc.). Most of the later writers have placed undue reliance on his statements, assuming that the truthfulness with which he "gave vent" to his own individual feelings and impressions, was the result of cool, impassionate observation. Anyone who has read attentively (and not merely glanced over at random for the purpose of obtaining quotations) his protracted "Mémoires," will become convinced that he is, in fact, one of the most unreliable eye-witnesses, as far as general principles are concerned. In every detail where his personal feelings are not involved or by which, even at the late date when he wrote, they were not involuntarily aroused, he is much more trustworthy than when he takes special pride or pains to be very explicit. Thus, it is curious to compare his description of "Wrathy Chief's" reception of Cortés with that given subsequently by the "Marquis del Valle" himself, ("*Carta Segunda*," Vedia I, p. 25). It was doubtlessly the greatest effort at pomp and display ever attempted by the Mexicans, since they went to meet and greet the most incom-

finery, when a number of articles were used to deck the " chief of men " as his official insignia, but the custom of speaking to

prehensible beings ever heard of by them. It is interesting to place both versions side by side. The translation is my own and I therefore beg for indulgence.

<table>
<tr><td>Cortés. Second Dispatch.</td><td>Bernal Diez de Castillo. Cap. 88.</td></tr>
<tr><td>

"At that place more than a thousand principal people came to greet and to speak to me, all citizens of the said city, and all dressed alike and according to their custom very richly, and when they came to speak to me, every one of them made, before coming up, a particular ceremony, customary among them, which consisted in each one of them putting his hand on the ground, kissing it; and in this manner I waited almost an hour until each one had made his ceremony." ". . . . . After we had passed that bridge, this lord Muteczuma came to receive us with about two hundred Lords, all barefooted and dressed in other livery or manner of clothing, also very rich after their custom, and more so than that of the others. They came in two processions, closely hugging the walls of the street which is very broad, fine, and straight, so that from one end of it the other end may be seen, and two-thirds of a league ("legua") in length, with very good buildings on both sides, dwellings as well as temples. And the said Muteczuma went in the middle of the street with two chiefs, one to his right and the other to his left. One of these was the same one who, as I said, had come to speak to me in the litter, and the other was the said Muteczuma's brother, lord of that city of Iztapalapa which I had left that day. All three were dressed alike, except Muteczuma who wore soles to his feet, whereas the other two chiefs had none and supported him by his arms. . . . ."

</td><td>

" When we reached the place where another pathway (dyke) branched off to Cuyoacan. . . . . . . many principals and caciques came, covered with very rich mantles, with ornaments and liveries, those of one cacique different from those of another, and the dykes were filled by them.   These great caciques were sent by the great Montezuma ahead to receive us, and as they arrived before Cortés they bid us welcome, touching the ground and kissing it in token thereof." "Thus we were detained a good while, and from there the Cacamacan, chief of Tezcuco, and the chief of Iztapalapa, and the chief of Tacuba and the chief of Cuyoacan went forward to meet the great Montezuma who approached in a rich litter, accompanied by other great Lords and caciques holding vassals.   And when we neared Mexico, where there were other small towers, the great Montezuma descended from his litter, and these great caciques took hold of his arms, advancing with him under a marvellously rich canopy of green plumes with large golden ornaments, much silver, and pearls and stones of " Chalchihuis " suspended from it as fringes, and very dazzling to the eye. The great Montezuma was very richly dressed after their custom, with cotaras on his feet (as they are called), with golden soles and much jewelry over them.   The four lords who came with him were also richly dressed, though not in the same manner as when they had come out to receive us,— as if they changed dress on purpose under way.   Besides these Lords, there came other great caciques who bore the canopy over their heads, and other many Lords preceded the great Montezuma sweeping the ground before him and placing ropes for him to step upon.   None of these Lords ventured to look him in the face, but all had their eyes cast down, except those of his relatives and nephews who supported him by the arms.

</td></tr>
</table>

him with downcast eyes was not so much a mark of particular
respect, as a thoroughly Indian habit of shy suspicion, common

A third eye-witness, *Andrés de Tápia* ("*Relacion*," etc., Col. de Doc's, II, p. 579),
simply says: "The said Muteczuma went in the middle of the street, and all the rest
of the people were along the walls, close to them, as such is their custom."

The version of Bernal Diez is corroborated by *Oviedo* ("*Hist. general*," etc., Lib.
XXXIII, cap. XLV, p. 500), from information derived by him of "some knights and
soldiers who had taken part in the conquest of New Spain" (Title of Chapter XLV, p.
494). But the old chronicler does not give the names of his informants.

The same question recurs here, which we have already discussed in regard to the
fights with the Tlaxcalteca ("*Art of War*," p. 155, note 205), and here again we reach
the same conclusion namely: that Bernal Diez de Castillo, "bent upon recollecting
personal incidents, and, from his subaltern position" less able to see closely, in this
instance, magnifies the importance of the action beyond the limits of truth.

It is easily noticed, how much more sober, and therefore less pompous, are the
statements of the Spanish commander and of his lieutenant, than those of the common
soldiers, including Oviedo's anonymous informants. And it should be remembered
that Cortés, who was the chief actor in the scene, certainly saw *more* of it and saw it
far better than any of the others. Furthermore, at the time he wrote his report (the 30 of
October, 1520, or only about one year after the date of the occurrence), Cortés had
personal and political motives to magnify and embellish the picture. If his statements,
therefore, fall far below those of his troopers in thrilling and highly colored details,
there is every reason to believe that they are the more reliable and trustworthy.

Referring, therefore, to the description by Cortés, we find, on the whole, nothing but
a barbarous display common to other Indian celebrations of a similar character.
Of the Mexicans themselves, a number of such receptions are related by aboriginal
authors. I particularly refer to *Tezozomoc*,("*Crónica*," etc., Cap. XXVII, pp. 41 and 42).
Upon the return of the Mexicans from their successful raid on Tecamachalco and
Tepeaca: "the Mexicans were received in triumph, with horns, trumpets (?), flowers,
and frankincense. The old men of the tribe, carrying censers and roses, stood in two
rows on each side of the way, their hair tied on the back of their heads with strips of
red leather, called cuauhtlalpiloni, with shields in their hands, rods — cuauhtopilli,—
and rattles, in token of old age and of being fathers to such braves. Between them
the Mexican troop had to pass,— and these are called cuacuacuiltzin,— taking in the
middle the captains, and the prisoners which they had brought from the four pueblos;"
also (Cap. XXIX), though it is less explicit, about the return from the foray against the
Huaxtecas; (Cap. XXXVIII p. 62), speaking of the return from the foray against
Huaxaca: "Then Moctezuma commanded to all the old men and to the principal Mexicans to go out and receive the returning warriors with much mirth and joy. They met
them in the road, and greeted them, incensing them with much copal, which is like
unto myrrh, and a mark of great honor, token of triumph in war;" (Cap. XLIX, p.
79): "At Mazatzintamalco (which has since become garden of the Marquis del Valle),
the old men, Cuauhuehueques, and the Mexican council were arrayed in line to receive
him, each one with his calabash-rattle, and armed with shields and macanas, wearing
ichcahuipiles, and with the hair tied up on the back of the head with straps of red
leather. Along the road there were, at intervals, bowers and huts decked with roses,
and the old men joined the procession which moved into Mexico-Tenuchtitlan, directly
up to the temple of Huitzilopochtli." This was when "Face in the Water" returned
from the raid against the Matlatzincas;—(Cap. LII, p. 85) when the same "chief
of men" returned, beaten and defeated by the Tarasca of Michhuacan, the same
reception was made to him, only with groans, and wails of grief and mourning; also
(Cap. LVIII, p. 96, Cap. LXII, p. 104, etc., etc.). It follows from the above that the
reception of Cortés and whatever barbarous display attended it, was strictly according
to established custom. Similar receptions were made to trading companies returning
with particular success. *Sahagun* (Lib. IX, cap. II, p. 339). "They went in procession like two files, one of priests and the other of chiefs, and they met them in

even now to much ruder tribes ;[250] and the ornaments and peculiar garments, like the head-dress so very appropriately designated by the Spaniards as a "half-mitre," and other articles already described by us on a former occasion were not worn by him alone, as the "Cihuacohuatl" enjoyed the same privilege.[251] This, and the burial-rites to which we cannot, here, refer in detail,[252]

the pueblo of Acachinanco," to the south of Mexico, in the direction of San Antonio Abad, says *Bustamante* (note a). This was while "Water-Rat" was "chief of men." That the "chief of men" moved alone, or with a small escort only, in the middle of the street, is very natural. He was the head of the official household and the chief war-captain of the confederacy. His particular duty it was, therefore, to greet the strangers. On any ordinary occasion it would have been misplaced, and against all rules of Indian etiquette, for the chief-officers of a tribe to go out to meet them; but in this case, wavering between fear and curiosity, an exception was made. It is worthy of remark that even when the "chief of men" returned at the head of a victorious war-party, the "snake-woman" is not mentioned as sallying forth to greet him in person.

[250] This custom of addressing people to whom some deference is due, has been noticed among numerous tribes of America. Among the Mexicans it was not at all an exclusive mark of deference towards the chief-officer. His interlocutors did not ook at *him*, neither did he look at *them*. See *Bernal Diez* (Cap. XCI, p. 86, Vedia II), *Clavigero* (Lib. VII, cap. XI, p. 473). The latter is particularly important, although he but copies *Torquemada* (Lib. XIV, cap. I, p. 535) in the main. As far as other tribes are concerned, I but recall here the Peruvian "Inca." See *Francisco de Jerez* ("*Verdadera Relacion de la Conquista del Perú y Provincia del Cuzco llamada la Nueva Castilla*," etc., etc., in Vedia, Vol. II, p. 331), when Hernando Pizarro met Atahuallpa for the first time: "los ojos puestos en tierra, sin los alzar á mirar á ninguna parte." Of the Indians of the gulf states of North America, it is said by *James Adair* ("*History of the American Indians*," p. 4): "They are timorous, and consequently cautious, ... exceedingly modest in their behaviour." See also on the Northern Indians, *Loskiel* ("*Geschichte der Mission der evangelischen Brüder*," Barby 1789, pp. 17 and 18). It would be superfluous to add further quotations.

[251] *Durán* (Cap. XXVI, p. 215, cap. XLIV, p. 357). *Tezozomoc* (Cap. XXXVI, p. 57, cap. LXIX, p. 115. etc.). *Durán* (Lámina 8, Trat 1°).

[252] That the burial of the "Cihuacohuatl" took place after the same manner as that of the "Tlaca-tecuhtli," is proven by the "*Codice Ramirez*" (p. 67): "Hiziéronse obsequias solemnísimas y un enterramiento mas sumptuoso que el de los Reyes pasados, porque todos lo tenian por el amparo, y muro fuerte del gran imperio Mexicano." *Durán* (Cap. XLVIII, pp. 381 and 382): "el qual despues de muerto, su cuerpo fué quemado y sus ceniças enterradas junto á los sepulcros de los Reyes, haciéndole las osequias conforme á persona tal se deuian, de la mesma manera que á los reyes se hacian y sus grandeças pedian." *Acosta* (Lib. VII, cap. XVIII, p. 496): "le hicieron exequias los Mexicanos, con mas aparato y demostracion que á ninguno de los Reyes auian hecho."

In connection with the burial rites it may be in place, here, to refer to a custom easily interpreted in favor of the assumption, that the "Tlaca-tecuhtli" was a monarch. It is the carving, in the live rock at Chapultepec near Mexico, of human shapes commemorative (or at least said to be) of each of these officers, towards the close of each one's lifetime. There can be no doubt as to the existence of such carvings. The last of hem, representing "Wrathy chief," was seen by *Don Antonio de Leon y Gama* ("*Descripcion Histórica y Cronológica de las dos Piedras que con ocasion del Nuevo Empedrado que se esta formando en la Plaza principal de Mexico, se hallaron en ella el Año de 1790*," Segunda Edicion; 1832, Parte Segunda, pp. 80 and 81), as late as 1753 or 1754, when it was destroyed ("picada") by order of the authorities. Another figure, intended for

again establishes the equality in rank of both officers, and it also dispels the notions of royal etiquette and magnificence with which, more particularly, the figure of " Wrathy chief" (Montezuma) has been surrounded in history.

The " chief of men" as head of the official household needed many assistants and subordinates. He required stewards for the care of the stores and their daily apportionment.[253] Especially did he need runners for the delivery of his messages. Such officers could be chosen by him and thus far, but no farther, did he enjoy the right of appointing subordinates.[254] But the appointment to a certain duty by the " chief of men," did not confer any hereditary rank or office. On the contrary, it is even probable that most of these posts were filled by outcasts, since this was, properly, the group from which the inferior servants for the transaction of tribal business could be selected without disturbing the balance of power between the kins.

The " Tecpan " being, as we have already stated, the " house of the community," that is the place where the business of the entire social cluster (as far as the tribe could represent it) was transacted, and, furthermore, it being proven that the same " tecpan"

"Face in the Water." existed a few years previous to that date. According to *Señor Don J. F. Ramirez* ("*Durán.*" p. 251, note 1 to Cap. XXXI), disfigured remnants, among which the sign "1 cane" (ce-acatl) is plainly visible, can yet be noticed in the rock at Chapultepec on the eastern side of that celebrated hill or isolated bluff.

Now it is equally certain, that such carvings were not only commemorative of the "Tlaca-Tecuhtli," but *also* of the "Cihuacohuatl." See *Durán* (Cap. XXXI, pp. 250, 251). A somewhat different version, is given by *Tezozomoc* ("*Crónica.*" Cap. XL, p. 65). It is remarkable, however, that comparatively little importance was attached to those funeral monuments. The place of Chapultepec itself, a very striking and conspicuous object and one with which many reminiscences were connected, was viewed as an object of "medicine." *Torquemada* (Lib. III, cap. XXVI, p. 303). That particular attention should be paid to the remains of an officer of high rank is very natural. It is found among the Iroquois, *L. H. Morgan* ("*Ancient Society.*" Part II, Cap. III, pp. 95 and 96, also, "*American aboriginal Architecture*" in *Johnson's Cyclopedia*). It would be useless to dwell further on the subject since it will be fully treated of in one of my subsequent monographs.

[253] It is not devoid of interest to notice, that this official household, in full "blast," appears only after the formation of the confederacy. *Codice Ramirez* (p. 65): " Puso assí mismo este Rey por consejo y industria del sabio Tlacaellel en muy gran concierto su casa y corte, poniendo oficiales que le servian de mayordomos. masetrsalas. porteros, coperos, pajes y lacayos. los quales eran sin número. . . . . ." This is not only confirmed by *Durán* (Cap. XXVI). *Tezozomoc* (Cap. XXXV and XXXVI), but even by *Torquemada* (Lib. II, cap. LIV, p. 169).

[254] This can easily be inferred from the fact, already established, that all the other kinds of officers of anything like important rank, were *elected* and not appointed. See also the passage, already quoted elsewhere, of *Durán* (Cap. LXIV, p. 498), which is very interesting in a general way.

was also the regular seat and place of office of the highest authority or " tribal council," it follows that peculiar and distinct relations must have existed between that council and the officer, whose duty it was to dwell at this same house. These relations are explained to us, partly, by the statement that the " chief of men" was placed there as a watchman, to guard tribal Interests in the midst of confederate business.[255] He was to be present, day and night, at this abode which was the centre wherein converged the threads of information brought by traders, gatherers of tribute, scouts and spies, as well as of all messages sent to, or received from neighboring, friendly or hostile tribes. Every such message came directly to the "chief of men," whose duty it was, before acting, to transmit its import to the "Cihuacohuatl," and through him to call together the "Tlatocan.[256] Thus the "chief of men" occupied an intermediate position between the confederacy and the tribe. He might, ex-officio be present at the deliberations of the council, but that presence was not obligatory ; and no decisive or commanding voice and vote was allowed him, beyond the weight that his reasoning and personal consideration for his merits and experience might carry.

Whenever any conclusion was reached, it became the " chief of men's" duty to provide for its execution. Thus, if traders returned illtreated, beaten, and bruised, and the Mexican council clamored for revenge, he sent his runners to the confederate tribes, calling upon them for assistance, as the contract authorized the Mexicans to do. Sometimes these messengers were chiefs, selected by the council itself.[257] The result of their mission was reported

[255] An attentive perusal of *Sahagun* (Lib. VI. cap. X) will convince the reader of the truth of this statement. See also *Durán* (Cap. XLI, p. 328; cap. LII, pp. 414 and 415) and *Tezozomoc* (Cap. LVI. p. 92; cap. LXI. pp. 100 and 101; cap. LXXXII, p. 144).

[256] *Durán* (Cap. XII. p. 109): " Vuelto á Tlacaellel, le mandó avisase á los de su consejo que ablasen. . . ." also (Cap. XVI, pp. 132, 134 and 138; cap. XXI, p. 182; cap. XL, p. 316; cap. XLI, p. 330; cap. LIII, p. 419, etc., etc.). " *Codice Ramirez*," (p. 66). *Tezozomoc* (Cap. XXI, p. 33; cap. XXXVIII, p. 60; cap. XL, p. 65; cap. XLII, p. 69; cap. LVII, p. 93; cap. LXVIII, p. 114, etc.). Besides, it must be inferred from the fact, already proven, that the " Cihuacohuatl" was the "foreman" of the council. In this capacity, it was to him that the "chief of men " had to communicate all business to be submitted to the council.

[257] Instances of that kind are found profusely noticed in the specifically Mexican chronicles. Extensive quotations would become too lengthy, I therefore limit myself to mere indications, leaving the reader to consult the authors in question. *Tezozomoc* (*Crónica,*" Cap. XXVII, p. 40, cap. XXVIII, p. 42, cap. XXXI, pp. 48 and 49, cap. XXXIV, p. 54, cap. XXXVII, p. 59, cap. LXXV, pp. 127 and 128, cap. LXXXVIII, p. 154, cap. LXXXIX. and XC, pp. 157 and 158). *Durán* (Cap. XVIII, pp. 156 and 157, cap. XIX, pp. 165 and 166, cap, XXI, p. 182, cap. XXII, p. 180, cap. XXIV, p. 201, etc., etc)

back to the " chief of men." [258] In case delegates arrived from other tribes, they had to be provided with lodgings. The " tecpan " was the place reserved for that purpose, and there they were accordingly quartered. They, consequently, first came into contact with the " chief of men," who was, officially, " mine host " for them, and who acted as inter.nediate between them and the supreme tribal authorities.[259]

No more striking illustrations of the foregoing can be found than the reception, by the Mexicans, of Cortés and his troops, at the pueblo of Tenuchtitlan. The house where the Spaniards were quartered was the " tecpan " or official house of the tribe, vacated by the official household for that purpose.[260] In sallying forth to

In addition to these authorities I add in a general way, *Torquemada* (Lib. XIV, cap. II, p. 537). This author has evidently either copied from, or at least used the same sources as *Fray Géronimo de Mendieta* (Lib. II, cap. XXVI, p. 129). My learned and highly esteemed friend, Sr. Icazbalceta, ascribes to the statements of both authors " a common origin " i. e. " Tabla de Correspondencias." (p 38). This common source, however, is found in *Zurita* (" *Rapport*," etc., pp. 118 and 119). From whom he, in turn, derived his information, has not as yet been ascertained.

[258] See the authors quoted above. Also *Clarigero* (Lib. VII, cap. XXV, p. 502).

[259] This follows from the facts already proven in regard to the duties of the " chief of men " as head of the official household. I would particularly refer to *Tezozomoc* (" *Crónica*," Cap. XCVII, pp. 172 and 173).

[260] " *Codice Ramirez* " (p. 87): " y con esto el gran Motecuczuma, por el mismo órden que vino se volvió con el capitan Don Hernando Cortés, al qual y á los suyos mandó que aposentassen en las casas reales, donde se les dió muy buen recaudo á cada uno, segun las calidades de las diversas gentes que iban con el capitan . . . . El dia siguiente el capitan Don Hernando Cortés hizo juntar á Motecuczuma, etc.. etc. . . . . en una pieza que en la casa habia muy á propósito para esto." . . . . ; (p. 88): " Porque acabada de hazer esta plática el buen capitan Don Hernando Cortés, los' soldados saquearon las casas reales, y las demas principales donde sentian que habia riquezas . . . . En este tiempo recelándose el Marquis no resultasse desto algun inconveniente prendió al gran Rey Motecuczuma, poniéndole con grillos, y á buen recaudo en las casas reales junto á su mismo aposento . . . . ;" (p. 89): " comenzaron á pelear con los españoles con tal furia que los hizieron retraer á las casas reales donde estaban aposentados." This is plain enough. It is commonly stated that the Spaniards were quartered at a great house belonging formerly to " Wrathy Chief's " father, " Face in the Water." The anonymous " *Fragmento No. 2* " (p. 139) has the following: " apartando la gente hasta que llegaron al palacio Real que habia sido de su padre de Motecuzuma Axayacatzin, y entrando en una gran sala en donde tenia Motecuzuma su estado, se sentó y á su derecha mano á Cortés, y hizo señas Cacama que se apartasen todos y diesen órden en aposentar los cristianos y amigos que traian en aquellos grandes palacios . . . . ." This anonymous fragment is evidently of Tezcucan origin. *Sahagun* (Lib. XII. cap. XVI, p. 24): " Luego D. Hernando Cortés tomó por la mano á Mocthecuzuma, y se fueron ambos juntos á la par para las casas reales;" (cap. XVII, p. 25): " De que los Españoles llegaron á las casas reales con Mocthecuzoma, luego le detuvieron consigo;" (Cap. XXI, p. 28): " Como comenzó la guerra entre los Indios y las Españoles, estos se fortalecieron én las casas reales con el mismo Mocthecuzoma . . . . ." (Id. p. 29, Cap. XXIII, p. 31. etc., etc.). These statements are very positive, and the less suspicious, since they represent traditions from three different sources, all evidently furnished by eye-witnesses, namely: *Mexican* (" Cod. Ramirez"),

greet the newcomers at the dyke, "Wrathy chief" acted simply, as
the representative of the tribal hospitality, extending unusual

Tezcucan (Fragment No. 2) and *Tlatilulcan* (Sahagun). The statements by Spanish eye-witnesses are of doubtful authority in this case, since none of them knew, or could know anything positive; and the pueblo was subsequently, so utterly destroyed that even its site could hardly be recognized. Nevertheless, the "old and new palaces of Montezuma" have become household words.

It is, nevertheless, interesting to compare the reports of eye-witnesses with the above quotations from aboriginal sources. *Cortés* ("*Carta Segunda*," Vedia I, (p. 25): "y tornó á seguir por ó la calle en la forma ya dicha, fasta llegar á una muy grande y hermosa casa, que él tenia para nos aposentar, bien aderezada." The house where "Wrathy Chief" staid with his household, appears to have been some distance from the Spanish quarters, since we read (p. 27): "dejando buen recaudo en las encrucijadas de las calles"—thus showing that crossings intervened. The following, however, is very plain, if not decisive ("*Carta Tercera*," p. 76): "E porque lo sintiesen mas, este dia fice poner fuego á estas casas grandes de la plaza, donde la otra vez que nos echaron de la ciudad, los españoles y yo estábamos aposentados; que eran tan grandes, que un principe con mas de seiscientas personas de su casa y servicio se podian aposentar en ellas; y otras que estaban junto á ellas, que aunque algo menores eran muy mas frescas y gentiles, y tenia en ellas Muteczuma todos los linajes de aves que en estas partes habia." This remark about the "principe con mas de seiscientas personas de su casa y servicio" evidently agrees with his previous statement concerning the household of "Wrathy Chief" ("*Carta Segunda*," p. 35): "La manera de su servicio era que todos los dias luego en amaneciendo eran en su casa de seisciento. señores y personas principales, los cuales se sentaban . . . . . . Y los servidores destos, y personas de quien se acompañaban henchian dos ó tres grandes patios, y la calle . . . ." Consequently, Cortés himself plainly confirms the native authors above quoted. *Andrés de Tápia* ("*Relacion*," etc., p. 579): "é hizo aposentar al marqués en un patio donde era la recámara de los idolos, é en este patio habie salas asaz grandes donde cupieron toda la gente del dicho marqués é muchos indios de los de Tascala é Churula que se habien llegado á los españoles para los servir." This eye-witness, therefore, does not mention either of the two "houses of Montezuma." The father of the tale is found in *Bernal Diez de Castillo* (Vedia II, Cap. LXXXVIII. p. 84): "E volvamos á nuestra entrada en México, que nos llevaron á aposentar á unas grandes casas, donde habia aposentos para todos nosotros, que habian sido de su padre del gran Montezuma, que se decia Axayaca, adonde en aquella sazon tenia el gran Montezuma sus grandes adoratorios de Idolos . . . . ."

Thus Cortés, who is the principal eye-witness in the case, unmistakably states that the Spaniards were quartered at the "tecpan." Of the other two conquerors, only the last mentions the Spanish quarters as being the "house of Montezuma's father," whereas Tápia is silent on the subject. Taken in connection with the assertions of the native writers, the statements of Cortés become of great weight.

It is but natural to expect (and the fact needs no proof) that the subsequent writers have followed either one or the other of the two versions. After having transcribed the letters of Cortés, *Oviedo* (Lib. XXXIII, cap. XLV, p. 500) mentions also: "apossentó aél é á los chripstianos, en unas casas que avian seydo de su padre," which statement he gathers from other conquerors (p. 494) whose names he fails to give; (Cap. XLVII, p. 507) he calls the said house "la morada de su abuelo." I forbear further abstracts.

Fortunately an official document of early date informs us of the exact situation of these two buildings. It is the "*Merced á Hernan Cortés de Tierras inmediatas á México, y Solares en la Ciudad*" (Col. de Doc's Icazbalceta, Vol. II, pp. 28 and 29). It bears date, Barcelona, 23 July, 1529, and conveys to Cortés: "los solares é casas son la casa nueva que era de Montezuma, que alinda por la una parte con la plaza mayor é la calle de Iztapalapa, é por la otra la calle de Pero Gonzalez de Truxillo, é de Martin, López, carpintero; è por la otra la calle en donde están las casas de Juan Rodriguez albañil; é por la otra la calle pública que pasa por las espaldas: è la casa vieja que era

courtesies to unusual, mysterious, and therefore dreaded guests. Leaving these in possession of the " tecpan," he retired to another of the large communal buildings surrounding the central square, where the official business was, meanwhile, transacted.[261] His return to the Spanish quarters, even if compulsory, had less in it to strike the natives than is commonly believed. It was a re-installation in old quarters, and therefore the " Tlatocan," itself, felt no hesitancy in meeting there again, until the real nature of the dangerous visitors was ascertained, when the council gradually withdrew from the snare, leaving the unfortunate " chief of men " in Spanish hands.[262]

We have qualified the position of the " Tlacatecuhtli " towards the council as intermediate between tribe and confederacy. In the latter body, he was but the general-in-chief and had no other duties or power.[263] Therefore, when Cortés seized the head-chief of Tezcuco, " Wrathy chief " had no authorlty to assure the Spaniards, although they called upon him for that purpose.[264] He ex-

de Montezuma, donde vivís, que alinda por la frontera con la plaza mayor é solares de la iglesia, y la placeta; por un lado la calle nueva de Tacuba, é por otro la calle que va de la plaza mayor ã S. Francisco; por las espaldas la calle donde están las casas de Rodrigo Rangel, é de Pero Sanchez Farfán, é de Francisco de Terrazas, è de Zamudio."

From these data it is easy to recognize in the present National Palace the site of the so-called " new houses of Montezuma," and in the buildings facing the " Empedradillo " the " Old houses." Both faced the central square of the pueblo.

The so-called " old houses " were also immediately in front of the central " house of God." It is said by Tezozomoc (Cap. LXX, p. 117): " Este templo y cerro estaba puesto adonde fueron las casas de Alonzo de Avila y Don Luis de Castilla, hasta las casas de Antonio de la Mota, en cuadro." Now according to *Icazbalceta* (" Los tres Diálogos," etc , notes to Sec'd Dialogue, p. 218): " La casa de Alonzo de Àvila estaba en la la calle del Reloj, esquina ã la de Sta Teresa la Antigua." Consequently the " old houses " were indeed those which Bernal Diez mentions as " where Montezuma at that time had his great adoratories." Now these " old houses " were, as we have seen, the " tecpan " or official house of the Mexican tribe. This again fully sustains our proposition that the Spaniards were quartered there, and that the official household had vacated it for that purpose.

[261] This fully explains the designation by, " New houses of Montezuma " mentioned in the preceding note.

[262] That the council met at the Spanish quarters, is plainly stated by *Bernal Diez de Castillo* (Cap. XCV, pp. 95 and 96, Cap. XCVII, p. 98). *Oriedo* (Lib. XXXIII, cap. XLVII, p. 509). That the members of the council gradually withdrew, is equally certain, from the fact that a successor to " Wrathy Chief " was elected, while the latter was still alive and a captive of the Spaniards.

[263] *Durán* (Cap. XLIII, p. 347). *Zurita* (" *Rapport*," etc., p. 11): " Le souverain de Mexico avait au dessous de lui ceux de Tacuba et de Tezcuco pour les affaires qui avaient rapport ã la guerre; quant ã toutes les autres, leurs puissances étaient égales, de sorte que l'un d'eux ne se mělait jamais du gouvernement des autres;" Id. (pp. 93 and 95). *Mendieta* (Lib. II, cap. XXXVII, p. 156). *Herrera* (Dec. III, lib. IV, cap. XV, p. 133). The two latter authors evidently have followed Zurita. See also note 4.

[264] See note 4. *Fragmento No.* 2, in " *Biblioteca Mexicana* " (pp. 142 and 143).

ercised no command over the other tribes except in the field. Still, his position, as confederate leader, was important enough to make the right to invest him with that dignity one of the conditions of the agreement under which the confederacy was formed. Hence the two head-chiefs of Tezcuco and Tlacopan are frequently mentioned as " electors " of the " chief of men." But their presence at the inauguration of every new officer of that rank did not imply the right to control his election.[265] It was a mere act of courtesy which the Mexicans returned, as often as their associates performed the same ceremony,[266] with this difference, however, that in the case of the Mexican chieftain, the two confederates appeared personally as being thereafter his military subordinates.

The military organization of the ancient Mexicans has already been described elsewhere,[267] and, so far, we have nothing to add to that picture. In it, as well as in social organization, the kin formed the basis, and since we have found, in the autonomous kin, that the military chieftains were the officers of justice, we are justified in looking for the officers of *tribal* justice among the chiefs of highest grade in the tribal forces. The " Cihuacohuatl" as ex-officio war-chief of the tribe could not, as we have already seen, officiate in that capacity ; but the " chief of men" was very distinctly clothed with the power to punish, even to such an extent as to impart to it the character of arbitrariness and despotism. If, however, we examine closely the instances reported, they appear to limit themselves : —

1. To cases of insubordination, unfaithfulness, or treachery within the official household :[268]

---

[265] " *Tenure of Lands* " (p. 417). *Zurita* (" *Rapport*," etc., p. 15): " Si le souverain de Mexico mourait sans héritier, les principaux chefs lui choisissaient un successeur dont l'élection était confirmée par les chefs supérieurs de Tezcoco et Tacuba." " *Codice Ramirez*" (pp. 66, 67 and 72). The chiefs, of Tezcuco and Tlacopan, are mentioned as " electors," but stress is placed only on the fact, that they " *crowned* the King." This evidently means investiture only. *Sahagun* (Lib. VIII, cap, XXX, XXXI, XXXII, XXXIII and XXXIV). Although very full of details, he plainly avoids mentioning the chiefs of Tezcuco and Tlacopan as taking part in the election (p. 318). *Durán* (Cap. XXXII. p. 255, XXXIX, pp. 302 and 303. Cap. XLI, p. 325).

[266] *Zurita* (p. 16). *Gomara* (" *Conquista de México*," Vedia I, p. 435). *Tezozomoc* (Cap. CI, p. 179).

[267] "*Art of War and Mode of Warfare of the Ancient Mexicans*," 10th Report Peabody Museum, 1877.

[268] Therefore the recommendation, by the " Cihuacohuatl," to the newly appointed servants and runners in the official household: " and behold that, where you enter, there are many valuable women, and also slaves, watch that you do not go astray, for at once you will be destroyed without the knowledge of any living soul . . . . ." *Tezozomoc* (Cap. LXXXIII, p. 146). It is evident that the " chief of men" had, in such

2. To cases of military insubordination, or treachery :[269]

3. To instances of great importance, demanding sudden action in order to avoid public danger.[270]

cases, the right of summary punishment, as well as in the case of unfaithful stewards or disobedient subordinates in general. Compare, on the same subject, *Durán* (Cap. LIII, pp. 419 and 420). The fact, that the "Cihuacohuatl" spoke to the young men, further shows that the exercise of such extreme power was known to, and sanctioned by, the council.

[269] Quotations are useless, the necessity for such a power being too plain. But it is well, here, to state that among much ruder tribes even, and where the democratic element was carried to its greatest extremes, arbitrary punishment by war-captains sometimes occurred. Thus it is asserted that, at the bloody engagement of Point Pleasant, Va., 10 of October, 1774, "Cornstalk," the great Shawnee war-chief, tomahawked one near him who had "by trepidation and reluctance to proceed to the charge, evinced a dastardly disposition." *Alex S. Withers* ("*Chronicles of Border Warfare*," Chap. VII, p. 129). It explains also the summary punishment of traitors and deserters, as well as of those who assumed the dress of the prominent war-chiefs during a raid or an engagement.

[270] The incarceration of runners or messengers may be (and has been to me in conversation by an aged friend) brought up in proof of the belief, that the "chief of men" had a despotic power. Instances of that kind are related by *Tezozomoc* (Cap. CVI, p. 189). This is the truly admirable description of the first news brought to México of the approach of European ships. It is too lengthy to be inserted here. A runner from the coast carried the news, and "Wrathy Chief" said to Petlacalcatl, take him to the cell made of logs (probably split logs, "tablon") and look after him. This was done to keep the news secret until the matter could be investigated, and was, therefore, a preliminary measure of policy. But, aside from the fact that the isolation rather than incarceration (since the latter would have been death) of a news-carrier was a matter of policy, and as such a *duty* of the "chief of men," it was also an established custom among the Mexicans. This is stated by *Sahagun* (Lib. VIII, cap. XXXVII, pp. 327 and 328): "Habiendo cautivado á alguno, luego los mensageros que se llamaban tequipantitlanti, venian á dar las nuevas al rey de aquellos que habian cautivado á sus enemigos, y de la victoria que habian obtenido los de su parte . . . . y el señor los respondia diciéndoles: "Seais muy bien venidos, huélgome de oír esas nuevas, sentad y esperad, porque me quiero certificar mas de ellas, y asi los mandaba guardar, y si hallaba que aquellas nuevas eran mentirosas, hacialos matar." *Torquemada* (Lib. XIV, cap. I, p. 536): "y que no le dejasen salir de Palacio hasta tener segundo Correo, que confirmase aquella buena nueva, que él havia traido. *Vetancurt* ("*Teatro*," Parte IIa, Trat. II°, cap. II, p. 381), almost a textual copy of the preceding author, as might be expected.

Among the many tales of prodigies, supernatural warnings, witchcraft, etc., etc., connected with the months and years immediately preceding the arrival of the Spaniards in Mexico, there is, also, one bearing a particularly pure Indian character. See *Durán* (Cap. LXVIII, pp. 524–530). *Tezozomoc* (Cap. CVI, p. 188 and 189). "Wrathy Chief," alarmed by mysterious prognostics, called upon all the old men, women, and the medicine-men, to report what they *might dream* or *had dreamt* within a certain lapse of time. It is well known what high value is attached by the Indians in general to *dreams*. There can be no doubt that, with the prevailing notion that dreams contained important and solemn premonitions, warnings from a higher source (*Sahagun* Lib. V), the request to communicate such dreams for the benefit of the tribe, to the "chief of men," was very natural. According to *Motolinia* ("*Hist. de los Indios de la Nueva-España*," Col. de Doc., Trat. II, cap. VIII, p. 130), certain men were particularly expert in explaining and interpreting dreams, so much so, that they were generally applied to for such purposes. If now, as the story in question has it, the said people refused to comply with such requests, the "chief of men" might, of his own accord

The power to appoint, which the " chief of men " enjoyed within the limits of the official household, implied, to the same extent, the power to remove and to punish. It was not even necessary to refer such cases to the action of the council.

In punishing summarily acts of insubordination, or of treachery, when committed during warfare, the " chief of men " acted as commander-in-chief and in strict compliance with the duties of that office.

Lastly, a certain amount of discretionary power was necessarily vested in the chief commander for the public good. Placed at the " tecpan " to " watch, guard and protect " the tribe and the confederacy, it was necessary to empower the " Tlacatecuhtlli " in cases of great urgency, to act " on the spur of the moment." It was not a privilege of royalty or a despotic right, but an obligation resulting from the nature of the office.

Consequently the " chief of men " was not, properly, the executioner of tribal justice either. This duty devolved upon other war-chiefs of lower rank, who, although superior in command to the leaders of the kins, when on the war-path, never otherwise interfered with the duties of the latter, any more than tribal jurisdiction conflicted with that of the autonomous kins. These chiefs were the " four leaders of the four great quarters of Mexico Tenuchtitlan," [271] or, as we have already intimated, of the four *phratries* into which the twenty kins had again agglomerated for religious and military purposes. These four " great quarters," named respectively, " Moyotlan," " Teopan," " Aztacalco " and " Cuepopan," [272] were not, as the current notion has it, so many governmental subsections, or wards of aboriginal Mexico. Shells

even treat them as traitors, and secure their persons to prevent injury to the public cause. All this, of course, provided the story be true!

The cases where secrecy is enjoined under penalty of death, are so plain that no illustration is needed. The " chief of men " had the right, in preparing general business, to give secret orders, to detail particular persons on secret missions. Anyone divulging the secrets entrusted to him, committed an act of treason, and therefore it was necessary that he should be chastised on the spot and on the spur of the moment, to obviate further mischief.

[271] *Art of War* (pp. 120, 121 and 122, especially notes 97, 99 and 101).

[272] The formation of these geographical circumscriptions I have already explained. The names can, in part, be etymologized. They are respectively: " Moyotlan " or place of the mosquito, from " moyotl," mosquito (*Molina* II. p. 58); " Teopan " or place of God, from " Teotl," God; "Aztacalco," "place of the house of the heron," from "Aztatl," heron (*Molina* I, p. 65 and II, p. 10), and " calli," house; "Cuepopan " or " place of the dyke," from " cuepotli," dyke (*Molina* I, p. 23, II, p. 26). All of which are, respectfully, submitted.

of as many original kins, common worship, perhaps, and common leadership in battle, were all that remained of the former organic cluster.[273] Rites of worship, as practised by a phratry, it is not the place here to investigate, and the position and functions of the phratry in warfare have already been discussed by us. The office of tribal executioners of justice, however, vested in the "four leaders" of the four phratries, deserves particular attention here.

The names of the four war-captains or rather their official titles, are: "man of the house of darts" (Tlacochcalcatl), "cutter of men" (Tlacatecatl), "bloodshedder" (Ezhuahuacatl), and "chief of the Eagle and prickly pear" (Cuauhnochtecuhtli). These officers are first noticed in the begnning of the fifteenth century, at the time the confederacy was formed.[274] They appear as immediate adjuncts or assistants — military lieutenants as it were — to the "chief of men" then promoted to the position of confederate commander, as well as of the "Cihuacohuatl."[275] Their

[273] These four geographical clusters, each comprising a certain number of original kins or calpulli, became known subsequently as the four Indian wards of Mexico, named respectively, San Juan (Moyotlan), San Pablo (Teopan), San Sebastian (Aztacalco), Santa Maria (Cuepopan). *Tezozomoc* (Cap. LIX, p. 98), *Vetancurt* ("*Crónica*," etc., p. 124), *Durán* (Cap. V, p. 42). That each of them comprised a certain number of kins has already been stated. The four chiefs are often mentioned as "councillors;" but their very position as immediate assistants to the "chief of men," is clearly established by the "*Codice Ramirez*" (pp. 57 and 58), which agrees with *Durán* (Cap. XI, p. 103) and also by *Sahagun* (Lib. XXX. p. 318): "Elegido el señor, luego elegian otros cuatro que eran como senadores que siempre habian de estar al lado de él, y entender en todos los negocios graves del reino," . . . This makes it evident that they must have been war-chiefs, and not representatives, in the supreme council, of an administrative circumscription superior to the "calpulli"—"barrio" or localized kindred group. The four "main quarters" therefore formed *military* bodies only, and this follows plainly from the detailed descriptions of warfare, so profusely given in the chronicles of *Tezozomoc*. The truth of this fact has been felt, though not fully understood, by *Clavigero* (Lib. VII, cap. VII, pp. 494 and 495) where he hints at the four chiefs (under various names) as so many "classes of generals." These four superior war-captains are, besides, found also in Michhuacan, "*Relacion, etc., etc., Mechuacan*" ("Primera Parte," p. 13): "tenia puesto cuatro señores muy principales en cuatro fronteras de la provincia," and in Peru, where they have been decorated with the titles of "vice-roy."

It is interesting to note here that the term "barrio" is applied by Spanish authors indiscriminately to the four great subdivisions and to the kins themselves.

[274] *Durán* (Cap. XI, pp. 97, 102 and 103), *Tezozomoc* (Cap. XV, p. 24) both place the organization by which these four chiefs appear prominent, immediately after the overthrow of the Tecpaneca, and before the confederacy with the Tezcucans and Tlacopans. *Ixtlilxochitl* ("*Hist. des Chichimèques*," Cap. XXXIV, p. 236) speaks in general terms of a "reorganization," after the confederacy had been formed. So does *Acosta* (Lib. VII, cap. XVI, p. 493), while "*Codice Ramirez*" (pp. 57 and 58) agrees with the two first.

[275] It is self-evident that these four chieftains were also inferior to the "snake-woman;" and this fact is amply illustrated. *Durán* (Cap. XVI, pp. 140 and 141) con-

office was, of course, elective and non-hereditary, and the election took place in the same manner and (sometimes, at least) at the same time as that of the " chief of men."[276] In case the latter was unable to lead the confederate forces on the war-path, and the " Cihuacohuatl" himself was not available either, then the posts of chief commander as well as of leader of the Mexicans proper, might be filled by one or the other of them.[277] This, however, was always a temporary situation, and there appears to have been no difference of rank between the four, since the Mexican

cerning "Ezhuahuacatl," Cap. XXII, p. 189): "y luego Tlacaellel, príncipe de la milicia, mandó en nombre del rey que fuesen apercibidos, etc., etc. . . ." "Llamó el rey á un señor que se llamaua Cuauhnochtli y hizolo general de toda la moltitud diciéndole que Tlacaellel era ya viejo y que no podria ya ir á guerra tan apartada, dándole todas las exenciones y autoridad que semejante oficio requeria, . . ." (Cap. XXXIV, p. 267, etc., etc.). *Tezozomoc* (Cap. XVII, p. 27), Tlacaellel, subsequently elected " Cihuacohuatl," was then only " Tlacochcalcatl," and he is, at that time, merely mentioned as "uno de ellos de los capitanes." Still (p. 28) he appears as "capitan general de ellos." (Cap. XXII, p. 34): "Respondió Tlacatleltzin y dijo: quiero dar aviso á Tlacatecatl, y á Tlacochcalcatl, para que publiquen luego en toda esta república esta guerra por los varrios, . . ." (Cap. XXVIII, p. 43): "mandaron el rey Moctezuma y Zihuacoatl, á los capitanes Tlacatecatl, Tlacochcalcatl, Cuauhnochtli, y Tilancalqui, que luego al tercer dia se apercibiesen y pusiesen en camino con sus armas y vituallas," etc., etc. This entire " Crónica" bristles with facts of that kind, too numerous to quote. The fact, amply proven heretofore, that the " Zihuacoatl" was also ex-officio head-war-chief of the tribe of Mexico, is alone sufficient to establish the inferiority of the four others. See " *Codice Ramirez*" (p. 67).

[276] In evidence of this there is the entire series of specifically Mexican authors, starting with the " *Codice Ramirez*" (p. 57): " Primeramente ordenaron que siempre se guardasse este estatuto en la corte Mexicana, y es que despues de electo Rey en ella, eligiessen quatro señores, hermanos ó parientes mas cercanos del mismo Rey, los quales tuviessen ditados de principes: los ditados que entonces dieron á estos quatro el primero fué . . . (follow the four names and titles). . . ." The same version has been adopted with more or less variation, by *Durán* (Cap. XI, pp. 102 and 103), *Tezozomoc* (Cap. XV, pp. 24 and 25), *Joseph de Acosta* (Lib. VI, cap. XXV, p. 441) and *Herrera* (Dec. III, Lib. II, cap XIX, pp. 75 and 76). Besides, there is the independent version of *Sahagun* (Lib. VIII, cap, XXX and XXXI, pp. 318 and 319), who is even too positive, stating, or at least leading to the inference, that at every election of a " chief of men," the four offices were also newly filled, and invested at the same time. This appears to be a misconception, explained by the Codice Ramirez and by Durán.

It may be in place here to refer to a different version, which reduces the number of these assistants to the " chief of men" to two only. We find it in *Gomara* (" *Conquista*," Vedia I, p. 442): " Las apelaciones iban á otros dos Jueces mayores, que llaman tecuitlato, y que siempre solian ser parientes del señor . . . ." and also in *Zurita* (" *Rapport*," etc.; p. 95). By reference, however, to *Sahagun* (Lib. VI, cap. XX), it will be seen that the celebrated Franciscan speaks of only two of the four which he mentions (Lib. VIII, cap. XXX). These two are " Tlacochcalcatl" and " Tlacatecatl" (" Tlacochtecutli" and " Tlacatecutli" by abbreviation), whom he again calls (Lib. VIII, cap. XXIV, p. 311) " principal captains, of which there were always two," while (Lib. IX, cap I, p. 336) he calls the same, " governors of Tlatilulco." The Tlatilulcan tradition appears very plainly in the writings of the learned friar, which writings have wielded such a vast influence in literature on aboriginal Mexico.

[277] " *Art of War*" (p. 122), *Sahagun* (Lib. VIII, cap. XXIV, p. 311), *Durán* (Cap. XXII, p. 189), *Clavigero* (Lib. VII, cap. XXI, p. 494).

chroniclers mention them indiscriminately as military captains of the highest rank. Still, while this fact remains undisputed, we notice among later authors that two of the four, namely: " Ezhuahuacatl " and " Tlacateccatl " are called : "judges." [278] How the duties of a judge sitting permanently, could be performed by a war-chief, is rather difficult to comprehend, whereas those of a chief executioner of judicial decisions agree well with those of a military office, in primitive society. " Cuauhnochtecuhtli " is positively stated to have been "chief executioner" ("alguazil maior") or sheriff."[279] The Codex Mendoza, however, makes all four equal, by calling each of them " executive officer." Samuel Purchas, in his "Pilgrimage," renders this incorrectly by "officer of dispatch." [280] Such was indeed their true position. What the " elder brother " was to the kin, the four great war-captains were to the tribe. To them the judicial decisions of the council were communicated through the " Cihuacohuatl " or the " Tlacatecuhtli," and *they* were intrusted with their execution. Consequently they superintended the maintenance of order and quietness at every place where the tribal authorities exercised control, as, for instance, in the markets, and in the central square encompassing the great "house of God." But they were also the immediate military assistants of the " chief of men," and as such, as far as he exercised any power to punish, they also acted as his " executive officers" when necessary.[281] It is doubtful, however, if the four leaders

---

[278] The " Tlacatecatl " is called a " Judge," second in jurisdiction only to the " Cihuacohuatl " by *Torquemada* (Lib. XI, cap. XXV, p. 352). The same author calls him a " valiant captain " (Lib. II, cap. LXXVI, p. 211). After this author, he has been called a Judge by *Vetancurt* (Parte IIa, Trat II°, cap. I, p. 370), by *Clavigero* (Lib. VII, cap. XVI, p. 481). It is singular to notice that for instance *Vetancurt* (Parte IIa, Trat. I°, cap. XVIII, p. 320) mentions that "Water-Rat" ("Ahuitzotl") was "Tlacatecatlo, captain general of the Mexicans." In this he follows *Torquemada* (Lib. II, cap. LXIII, p. 186), who, in turn, agrees with his predecessor, *Mendieta* (Lib. II, cap. XXXV and XXXVI, p. 151). The latter is particularly explicit. His statements agree with those of the *Codex Mendoza* (plates XIII and XVIII). "Ezhuahuacatl" is also represented as "alcalde" in the *Codex Mendoza* (plate LXIX, tercera Partida, No. 18), which again represents him as "executor" (plate LXVI, tercera Partida, No. 10). All this tends to show that these officers, besides being principal war-captains, were also executors of judicial decrees.

[279] *Ramirez de Fuenleal* (*Lettre*, Mexico, 3 Nov., 1532, " *Premier Recueil*," etc.. p. 248): " Un officier, nommé Guamuchil. remplit les fonctions d'alguazil mayor. . ." *Torquemada* (Lib. XI, cap. XXV, pp. 352 and 353), *Vetancurt* (Vol. I, p. 370, etc.), *Clavigero* (Lib. VII, cap. XVI, p. 481). The " *Codex Mendoza* " (plate LXVI, tercera Partida, No. 7) calls him "executor," like " Tlilancalqui " and " Ezhuahuacatl."

[280] *Codex Mendoza* (plates LXVI and LXVIII). In the latter he calls them " Valientes." For the interpretation of Purchas see *Kingsborough* (Vol. VI, pp. 73 and 74).

[281] Instances of that kind are frequently found, both in Durán and Tezozomoc.

had the right to appoint the assistants whom they needed, beyond sending out subordinates, or rather detailing them on particular errands. As to watchmen in the market-places,— the officers who circulated about preserving peace and order there — they were placed at their posts by the tribe. But it was their duty to report to the chief executive officers, nay, to apply to them for assistance, whenever anything happened which required the exercise of higher power. On the other hand, these subalterns obeyed their orders in the interests of tribal business.

We have already noticed that, among the four, " Cuauhnoch-tecuhtli" is most distinctly mentioned as judicial executioner, even prominently before the others. But this officer again is lost sight of at the election of a " chief of men." Then another looms up in his place. This is the " man of the black house," Tlilancalqui. It appears that each of the three first-named positions namely : " Tlacochcalcatl," " Tlacateccatl," " Ezhuahuacatl," was, together with the last-named " Tlilancalqui," a preparatory stage for the office of " chief of men."[282]   " One of these four had to be elected king " says the Codex Ramirez.[283]   While it is difficult to

[282] This statement rests upon the authority of the " *Codice Ramirez* " (p. 58). which document agrees almost verbally with *Durán* (Cap. XI, p. 103). Aside from *Tezozomoc* (Cap. XV) and *Acosta* (Lib. VI, cap. XXV), who both, though rather vaguely, confirm the above, there are other indications confirming it. For instance: *Codex Mendoza* (plate XI, interpretation or rather text) : " Yten el dicho Tiçoçicatzi fue por estremo valiente y velicoso en armas, y antes que subcediese en el dicho señorio, hizo por su persona en las guerras cosas hazañosas de valentia, pordonde alcanzó tomar dictado de Tlacatecatl, que tenia por titulo de gran calidad y estado, y era el punto de que en vacando dicho señorio, el tal punto y grado subcedia luego en el dicho señorio, lo qual ansimismo sus antecesores hermanos altras contenidos, y padre, y aguélo tuviéron el mismo curso de los titulos y dictado, por donde subiéron à ser señores de México." Again (plate LXVIII, tercera partida), no difference is made between " Tlacatecatl " and " Tlacochcalcatl ;" both are called " valientes " and " capitanes de los exercitos Mexicanos." *Torquemada* (Lib. II, cap. LV, p. 172): "y que Axayacatl, Hijo de Teçoçomoctli (Señor Mexicano) era Hombre Valeroso, y de mui gran fuerte, para el Reinado, fue de comun consentimiento, pasado á esta Dignidad, de la que tenia de Tlacuhcalcatl, y Capitan General, y hecho Rei." (Cap. LXIII, p. 186): "Ahuitzotl, Hermano del Difunto, y de su Antecesor Axayacatl, era Tlacatecatl, ó Capitan General de los Mexicanos. . . ." Thus he acknowledges that both Tlacatecatl and Tlacochtecatl were alike eligible. It is but natural to read similar assertions in *Vetancurt* (Parte IIa, Trat. I°, cap. XVI, p. 305, cap. XVIII, p. 320), and *Clavigero* (Lib. IV, cap. XVIII, p. 283, cap. XXII, p. 287). This author speaks of the different " chiefs of men " having been " generals in chief " of the Mexicans. Now since (Lib. VII, cap. XXI, p. 494) he states that the " Tlacochcalcatl " was the " principal " among the war-captains, it follows, that the chiefs named by him had all attained that rank. But we know that other authorities frequently give them another title also, therefore the conclusion is but natural that there were *several* head-chiefs for military purposes, etc., from whom the " chief of men " might be chosen.

[283] " *Biblioteca Mexicana* " (p. 58).

conceive why the captain " Cuauhnochtecuhtli " should *not* be one of the privileged four, it is easy to understand why the " man of the black house" should be of that number. The dark house, "Casa Lobrega" of Nuñez de la Vega, in Chiapas, plays a conspicuous part in the worship, or " medicine " of the aborigines of Mexico and Central America.[284] The " man of the black, or dark house," was therefore an intermediate between "medicine" and tribal government. As such, he appears to occupy a stage preparatory to the high office of " chief of men," and represents. together with the " satraps and papaoaqui" named by Sahagun,[285] the element of medicine or worship in the election of that officer. " Tlilancalqui " is occasionally, though rarely, mentioned as a war-chief,[286] but missions of importance appear to have been intrusted to him ; and Joseph de Acosta calls the three other chiefs " warriors,"[287] to his exclusion ; and finally, he is made a confidential advisor in times of great public danger. This is about all we know of this office, in relation to the government of the Mexican tribe.

The fact, amply proven as it is, that the " chief of men " had to be selected from among the four chiefs and officers enumerated, bears directly on the nature of the dignity with which the " Tlacatecuhtli " was invested. It fully disposes of the assumptions, that this officer was anything but an Indian war-chief of the highest order, or that heredity was attached to the office, though it does not disprove succession of office limited to any single *kin*. While it thus explains many incidental features of organization and government, it leads us back to the office of "chief of men" and through it, recalls some of the fundamental attributes of the tribe.

[284] *J. H. von Minutoli* ("*Beschreibung einer alten Stadt in Guatemala,*" etc., "*Teatro Critico Americano.*" by *Felix Cabrera,* German translation, p. 31): "house of darkness which he (Votan) had built in the space of a few respirations." But the dark house is yet more positively noticed in Guatemala. *Popol Vuh* (Part II. chap. II, p. 85): "Gekuma Ha," from "Gek" black, "*Grammaire QQuicheé*" (p. 180). Also (Chap. VIII, p. 147, cap. IX, pp. 148 and 149). It is interesting to notice, in connection with this, that the same gathering of aboriginal traditions also mentions (p. 81) a house filled with lances (darts): "R'oo chicut Chayim-ha u bi, utuquel chakol chupam zaklelohre chi cha. chi tzininic, chi yohohic, chiri pa ha." (Cap. IX, p. 154): "qate chicut ta x-e oc chi qaholab pa Chaim-ha." This corresponds with the Mexican "Tlacochcalcatl." Again we are treated (p. 85) to a "house of tigers" also repeated (p. 154), and it is easy to recognize in it a counterpart to the "Tlacatecatl." Thus again the analogy between the Guatemaltecans and the Mexicans, appears sustained to some extent.

[285] "*Historia general,*" etc. (Lib. VIII, cap. XXX, p. 318).

[286] By *Tezozomoc.* Quotations are superfluous. See his "*Crónica.*"

[287] "*Historia natural y moral de Indias*" (Lib. VI, cap. XXV, p. 441).

We have already stated that the tribe was a voluntary association of kins for mutual protection. Though this was undoubtedly the original purpose, it becomes evident that, in course of time and as a result of success in warfare, the tribe, as a military organization, grew into a cluster for procuring and increasing subsistence.[288] This was achieved by gathering booty in successful raids, and by imposing tribute upon tribes whose military power had been overcome in such dashes and forays.

Previous to the formation of the confederacy, but few tribes had been conquered by the Mexicans.[289] In fact, it was the nearly equally balanced power of the Pueblos occupying the lake basin, that made the formation of that confederacy possible. Such a course was necessary to prevent them from destroying each other for the benefit of expectant neighbors.[290] But when once this confederacy was formed, then their joint efforts were directed to conquest, and to the acquisition of the means of subsistence through tribute. As the imposition of tribute was a military measure, so, also, its collection was in the hands of the *military* branch of the tribal government. This is evident from the fact that the kins had delegated to the tribe all authority over outside matters.[291] Hence the "chief of men" became the official head of tribute-gatherers.[292]

[288] "*Art of War*" (pp. 96, 97 and 98, also notes).

[289] The number and names of these tribes are yet undefined. The specifically *Mexican* sources insisting upon a *conquest* of Tezcuco (by force of arms) by the Mexicans, it follows that, according to the *Codice Ramirez* (pp. 51 to 61), the tribes subjected before that supposed event, were the Tecpaneca, the Xochimilca, and those of Cuitlahuac, or the settlements to the west and southwest. *Durán* (Cap. IX to XV) and *Tezozomoc* (Cap. VIII to XX) concur; so does, of course, *Acosta* (Lib. VII. cap. XII to XV). The *Codex Mendoza* (plates V and VI) adds to the above the pueblos of Chalco, Acolhuacan and of Quauhnahuac (Cuernavaca). If we compare it with the *Tezcucan* tradition, as reported by *Ixtlilxochitl* ("*Hist. des Chichiméques*," Cap. XXXI, p. 216) we notice that it is claimed for that tribe, that it assisted the Mexicans in the conquest of Xochimilco and Cuitlahuac, although the formal confederation took place (according to the same authority. Cap. XXXII) some years later. According to *Torquemada* (Lib. II, cap. XLII. pp. 148, etc.), *Vetancurt* (Parte IIa, Trat. 1°, cap XIV, p. 291), the Xochimilcas were conquered by the confederates. According to *Veytia* ("*Historia antigua*," Lib. III. cap. I, p. 150), the Tezcucans subjected Xochimilco. *Clavigero* (Lib. IV, cap. V, p. 253) agrees with the Mexican version.

[290] "*Codice Ramirez*" (p. 61).

[291] This resulted from the constitution of the tribe, as an association of kins for mutual protection and sustenance.

[292] *Tezozomoc* (Cap. X, p. 18): "y aunque envian á darlo á Ytzcoatl era para todos los Mexicanos en comun." The fact that the gathering of tribute was directly controlled by the "chief of men" is so generally admitted that it hardly needs any further proof. *Ramirez de Fuenleal* ("*Lettre*," etc., p. 248, 1er *Recueil*) ascribes the gathering of tribute to an officer whom he calls "tecuxcalcatectli." This should be, properly,

Whenever any tribe, with or without a struggle, yielded to the warlike power of the Mexicans and their associates, the amount and kind of articles to be delivered, as tribute, at fixed periods, was at once determined between " the parties.[293] For the faithful performance of that contract, the vanquished stood in daily peril of their lives ;[294] and in order to watch them constantly, and to regulate the delivery and transmission of the tribute, special officers were maintained among the conquered pueblos by their conquerors. These officers were called " gatherers of the crops," calpixqui. Each one of the three confederates sent its own " calpixqui " among the tribes which had become its exclusive prey, and. where, as sometimes occurred, one pueblo paid tribute to all three confederates, it had to submit to the residence in its midst, of as many representative gatherers of duties.[295]

"tlacochcalcatl-tecuhtli." But we know that the duties of the latter officer were quite different. Still, the collection of tribute being a branch of military life, the mistake is easily accounted for. The military chronicles of the Mexican tribe teem with instances where the stewards are described as under direct orders of the "chief of men," as in *Zurita* (pp. 68, 69, 70). It may also be inferred from the exaggerated statements about the tribute system among the Tezcucans, contained in *Ixtlilxochitl* ("*Hist. des Chichimèques*," Cap. XXXV, pp. 239–241).

[293] I refer to the following passages of *Tezozomoc* ("*Crónica*," Cap. IX, p. 16, Capture of Azcaputzalco; Cap. XV, p 24, Cuyuacan; XVII, p. 28, Xochimilco; XVIII, p. 29, Cuitlahuac; XXVI, p. 40, Chalco; XXVII, p. 41, Tepeacac and Tecamachalco; XXIX, pp. 44 and 45, Tziccoac and Tucpan; XXXII, p. 50, Ahuilizapan, and the Totonaca; XXXVIII, p. 52, Coayxtlahuacan; XXXVIII, p. 61, Huaxaca; Cap. LXI, p. 102, Chiapan and Xilotepec; Cap. LXV, p. 110, Cuextlan; Cap. LXXII, p. 122: Teloloapan; LXXVI, p. 130, Tecuantepec and others; LXXIX, p. 136, Xoconuchco; LXXXIV, p. 148, Nopallan; LXXXVIII, Xaltepec; XCI, p. 159, Quetzaltepec). *Durán* (Cap. IX, p. 77; X, p. 94; XII, p. 112; XVII, p. 151; XVIII, p. 159; XIX, p. 171; XXI, p. 185; XXII, p. 191; XXIV, p. 205; XXXIV, p. 269; XLI, p. 331; XLVI, p. 373, etc.). These passages fully illustrate the manner in which the tribute was imposed on the vanquished, at the close of a successful foray. *Ixtlilxochitl* ("*Histoire des Chichimèques*," Cap. XXXVIII, pp. 271 to 273). *Sahagun* (Lib. VIII, cap. XXIV, p. 313): "Habiendo pacificado la provincia, luego los señores del campo repartian tributos á los que habian sido conquistados. . . ."

[294] *Durán* (Cap. LIII, p. 423), Also the complaints of the Indians of Cempohual and Quiahuiztlan (Totonaconas) (on the coast), to Cortés, about the dread in which they continually stood of being overrun again by the Mexicans and their confederates. (*Cortés* "*Carta Segunda*," p. 13, Vedia I), *Bernal Diez* (Cap. XLV, p. 40; XLVI, p. 41, Vedia II), "*Real Ejécutoria, etc.*" (Col. de Doc's II, p. 12).

[295] This results from the "articles of agreement" of the confederacy. See besides: *Zurita* (p. 67). *Hernando Pimentel Nezahualcoyotl* ("*Memorial dirigido al rey, etc.*" "*Géografia de las Lenguas*," Orozco y Berra pp. 244 and 245) also states: "The pueblos whose tributes were distributed among Mexico and Tezcuco and Tacuba were the following: Coayxtlavuacan, Cuauhtuchco, Cotlaxtlan, Avliçapan, Tepeaca." Against this there stands the version of *Sahagun* (Lib. XII, cap. XLI, p. 59): "Luego alli habló otro principal que se llamaba Mixcoatlaylotlacauelitoctzin, dile al señor capitan, que cuando vivia Mocthecuzoma el estilo que se tenia en conquistar, era este, que iban los Mexicanos, y los Tezcucanos, y los de Tlacupan, y los de las Chinampas, todos

Thus the Mexicans had a number of such officers scattered among tributary settlements. The " chief of men" controlled their actions, but his power did not extend over the " calpixca" of the tribes of Tezcuco and Tlacopan. He could not even appoint the stewards sent to dwell among the tributary foreigners,[296] this power being vested in the council alone.[297] Such an office was by no means a post of honor and enjoyment. On the contrary, there was no more responsible or dangerous duty within or without the tribe. The " calpixqui" while he had not the slightest authority to meddle with the affairs of the tribe where he lived,[298] was expected to watch closely the dispositions and incli-

juntos iban sobre el pueblo ó provincia que querian conquistar, y despues que lo habian conquistado, luego se volvian á sus casas, y á sus pueblos, y despues venian los señores de los pueblos que habian sido conquistados, y traian su tributo de oro y de piedras preciosas, y de plumages ricos, y todo lo daban à Mocthecuzoma, y asi todo el oro venia ă su poder." This plain and very natural statement, from a Tlatilulcan chief who afterwards became "·gobernador" of Tlatilulco (*Sahagun*, Lib. VIII, cap. II, p. 274), has been twisted by *Torquemada* (Lib. IV, cap. CII, p. 572), so as to say among other things: "·and they had the tributes gathered at Mexico, and here it was distributed among the three Lords according to the directions given by him of Mexico." *Torquemada* has, in this instance, evidently changed the text of his predecessor. There is also an undeniable confusion here between booty and tribute. The former had to be divided among the conquerors while they were yet together; the latter occurred regularly afterwards, and hence did not need to go through the hands of Mexicans again. The story of Torquemada is corroborated by *Ixtlilxochitl* ('*Hiot. des Chichimèques*," Cap. XXXIX, p. 282), who clearly says that "Fasting Wolf" put stewards only when the tribute belonged to his tribe, but that the whole tribute was brought to Mexico and there " the agents of the three chiefs divided it among themselves. Finally, we have the obscure statements of *Ramirez de Fuenleal* (pp. 244, 247, in 1er Recueil of Mr. Ternaux).

[296] The " Calpixcayotl" was a permanent office, not a temporary duty or mission; consequently its incumbents could not be appointed by a single war-chief. There is evidence to that effect. According to *Durán* (Cap. XVIII, p. 164), after those of Tepeacac had been conquered, " Cihuacohuatl" placed a steward in their midst: " Mirá que en ello no aya falta ni quiebra; y para questo mejor se cumpla, os quiere poner un gobernador de los señores Mexicanos, al qual aueis de obedecer y tener en lugar de la real persona, el qual se llama Coacuech, y con esto os podeis ir en norabuena ă vuestras tierras y ciudades porque al rey no le podeis hablar." (Cap. XXI, pp. 186 and 187). The steward for Cuetlaxtlan was chosen by the " Snake-woman;" or at least his choice was proclaimed by that officer. (Cap. XXIII, p. 199): "Acauado el sacrificio y despedidos los güéspedes, Tlacaelel, con consejo del rey, enuió un virey á Coaixtlavac para que tuviese cargo de aquella provincia y de los tributos reales, el qual se llamaua Cuauxochitl. . . . ."

[297] This results from the fact that the " Cihuacohuatl" announced the newly chosen " Calpixqui." In this case he plainly acted as *foreman of the council*, proclaiming their choice.

[298] I have already, in note 4, disposed of the statements of *Sahagun* (Lib. VIII, cap. XXIV, p. 313): " y luego elegian gobernadores y oficiales que presidiesen en aquella provincia, no de los naturales de ella, sino de los que la habian conquistado." In further explanation thereof, I beg to call attention to some statements of the interpreters of the *Codex Mendoza* (plates XX and XXI): " Los pueblos figurados en los dos planos siguientes, resumidos aqui, son diez y ocho pueblos, segun que están entitulados. Por

nations of those by whom he was surrounded and to report forthwith any suspicious movements or utterances that came to his notice. Thus he appeared, in the eyes of the people among whom he resided, as a spy, whose reports might, at any time, bring down upon them the wrath of their conquerors. Again, it was his duty to control the bringing in of the articles promised as tribute, at stated times. Consequently he was the hateful tax-gatherer, the living monument of their defeat with all its unfortu-

los Señores de Mexico tenian puesto un gobernador llamado Petlacalcatl, aunque en cada un pueblo tenian puesto un Calpixque, que es como Mayordomo, que tenian à cargo de hacer recojer las rentas y tributos que los dichos Señores tributaban al Señorio de México y todos los dichos mayordomos acudian al dicho Petlacalcatl, como su governador;" (plates XXII and XXIII): " . . . . tenian puestos Calpixques, en cada uno de ellos, y en lo mas principal dominaba sobre todos ellos un governador, para que los mantubiese en paz y justicia, y les hiciese cumplir sus tributos y porque no se rebelasen;" (plates XXIV and XXV): "Y á que fuesen bien regidos y governados, los Señores de Mexico en cada uno de ellos tenian puestos Calpixques, y sobre todos les Calpixques un governador, persona principal de México, y ansi mismo los Calpixques eran Mexicanos, lo qual se hacia é probeya por los dichos Señores y á seguridad, para que no les rebelasen, y ă que les administrasen justicia y oyesen en policia." It follows from the above that the "Governors" were placed, not so much over the tribes, as over the "calpixca" themselves, and indeed the "Petlacalcatl," "man of the house of chests," was the head-steward, to whom all the other stewards had to direct their consignments of tribute. Consequently, it is not to be understood as "governor of a province," but only "governor of the stewards," which is totally different.

Besides, there is positive evidence to the effect, that the Mexicans and their associates never interfered with the autonomy of tributary tribes. *Andrés de Tápia* ("*Relacion*," etc., p. 592): "Los que tomaba de guerra decian tequitin tlacotle, que quiere decir, tributan como esclavos. En estos ponia mayordomos y recogedores y recaudadores; y aunque los señores mandaban su gente, era debajo de la mano destos de México. . . . *Zurita* ("*Rapport*," etc., p. 68): "Les chefs, restant seigneurs comme avant la guerre, conservaient la jurisdiction civile et criminelle dans toute l'étendue de leurs domaines."

When the tribes of the gulf coast (the Totonacas, etc.) arose against the Mexicans, murdering the stewards who had been placed among them, they were speedily overcome again, and when they attributed their revolt to the intrigues of their head-chiefs, asking the Mexicans to punish them for it, the Mexicans replied, according to *Durán* (Cap. XXIV, p. 204): "nosotros no traemos autoridad para matar á nadie sino es en guerra: vuestros señores no han parecido en esta guerra ni los emos visto, pero no por eso se escaparán, pues vuestras razones y deseo y lo que pedís, se dirá al rey nuestro señor Monteçuma, y él mandará que se execute lo que nosotros dexaremos ordenado, y luego sin mas dilacion los traed aqui á todos ante nosotros y á muy buen recaudo." Afterwards: "enviaron á Cuaunochtli y ă Tlilancalqui, que eran de los mayores oydores del consejo supremo, para que executasen aquella justicia." The two chiefs were cruelly butchered (p. 206). This story is also related by *Tezozomoc* (Cap. XXXV, pp. 55 and 56), and it is evidently the instance referred to and illustrated by the *Codex Mendoza* (plate LXVII). The foregoing tells us that even in a case of dangerous treachery and rebellion such as the above, the Mexicans did not claim the right to interfere in the internal affairs of the conquered tribe, of their own accord, but that it required the positive request of that tribe to cause them to act in the premises. Furthermore, the position of the "chief of men" as military executor is clearly defined: "y el mandará que se execute lo que nosotros dexaremos ordenado." A very important statement!

nate results. It certainly required men of capacity and experience to fill such a position, and we need not wonder, therefore, if the "calpixca," whom Cortés met among the Totonacas of the coast, wore the distinctive tokens of chiefs.[299]

The conditions of tribute were various. Some tribes delivered their contributions every eighty days, whilst others sent them in annually.[300] In most cases, they had to be carried to Mexico-Tenuchtitlan by the tributaries, or at least, the delivery was at their charge.[301] This was done frequently by prisoners of war, made by the tributary pueblo and sent as part of the tribute itself.[302] The "calpixqui" superintended this intercourse, he verified the articles received, and again dispatched them, properly, to the "seat and home" of the Mexicans. All this necessitated

[299] *Bernal Diez de Castillo* (Cap. XLVI, pp. 40 and 41).

[300] The most complete record of tributes which we possess, until now, is contained in the so-called *Codex Mendoza* (Parte Segunda, plates XIX to LVII, inclusive). A full discussion of the multifarious details thereof is impossible here. It would require an essay by itself, which, however instructive it might be, would largely exceed the limits of this paper. Of course, not all the authorities agree with them. I merely refer, in addition, to *Durán* (Cap. XXV), *Oviedo* (Lib. XXXIII, cap. LI, pp. 535, '6 and '7), *Clavigero* (Lib VII, cap. XV), *Ixtlilxochitl* ("*Hist. des Chichimèques*," Cap. XXXV), the latter as well as *Torquemada* (Lib. II, cap. LIII, pp. 167 and 168) confining himself to the Tezcucans and their tributaries exclusively. See furthermore, *Zurita* (pp. 246, 247 and 248), *Ramirez de Fuenleal* (Letter, p. 251). It is also interesting to consult the statements gathered on the tribute question, from tribes subject to the Mexicans. See, on *Chalco*, *Fray Domingo de la Anunciacion* (Letter dated: Chalco, 20 Sept., 1554, 2d "Recueil" of Mr. Ternaux-Compans. pp. 333 and 334): on *Matlatzinco*, *Zurita* (pp. 394-397), *Herrera* (Dec. III, lib. IV, cap. XVIII, p. 140). The latter mostly copies from Zurita. Finally, much information as to the details can be gathered from the "*Codice Ramirez*" (pp. 63 and 65), and especially from the traditions on the forays and dashes of the Mexicans contained in the specifically Mexican sources already quoted.

[301] *Tezozomoc* (Cap. XXVII, p. 41, Cap. XXXIII, p. 52, Cap. LXI, p. 102, etc., etc.), *Durán* (Cap. LXIX. p. 171): "Pues mirá que lo aueis de llevar á México vosotros mesmos. Ellos respondiéron que les placia de lo lleuar allá y seruillos, ..." (Cap. XXII. p. 191): "y que se obligasen á traello á México. . . ." (Cap. XXIV, p. 206, Cap. XXV, p. 203, etc., etc., etc.)

[302] *Durán* (Cap. XXV, pp. 212 and 213). Such female slaves became concubines. The various tribes exchanged also their prisoners of war, one tribe buying (exchanging for products of the soil or for manufactures) of another those prisoners which it had received as such tribute, and also presenting each other on solemn occasions with such prisoners. There are many illustrations of this to be found. Thus the markets of aboriginal Mexico also had "slaves," for sale, who were obtained in this manner. They were not numerous, and did not form a class, only an object of medicine subject to exchange and barter. *Cortés* ("*Carta Segunda*," p. 35, Vedia I) only speaks of "bonded people" standing in the markets" or "outcasts" ready to "bind" themselves — "to let." But *Bernal Diez de Castillo* (Cap. XCII, p. 89, Vedia II), evidently describes such unfortunate people: "é traianlos atados en unas varas largas, con collares á los pescuezos porque no se les huyesen, y otros dejaban sueltos." The same author (Cap. XLVI, p. 41) mentions the demand made upon the "Totonaca's" of the coast by the Mexican "calpixca" for "twenty Indians of both sexes to pacify their Gods therewith." This is confirmed in a general way by *Cortés* ("*Carta Segunda*," p. 13, Vedia I).

assistants at his disposal — runners — who not only accompanied the convoys of tribute, but through whom a regular communication might be kept up with the Mexican tribe. On the strength of this, it has been fancied that not only a road-system analogous to that of the Romans, pervaded the entire area of actual Mexico, but that a perfect postal system was in full and successful operation. In regard to the first assumption we beg to refer to the letter of the Licentiate Salmeron, dated Mexico, 13th August, 1531, and directed to the council of the Indies:[303] "I believe that all through the land roads should be opened which would be practicable both for beasts of burthen and for carts. It would greatly increase the security of our possessions. Since the Indians had no beasts of burthen, their paths were straight and narrow, and so direct that they would not deviate an inch in order to avoid climbing the most rugged mountains." Over these Indian trails, where occasionally heavy culverts of stone, filled up gaps and spanned narrow ravines,[304] the tribute was forwarded to the pueblo of Tenuchtitlan, and the necessary runners moved swiftly, to and fro, as occasion required. But there was no regularity in this intercourse. There were no relays, and the Indian messenger relied, in order to traverse the wide belts of waste lands between tribe and tribe, upon his own endurance and upon the bag of provisions which he carried along.[305]

On solemn occasions, the convoys of tribute were not merely escorted by runners and watchmen detailed for that purpose by the " calpixqui," but that officer, himself, accompanied them and entered Mexico-Tenuchtitlan at their head.[306] The articles were . carried to the " Tecpan" and then the duties of the " chief of men " in regard to tribute in general ended. For this tribute was not due to him, but to the tribe, and it was the tribal representa-

---

[303] " *Second Recueil de Pieces sur le Méxique* " (H. Ternaux-Compans, pp. 191 and 192).

[304] The collection of Lord Kingsborough has, among others, the pictures of so-called bridges. Anyone can see at a glance that they are mere heavy culverts. *Mr. H. H. Bancroft* (" *Native Races*," Vol. IV, p. 528) figures a bridge at Huejutla, but his argument in favor of its being an aboriginal construction appears to me very unsatisfactory. The masonry covering the mound at Metlaltoyuca shows, according to his own words (Id. p. 461): " there is no evidence that the arch was intentionally self-supporting."

[305] We must always discriminate between delegates, entrusted with certain business to transact, and therefore also clothed with a certain authority, and mere *runners*. ("Correos"—" Yciuhca titlantli" *Molina* I, p. 30, from " Iciuhca "—quick and " titlantli "—he who goes on an errand, II. pp. 32 and 113). The latter are very well described by *Torquemada* (Lib. XIV, cap. I, pp. 535 and 536), although he presupposes relays at regular intervals. This was not the case, as the march of Cortés amply proves

[306] " *Codice Ramirez* " (p. 63).

tives to whom it was delivered.[307] If the gathering of tribute thus required a set of officers necessarily placed beneath the orders of the military chieftain, another set was needed for its preservation and judicious distribution. If the one consisted of stewards dwelling outside of the pueblo, the other was composed exclusively of home-stewards. Every convoy was therefore " consigned " to a proper officer, whose duty it was to receive it and then abide the directions of his superiors as to its apportionment.[308]

We have already mentioned the " Cihuacohuatl " as the officer, who was responsible to the council for the administration of the stores and the proper distribution thereof, though he had beneath him another officer, to whom this duty was really and practically assigned. Torquemada and those who have followed his school, call this subordinate " great crop-gatherer," " Hueycalpixqui,"[309] whereas Tezozomoc and Durán apply to him the title of " man of the house of chests" " Petlacalcatl "[310] In both cases, however, he is represented as " chief steward," to whom all the others should render account. He superintended the distribution of the tribute,[311] and to him the kins came for their share — perhaps the largest of all. Unfortunately, we are unable to establioh the principles upon which the division took place. All that we know is, that the tribe received one portion and the kins or " calpulli" the other, and that the " man of the house of chests," under whose eyes the distribution took place, afterwards looked to those stores, in particnlar, which were reserved for the tribe, i. e. : for the demands of the tribal government.[312] Therefore, the " man of the house of chests " frequently appears to be under the direct orders of the " chief of men," who could apply to him, more particularly, for such articles as were required for the exercise of tribal hospitality including gifts, and for displays of finery on particularly solemn occasions.[313] It is true that, as we have elsewhere shown, particular tracts of land, " tecpan-tlalli," were reserved among tributary tribes for the demands of the official

---

[307] *Tezozomoc* (Cap. X, p. 18), *Herrera* (Dec. III, lib. IV, cap. XVII, p. 138).

[308] *Tezozomoc* (Cap. XXXII, p. 51): "A los dichos pueblos fué un mayordomo para cobrar este tributo, como para todos los demas pueblos, que en Mexico havia un mayordomo, y otro en el mismo pueblo para mayor sugecion y vasallage."

[309] *Torquemada* (Lib. XIV, cap. VI, pp. 544, 545), copied by Vetancurt (Parte IIa, Trat. 11°, cap. 1°, pp. 370 and 371), *Clavigero* (Lib. VII, cap. X, pp. 468 and 469).

[310] Also by the *Codex Mendoza* (Interpretation to plates XX, XXI, etc.).

[311] See note 309, also *Tezozomoc* and *Durán.*

[312] This is so frequently mentioned by *Tezozomoc,* that I forbear detailed quotations.

[313] *Tezozomoc* (" *Crónica Mexicana,*" sundry places, too numerous to refer to).

households,[314] still, on many occasions, whether festive or in the hour of need, the crops raised thereon would not be sufficient, and thus other stores were laid up and held for prudential reasons.[315] Over these stores the "Petlacalcatl" presided. This officer was, in all probability, appointed by the council, and he was accountable in the first place to the "Cihuacohuatl," who kept a register or list of the articles received as well as of their apportionment. These rude paintings on prepared skin, or tissue, have given rise to the fable that "archives" existed at the aboriginal pueblos of Mexico, Tezcuco, and Tlacopan.[316]

The stores required for worship and for the support of the "medicine-men" were, as far as the central or tribal "house of God" was concerned, also, taken from this tribute, and assigned to the "medicine-men" according to their need. But the bulk of the tribute, presumably, went to the kins, who apportioned it among their members, after reserving the necessary quota for their government and for worship. In this manner the proceeds of tribal association finally reached the individual,— not through the tribe unless he was an outcast, but through the kin,— and thus the latter again appears as the working unit of organized society, even in the vital matter of subsistence.

The procuring of subsistence, by means of warfare, is the widest field of tribal action known to aboriginal Mexico. It links together kin and tribe, and furnishes a *raison d'être* for the highest known form of tribal society — the confederacy.

After what has been said in this and the preceding essays, it is superfluous to recur, in detail, to the confederacy formed by the three "Nahuatl" tribes, of Mexico, Tezcuco and Tlacopan. Its "articles of agreement" have been stated elsewhere; and we know the prominent position, in a military point of view, occupied by the Mexican tribe in this partnership, formed, as it was, for the purpose of war and plunder. All that remains for us to emphasize is the fact, that this inter-tribal connection in the Mexican valley did not extend further than a tri-partite association for the aforesaid purposes. There was no interference on the part of the conquerors, in the affairs of the conquered, no attempt gradually

---

[314] "*Tenure of Lands*" (pp. 419 and 420).

[315] See the concurrent reports about the great drouth, while "Wrathy chief who shoots arrows heavenward" ("Montezuma Ilhuicamina") was "chief of men."

[316] This very interesting and important question will soon be fully discussed by a very competent authority. I consequently forbear entering into any examination thereof.

to cast the heterogeneous elements into one uniform mould, because there was no idea of any form of society other than that based upon kin, and of this, the tribe, characterized by independent territory, a dialect of its own and a common name and worship, formed the highest governmental expression.

We have thus, involuntarily almost, retraced our steps to the point of departure and justified, as we believe, our original propositions. We have tried to show that there was, in aboriginal Mexico, neither state, nor nation, nor political society of any kind. We have found a population separated into tribes representing dialectical variations of speech, each tribe autonomous in matters of government, and occasionally forming confederacies for purposes of self-defence and conquest. Out of that confederacy, brought so prominently forward by the events of the Spanish conquest, we have selected on account of its military pre-eminence, one tribe,— the ancient Mexicans — and we have shown that it was an organic body composed of twenty autonomous kins for purposes of mutual protection and subsistence. A social organization resting upon such a foundation must, of necessity, have been a democratic body. Indeed, we have found that each kin was governed by strictly elective officers, subject to removal at the pleasure of their constituents; that the twenty kins, for their mutual benefit, had delegated their powers to transact business with outsiders to a council of the tribe, in which every kin was represented by one member and consequently, had the same voice and vote as either one of the others. The execution of the decrees of this council was left to elective officers, whose power was limited to military command, and whom the tribe might depose at pleasure. With the exception of some very inferior positions, these officers had not the power of appointing others to office, not even their assistants of high rank. The dignity of chief, so commonly transformed into hereditary nobility, has been found to have been, merely, a reward of merit and carried with it no other prerogatives than personal consideration and occasional indulgence in finery. Taking all this together, and adding to it the results of our investigations into the military organization of the ancient Mexicans, as well as of their communal mode of holding and enjoying the soil, we feel authorized to conclude *that the social organization and mode of government of the ancient Mexicans was a military democracy, originally based upon communism in living.*